Never Say Die

Never Say Die

New Adventures
from the Country Vet

Dr. David Perrin

Illustrations by Wendy Liddle

Have a good read.

[signature]

December 2, 2016

DAVE'S PRESS INC.

Published by Dave's Press Inc.
Box 616, Lister
British Columbia
Canada V0B 1Y0

Cover and book design by Warren Clark
Illustrations by Wendy Liddle
Edited by Betsy Brierley
Proofread by Elizabeth McLean

Printed and bound in Canada

Library and Archives Canada Cataloguing in Publication

Perrin, David, 1948–
    Never say die: new adventures from the country vet / David Perrin.

    ISBN 0-9687943-5-1

    1. Perrin, David, 1948-. 2. VeterinariansBritish Columbia—
Biography. 3. Animals—Anecdotes. I. Title.
SF613.P47A3 2006   636.089'092   C2006-905885-7

To my children:

Joan, Marshall,

Gordon and Alicia

Acknowledgements

Almost every day of the year I spent in Hawaii, I walked barefoot along the same two-and-a-half-mile stretch of beach. Most days, the sand that faced the pair of half-moon bays was packed as hard as pavement and walking was easy. After storms stirred things up, the going was tougher and each step would see me sinking ankle deep in the newly churned material. On those days, my negative inner chatter would try to convince me into only going partway. Invariably, once I reached the first point and could see the waves crashing into the rock cliffs at the far end of the second bay, I ventured on.

Writing this book was much like walking that stretch of beach—some days, continuing on wasn't the easy thing to do and my mind looked for almost any excuse to give up the journey. At times like that, emails and letters from readers and encouragement from friends and family kept me plugging on.

I'd like to thank my readers for taking the time to write me, expressing opinions about my work, and sharing its effect on their lives. I'd like to thank my sisters Kay Rizzotti and Audrey O'Hearn for keeping track of me, my children Joan, Marshall, Gordon, and Alicia for keeping me a big part of their lives, and my friends for their part in nurturing our relationships.

As with all my other books, my editor Betsy Brierley, my illustrator Wendy Liddle, my designer Warren Clark, and my proofreader Elizabeth McLean extended themselves beyond my expectations. I couldn't have asked them for more.

Contents

A Case of Indigestion

"Doris! What have you done to me now?"

Doris calmly placed a patient record in its folder and closed the file drawer. "What do you mean?"

"What's this about a snake?" I pointed accusingly at the appointment book.

"It's a garter snake," she explained lamely.

I screwed up my face. "A garter snake! Are you kidding me? Who in his right mind would bring in a backyard snake?"

"A young fellow from the Wildlife Centre called right after we opened...He said something about a snake swallowing a sunfish."

"Are you guys at it again, Doris?"

I studied her face carefully to see if "the girls" were pulling another fast one on me. Many times in the four years since I'd recruited her as my receptionist, Doris and her cohorts had orchestrated practical jokes with me in mind. In this instance, I couldn't detect any indication of monkey business.

"I never learned anything in college about treating snakes with indigestion," I said.

Doris smiled. "You're the vet, remember...I'm the granny you hired to answer the phone. You told me I could sit around and knit the rest of the time."

Sensing I was on the losing end of the conversation, I chose to cut my losses. I shook my head absently and mumbled my way to the kennel room to check on the hospitalized patients. I paused in front of Hank's kennel. He was going home again without a diagnosis and leaving me totally baffled. This was the third time he had been presented to the clinic with the nebulous history of "not doing well."

The dog was an enigma and more than just a problem to me, his veterinarian. Most times, owners had pets that matched their personalities. Somehow, Hank didn't remotely fit the family that had adopted him. This overweight cocker would rather sleep away the day than play ball with Jim Forner and his three children.

I plucked Hank's medical record from the chart rack and perused it again. What was I missing? I had convinced myself that he presented a classic case of hypothyroidism. He was the right breed and his history was highly suggestive of it.

Hypothyroidism in the dog was usually characterized by obesity, lack of energy, and rough hair coat. Many hypothyroid cocker spaniels also had seborrhea oleosa, a skin condition characterized by a greasy, foul-smelling hair coat that left a disgusting scent on your hands long after you finished handling the dog. Hank certainly never had that problem. His hair coat was soft and sleek. The odour the family complained about was not from his skin but his bowels. According to Jim Forner, Hank was constantly farting. Sometimes, for self-preservation, the entire family would have to evacuate the room.

I stared at the card again trying to will the numbers to change. Doris had taken the call from the lab in Langley while I was doing herd health at Tsolum Farms. Why couldn't the numbers have cooperated for a change? At the 1976 veterinary conference in Vancouver, an endocrinologist had made a presentation on hormonal imbalances in dogs. He had stated emphatically that many dogs with T4 levels at the low end of the acceptable range were actually hypothyroid. He maintained that these animals should be put on thyroid supplements even if the lab called their results normal.

I had been so confident of Hank's diagnosis that I'd already calculated the dosage of Eltroxin he'd require, certain it would be the
answer to his problem. I shook my head at the number—it was
solidly within normal range.

I'd wait for the rest of the report to come back by mail before
I sat down and talked to Jim. I wasn't looking forward to that
meeting. The man was regretting that he'd taken this dog into his
home, and I was worried he'd soon regret choosing me as his
veterinarian.

Grabbing a thermometer from the antiseptic bath, I shook it
down and opened the door to Hank's kennel. He lifted his head to
look absently at me as if mildly irritated that someone had the
nerve to interrupt his slumber. As I lifted his stubby tail and
slipped in the glass rod, he laid his head down with a sigh.

"What's with you, old man? If we don't find out soon, your
master will be dumping both of us."

His tail twitched once in response to my admonition. I ran my
hands over his body, retracing familiar territory in search of something out of the ordinary. Other than a very generous distribution
of blubber, everything appeared normal. With my hands on either
side of the dog's abdomen, I methodically palpated my way
through his viscera, searching for something of interest.

After several minutes in this fruitless pursuit, I removed the
thermometer and looked at it in disgust—38.5. Again, right on
normal. I closed the kennel door. "Hank, you're just a lazy old
bugger."

He sighed and closed his eyes.

Later that morning, I was removing the surgical drapes from a cat
we had spayed when we heard the door open in the reception area.
Doris left to see who it was while I unhooked the hose of the anesthetic machine from the endotracheal tube. I had the drapes in the
laundry basket and the cat in the recovery kennel by the time she
returned.

"Your new patient is here, Doctor."

I removed the tube from the cat and pulled out her tongue to make sure her airway was clear. The queen snorted a few times, sneezed, and emitted a deep-throated meow. She lay on her side, growling with each breath and kneading the air with her talons.

"I'll look after her now, Dave. I don't think you'll be requiring my services out there."

"How big is the snake?"

"How am I supposed to know?" Doris retorted. "I hate snakes! If I saw one in the orchard, you couldn't beat me to the house."

I took one last peek at my patient, then passed through to the exam room. A tall, lanky lad in his early twenties stood patiently leaning on the table, a cardboard box in front of him. He was blond with a scraggly, rather sparse beard and a pointed nose. As I approached, he extended his right hand.

"Matt Hellier...I'm here in Creston trying to complete the research for my master's degree at Simon Fraser. I'm studying the movement of garter snakes at the Interpretation Centre."

"Oh, isn't that a great way to spend the summer...Glad to meet you, Matt."

"This guy was my first specimen," he went on. "He has a radio transmitter implanted in him, and I've been following him most of the summer. He might not look like much, but the amount of time I've been working with him makes him a pretty valuable snake to me." He fumbled with the few hairs of his moustache, twisting the ends pensively.

"I've never seen anything quite like this," he said, opening the cardboard box and withdrawing a grey-green snake. The creature wriggled unproductively as its body dangled from Matt's finger-tips. Its flame-red tongue waved from its open mouth as if trying to glean information about the new surroundings. It was three feet in length and typical of the snakes I had played with as a kid, with one exception.

About a third of the way along the reptile's sleek body, a

series of sharp protuberances jutted through the skin.

"He obviously swallowed a sunfish backwards," my client observed.

I took the animal from him and gently prodded the foreign body. Prickly spines poked through the creature's side, leaving long rents where they had torn the gut, muscle, and skin.

"Isn't that something!"

"Of all the snakes this could have happened to, wouldn't you know it happened to mine…I was hoping to track him through the entire year."

I placed the snake in the box. It raised its head to scout the surroundings, then slithered into the corner to coil up in a ball. The wounds didn't seem to be an impediment to its movements.

"It certainly isn't slowing him down," I observed. "I may just be able to snip off these spines and let him pass the rest. Reptiles are not anywhere near as susceptible to infections as mammals."

"Could you get some X-rays of him so I can present this as part of my thesis? I'm not sure how I can work it in, but I'd really like to have proof of this. I've already taken pictures but keep thinking that an X-ray would be really cool."

"We can do that," I replied. "I'm sure I'll have to do some experimentation to get the right exposure…but we can manage." I prodded the area adjacent to the wounds, convinced that I'd be able to snip the spines with a pair of side cutters. "Leave him with us for a bit. I'll see what we can do."

After Matt left, I found Doris in the kennel room. "I need your help to get some X-rays of this snake."

She watched warily as I approached with the cardboard box. "You keep that bloody thing away from me, Dave…You know I hate snakes."

"Aw, Doris, he's kinda cute. And besides, you don't have to handle him. All you have to do is push the button."

With my hands in bulky lead gloves, I knelt on the floor and fumbled to stretch our patient across the film plate. I was determined to get just the right angle to display the spines of the sunfish protruding through the reptile's sides.

There were a lot of similarities between taking X-rays and taking black and white photos. The main difference was that in a camera, a film was exposed to varying intensities of light waves, whereas in an X-ray it was being exposed to varying intensities of X-rays. Because X-rays had a shorter wavelength and a higher energy than light rays, they had the ability to penetrate through tissues of the body where light rays were blocked. Because bones and cartilage were composed of bigger atoms like calcium, they tended to be much better at absorbing X-ray photons and not allowing them to reach the film. Just looking at this snake, I didn't expect that either he or the sunfish would have a lot of calcium atoms to block X-rays. I set the dial for very low penetration—the lowest I had ever attempted—hoping I was guessing correctly.

"Now, Doris."

The moment the machine clunked, I juggled the snake back into the box and handed the plate to Doris.

"See how that looks."

Giving the box a wide berth, Doris headed for the darkroom. I laid my long frame on the floor, stuffed the X-ray gloves under my head for a pillow, and closed my eyes.

The last few weeks had been trying. I was working alone again and dealing with a constant flow of commentary from clients about how it was too bad things couldn't have worked out with Cory, my former friend from veterinary college. I had become accustomed to wagging my head and mutely agreeing with them. It was hard, knowing full well they were all aware of how Cory had ended up with the woman I had hoped would be my partner. During the last summer, Marcie had been a student and had accompanied me on some rounds to clients. I could tell she'd make a good country veterinarian.

At least I had reached the point where I could sleep again. For weeks all I could do was lie in bed listening to the snores of my

German shepherd, Lug, while I fumed on about how unfair life could be. I had almost become resigned to the fact that Marcie and Cory were moving away and she would be out of my life permanently, when my realtor friend, Gordon Veitch, asked me to stop by.

"You won't like this, Dave, but Cory and Marcie are setting up practice in Creston. They've bought property in Canyon for a house, and rented that old building across from the post office for a clinic." Gordon paused to let the realization sink in. "He was apparently hoping I'd give him a hand with his wiring."

I stared numbly at Gordon for more than a minute, trying to ignore the sick feeling in my gut. When I rushed from his office, he called after me. I could still hear him shouting my name as I bolted through a red light on 12th Avenue and hurried on to the clinic. Wasn't it bad enough that Cory had won the woman I had my heart set on? Now he wanted not only my clients but my best friends, too. It was amazing he'd left me with Doris. That led me to pondering the ultimate humiliation. Maybe he had asked her to go with him, too. Was there one more shoe to fall?

I focused on the sounds of the stainless steel lids rattling in the darkroom as Doris processed the X-ray. She'd be putting the film in the developer now and setting the timer for three minutes. The drawer squeaked as she opened it; she was removing the box of film to reload the cassette.

A tandem truck screeched to a halt at the crosswalk in front of my building. The engine revved as the vehicle rolled off in the direction of Cranbrook, and I listened as the driver shifted once, twice, then a third time in his retreat. I followed the growl of the diesel engine until it blended into the general din of Canyon Street.

I was anxious to move out of downtown and live on my farm. Lister was so beautiful and quiet. Although I had become used to sleeping with a chorus of barking dogs and squealing tires, that didn't mean I should accept it as a given. How much more restful it would be to listen to the sound of the wind in the bull pines and frogs croaking in the creek.

Cory and Marcie were already building on their property. Just after dusk the evening before last, I had driven down the road past where Gordon told me they had bought acreage. In the fading light, I could make out plywood forms and newly excavated earth. Building materials were stacked all around. Why should I stare at four ugly walls in this rickety old building when they had a panoramic view of the gorgeous Skimmerhorn Mountains?

I had to do something with that property of mine. Although I was still feeding a few cattle with the hay I got from sharecroppers, I had to do more. With Keith Marling and I already practising in town, and the added competition from two more vets, I'd likely need to supplement my income just to survive. I had a tractor. Surely I could buy some other machinery cheaply and do some real farming.

The alarm rang, signalling three minutes in the developer. There was a rattling of lids as Doris retrieved the film and rinsed it in the water bath. There was more clanging as she lifted and replaced the lid from the fixer tray.

I pondered how much a used hay swather and baler would cost me; I could probably find something affordable. I'd be hard-pressed to have enough room in my sheds if I put all the hay up myself, but maybe a lean-to would handle the extra bales. I paused in my musing to chastise myself. How could I buy machinery and build a house at the same time? Marg Rogers, my bookkeeper, was already having to be creative to make ends meet. I had cleared all the underbrush from a spot right across from the Ivany farm, thinking it would be an ideal place to set up a trailer or a Quonset hut to live in until I could afford to build a decent house.

The tank lid in the darkroom rattled, and the darkroom door opened.

"Well, don't we have it cushy?" said Doris.

I opened my eyes. She was standing over me. In her right hand she held the still dripping X-ray. I clicked on the light of the view box and groaned when I held the plate up—the shot was totally burnt. A faded stripe across the darkened film was all there was to represent the snake. I had to use my imagination to visualize where the spines of the sunfish should have been.

It wasn't until the third shot that I was satisfied with the radiograph. Still in a quandary about how to handle our patient's wounds, I kept digging into my memory banks for anything about snakes. Although I wasn't certain of the details, I recalled a conversation with a client by the name of John Hopcraft who had recently moved to the valley from Kenya. While Doris was developing the second X-ray, I dug out his card and dialled him up.

"John, do you remember telling me a story about a snake that had a horn sticking through its side? I know this is kind of a strange call, but I have a vague memory about it."

"I well might have, Dave. We had quite a few African rock pythons in Kenya. What's the problem?"

"A fellow from the Wildlife Centre has brought me in a garter snake that's swallowed a sunfish and managed to get punctured by the spines."

"Isn't that the strangest thing…Well, a lot of strange things can happen with snakes. Once when we were at home on the farm one of the men came in hollering about a big python taking down one of our fat-tailed sheep. By the time I got there she was dead, and all we could do was watch him unhinge his jaw and stretch it over her head. It's quite the thing to watch a python slither away with that bulge dragging along the ground."

"I should say," I responded, thinking that I'd appreciate Doris's dread of snakes better if I had a critter like that in my backyard.

"But the story you must be thinking of happened at my uncle's place. The kids saw a big python take the family's pet spaniel. When we got there, the snake was gone. We followed a strange mark on the ground—like one you'd make by dragging a stick

9

along in the dirt. When we caught up to the python, my uncle was upset enough to shoot him. It was after we cut his dog out to bury him that we noticed a pair of horns sticking through the snake's side. Apparently, he had eaten a dik-dik. That's a little antelope not much bigger than a jackrabbit, around seven or eight pounds. I don't know what would have eventually happened to the horns, but they didn't seem to be bothering the snake much. His side didn't look infected or anything."

I thanked John and hung up the phone, determined to snip off the sunfish spines as close to its own vertebrae as possible. I had the side cutters laid out on the table and was wondering how to coerce Doris into holding the snake when the telephone rang.

Doris answered. "Hello, Creston Vet Clinic…Hi, Ben…Yes, yes, he is. Let me see if he can put aside what he's doing to talk with you." She held the phone in the air and raised her eyebrows. "It's Ben Ahlefeld."

I put the snake back in the box and went to the phone. "Hello, Ben."

"Did I catch you at a bad time?" he asked.

"Not really. There always seems to be something brewing around here."

"I have this lame cow we brought in from pasture…" Ben paused and I waited for him to go on. "We wasted the whole morning trying to corner her calf without catching the blame thing. I brought the cow home by herself and unloaded her, but I can't figure out for sure what's wrong. Could you come down and have a look at her? I hate to keep her separated from her calf any longer than necessary." He continued apologetically. "I know it's close to lunch and all, but I have her in the chute if you could come right away."

"Okay, Ben…I'll be right out."

I was on my way out the door when Doris hollered at me. "You do something with the darned snake before you go!"

"He's in a box. What are you worried about?"

"There's a hole in the bottom of that box big enough for him to slither out of. I saw it when you had him out. I don't want anything to do with him!"

To pacify my loyal assistant, I took the box into the ward and tried to fit it in a kennel. As it turned out, the box was too wide. I considered just closing the door and leaving the box in the corner, but Doris was right—there was a small hole where the cardboard was folded together that the snake could theoretically work its way through. If that happened, it could easily squeeze under the door. I considered cutting the side out of the box, wiring it to the bars in a kennel, and letting the poor creature loose inside, but it would take too much time. Ben and his lame cow were waiting for me.

In search of something to put the snake in, I rummaged through a tub of miscellaneous blankets I had purchased from the thrift store to bed the kennels. I was about to give up and start cutting cardboard when I found what I really needed—a pillowcase. I smiled as I stuffed my patient in the bottom and tied the top in a knot.

"I'm off, Doris…and your snake's in a kennel."

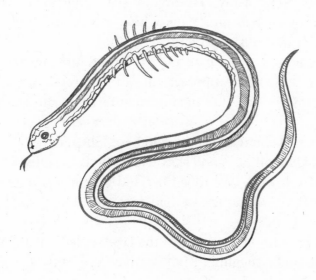

Ben was waiting for me as I drove into his yard on the outskirts of town. Lug whined as I pulled into the drive, thinking that he might get the opportunity to run around. Ben's aged collie rushed at the truck, barking in a shrill tone. Fearing a confrontation, I pushed Lug off the seat and made him sit on the floor.

Ben had done a miraculous job of rejuvenating this farm since I had moved to the valley. When I first met him, he, his wife Sheila, and their two children lived in a squat building with hideous asphalt siding. During the last two years he had built a new house, a new barn, and a set of corrals that was a treat to work in. Since my last visit, he had completed a circular drive to access both the barn and his new home.

"Boy, haven't you been busy," I said.

"Coming right along, isn't it?" he responded proudly. "We moved into our new house last weekend." He motioned to the spacious split-level home on the edge of the knoll. "We've got to finish the calving pens in the barn and build a new hay shed...then we'll be pretty much finished."

"I wish all my clients would get the same building bug," I joked.

Ben smiled sheepishly. "I'm tired of struggling and calving out cows in the wind and rain. This winter it'll be different. It was either this, or quit raisin' critters."

He swung open a new gate and I followed him down a lane to the squeeze. As we approached, an impressive Charolais Hereford–cross rattled the metal structure in an attempt to get free.

"I'm worried about this cow," said Ben. "She raised my best calf last year and was off to a good start with this year's heifer. I noticed her limping last week. We roped her and gave her a shot of long-acting penicillin, thinking she had foot rot...but it didn't do a damn bit of good."

I stood next to the chute until the cow settled down. With all her dancing and struggling, I noticed how diligently she avoided putting weight on her left front foot. She shook her head and rattled the metal cage as I prodded her shoulder and slowly worked my way down the leg.

"She was lyin' right next to the corral when we went out to check her. We got her up and she just held that front foot off the ground. Took us ten minutes to drive her the fifty feet to the pen."

There was no swelling in the cow's shoulder or lower leg and no evidence of puffiness between the claws where the organism that causes foot rot usually gained entrance.

"Let's get her foot up here where I can get a close look at it."

Ben removed the pins that held a bottom panel in place; it fell outward, exposing the cow's lower limbs. I slipped a cotton rope around her pastern, wrapped the rope around the upright of the chute, and hefted. After considerable thrashing and banging, the critter finally quit and stood with her sore foot elevated. I pulled it over and tied it to the bar of the chute. It was immediately evident what was causing the animal's discomfort. A large part of the sole on the outer claw of her foot had separated. I pulled my hoof knife from my back pocket and began paring away dead and infected tissue.

"What would have caused that?" Ben asked.

"It probably started with a sole abscess. We see more of this sort of thing in the dairies when the cows are always standing on concrete."

By the time I had finished removing the dead material from the infected area, a large part of the sole was pink and bleeding without protective horn to cover it.

"How's she ever going to walk on that?" Ben asked mournfully.

"We'll bandage it and make a bit of a shoe for the other claw. Have you got some three-quarter-inch plywood and a table saw handy?"

Ben nodded.

"A piece of cardboard?"

"Some in the shop."

13

He took off in the direction of one of the new buildings while I scraped away a gob of blood and finished paring the foot. Within a minute, Ben had returned. The cow stood shaking as I traced the pattern of her good claw onto the cardboard.

"We need a plywood shoe that size," I said, handing the tracing to Ben.

While he went to cut the shoe, I lowered the cow's leg to give her a rest. After waving her foot in the air and struggling fruitlessly against the head gate, she reluctantly stood still and let the foot rest on the bottom of the squeeze.

"Why did I cut a shoe to fit her inside claw when you did all the cutting on the outside one?" Ben asked.

"We'll wrap this claw to keep it clean and protected, and put the shoe on her good claw. That way, the wound will be clean and up off the ground where there's no pressure on it. Hopefully, by the time the tape wears out and the plywood falls off, her other sole will be healed."

I tore the plastic wrap from a roll of Elastoplast and packed the bottom of the injured foot with gauze soaked in an antibiotic preparation called Furacin. I wrapped the claws in a figure-eight fashion. When we finished and gave the cow her foot, she tentatively put it to the ground. With the good claw elevated almost an inch, the injured one dangled beside it. Satisfied with the result, I handed Ben six huge pills called Spanbolets. Then I manipulated a long metal tube, a Frick speculum, into the cow's mouth and over the base of her tongue.

"Pop one in, Ben." Moving the speculum back and forth, I waited for the cow to swallow the three-inch pill, then gave her the others one at a time. "These pills will roll around in her rumen and slowly wear down over the next six days. They should give her therapeutic levels of sulfas until the foot is healed."

"So I can take her back to her calf?" my client asked hopefully. I nodded.

After we released the cow, Ben showed me through the new

barn. He enthusiastically pointed out where he was going to put calving pens and where there'd be a chute the whole length of the barn to make sorting cattle easier. How I wished all my clients would follow Ben's lead.

The whole time we'd been working, I could hear the shrill bark of Ben's old dog. As annoying as it was, I was more concerned that it was being joined by a deep, angry voice that was obviously Lug's. He was not sitting on the floor where he'd been told to stay.

We were on the way back to my truck when we passed the little asphalt-shingled house that the Ahlefelds had started from.

"It's too bad I don't have more ambition," Ben lamented. "If I wasn't so tied up with all the other building, I'd tear this place apart for fence posts."

"Fence posts?"

"Yeah. It's actually a log house—mostly fir and larch. Sheila tells me it was built as a way station to feed the men working on the old Bedlington-Nelson Railway that used to run between Kootenay Lake and Idaho. It's apparently one of the oldest buildings in the area—built somewhere before the turn of the century."

"Really?" I mused.

"Sheila's mother got tired of living in a log house back in the fifties and talked her husband into covering it. Asphalt siding was all the rage in those days."

I studied the little hip-roofed building with different eyes. If the logs were exposed, it could be kind of cute. My mind started buzzing.

"Do you mind if I pry one of those shingles off to have a look at the logs, Ben?"

"Go ahead. The Creston Fire Department will be here Friday night to burn it down. They want to use it for practice. I'd have left it here, but regional district bylaws won't allow for more than one house on the same property. I had to tell them I'd tear it down before I could get the permit to build my other one."

I worked my hoof tester under one of the asphalt shingles and

15

pried it loose. Beneath it was a flattened log, weathered as black as if it had been burnt. Ripping off one panel of siding after the other, I had soon exposed the logs right to ground level. Although the bottom log had rotted where it had been exposed to moisture, the others looked sound. I rapped the exposed wood repeatedly with my hoof tester and was reassured by the solid thump. With my hoof knife, I scraped at the darkened surface. A fraction of an inch beneath the weathered black, the wood was a deep reddish-blond.

"Ben, would you consider letting me tear this building down? I've heard of people numbering each piece and moving log houses…Maybe I could make something of it."

"So long as you get right at it and clean up the mess when you're done, I can't see it'd make much difference to us," Ben said. "Let me talk to Sheila and I'll call you later. She loves the new house, but she's been a bit down at the thought of her old family home going up in smoke."

I arrived back at the office with my mind in a whirl. Thoughts of my new project soon displaced my anger with Lug. As I scrubbed his slobber off my windows, all I could think about was getting started on my house. I kept trying to picture what it would look like—where on my property I'd put it.

I hadn't given a thought to the snake. Matt would be here any moment, and I was still up in the air about how to treat his research subject. I pulled off my boots and coveralls and headed to the kennel room to retrieve my patient.

I pulled up short. The kennel was empty. In a panic, I searched all the compartments. The cat we had spayed in the morning was huddled in the corner behind her litter box. One of yesterday's dog spays and the neuter were still here. The other dog was missing and her kennel was open.

Just then the door opened and in charged the missing Labrador retriever on the end of a lead. Allan, the kennel boy, was here over lunch hour giving the dogs their midday exercise.

"Where's the snake, Allan?" I asked.

"Snake?" The boy frowned and shrugged his shoulders. "I didn't see no snake."

"I put it in a pillowcase so it couldn't get away and left it in that kennel." I pointed to the cage in front of me.

Allan's face turned ashen. Dropping the leash, he dove for the drier. The machine stopped its thumpety-thump-thumping as he wrenched the door open.

"I didn't know! Really..." he moaned.

Digging madly through the clothes in the chamber, he pulled out blankets, a pair of coveralls, and finally, a pillowcase with a knot tied in it.

I felt sick. I took a deep breath and retrieved the bag from his outstretched hand. I went into the surgery and picked open the knot at the top of the pillowcase. Doris joined me as I dumped the contents onto the surgery table next to the side cutters that I had left laid out and ready. I was prepared for the worst.

The creature landed with a plop. Doris screamed as it raised its head and stuck out its long red tongue. I grabbed the snake a fraction of a second before it could slither over the edge of the table, and breathed a sigh of relief that it had survived the ordeal.

"Look!" Doris exclaimed. "The spines are gone."

I stared in amazement at the sites where the spines had protruded. The only evidence that they had ever existed was a series of small rents in the reptile's skin. The majority of the bulge, which was the sunfish, had already passed farther down the snake's body.

I could see the headlines in the *Canadian Veterinary Journal*: "Garter snake punctured by sunfish spines." I would be quoted as to the non-surgical repair procedure: "Wash on gentle cycle. Place five minutes in the drier."

Attack of *Dermacentor andersoni*

Wiping sweat from my brow with my shirtsleeve, I stood back and surveyed what I'd accomplished. It was after nine and daylight had faded to the point where it was almost impossible to continue working. I'd been at the Ahlefeld farm for three hours. My shoulders were aching from swinging the sledge, but I hated to quit. I so wanted to see what the interior of my new home was going to look like. The log structure that was close to a hundred years old was now mine, and I was full of ideas. Although I'd decided there'd be no partitions in the log portion of the building, the other details, including the exact location to place it on my Lister farm, were sketchy.

I reefed on a two-by-four I had pounded free. With a screech, the rough-sawn timber relinquished its hold on the bottom plate but hung tenaciously from several spikes at the top. Grabbing the claw hammer, I pulled a dangling nail, then yanked back and forth until the upright pulled free. I dragged the two-by-four out the back entrance and stacked it in a pile with the rest of my salvage. I was determined to save as much of this material as possible to reduce the cost of rebuilding.

From the moment Sheila Ahlefeld called to tell me I could have the old house, I had been calculating how I was going to get the job done. My contractor friend, Jack, was almost finished the

19

project he was working on, and we were going to get together sometime this week to check out possible building sites. I was hoping he could give me some practical advice as well as a rough idea of the cost of pouring a foundation.

The previous day, it had been after two in the morning when I quit doodling on my notepad and fell into bed. Although I was still uncertain as to what I did want, I had left a wastebasket full of crumpled pages and ideas that didn't make the cut. I sighed as I looked up at the structure. As it stood, it certainly wouldn't be more than a temporary step on the way to building a house I'd want to live in. With all the partitions removed, I'd be left with eight hundred square feet on the main floor to fit in a living room, a kitchen, and a bathroom. No matter how I drew the plans, I couldn't visualize something I'd be happy with if I didn't design some sort of addition.

I took in the silhouette of the hip-roofed structure against the darkening sky. How could I build onto an antique log home without making it look like a shanty? I thought back to the few log homes I had seen with additions and couldn't remember one that really worked. The only thing that went with logs were other logs, and how in the world could I make new logs resemble these ones? It'd take me forever to flatten, notch, and blend them in with the others.

Like the Ahlefelds, I had to abide by regional district bylaws and could build only one permanent residence on my eighty-acre property. Unless I came up with a floor plan that worked, this place would be destined for a shop or storage facility.

I circled the little house trying to visualize an added wing. After a second lap, I decided it would have to extend out what now was the front door, so it could butt into the existing structure in the form of an L. Trying to continue the present line would make the building look more like a silo than a house. The addition had to do something to minimize the current dumpy appearance. I wandered back into the area that was once the kitchen. I had managed to clear it to the original bathroom wall. I tried to imagine what the place would be like without the dangling wires and cast-iron pipes. My attention wandered toward the ceiling. I'd definitely need different floor joists for the second floor. These were rough-sawn two-by-sixes, supported by the very walls I was tearing out.

Ripping the old lath and plaster from the inside of the kitchen wall had been truly inspirational. When I saw the rich red colour of the logs that had been protected from the weather, I realized the tremendous potential of my new project.

Back at the office Lug was at the door to greet me. His body swayed in harmony with the wag of his tail as he whined and enthusiastically nuzzled my hand. He had obviously forgiven me for leaving him at home. He and Ahelfelds' old collie seemed incapable of coming to a truce, and it was just easier to avoid the hassle.

"Pretty soon, old boy, we'll have a place of our own where you can run."

I checked the answering machine and heaved a sigh of relief when there were no messages. I turned it off and trudged upstairs to the bathroom. As the water ran into the tub, I looked in the mirror. My face was streaked with dirt and my long brown hair was matted with cobwebs and sprinkled with bat droppings. Maybe Doris was right—it might be time to go for a shorter, more professional hairstyle. I stripped off my clothes and experimentally stuck a toe in the water.

I groaned as I slipped into the warm water and felt it caress my aching body. Lifting poodles onto exam tables and sticking my arms up cows' butts left me unprepared for three hours of swinging a twelve-pound sledge—this little house project was going to get me into shape. I sank into the water until all that protruded was my snout.

Trying to stop my jumbled rush of thoughts, I focused on the flow of air as it entered and left my nostrils—the way they had taught me to breathe at the ashram. An image of a quaint log home surrounded by majestic trees drifted into my mind. Forcing my attention back to the ebb and flow of my breath, I tried to become one with the water. I turned the hot water tap with my toes and listened to the popping of the soap bubbles.

The telephone rang a third and fourth time before commanding my attention. With reluctance, I dragged myself from the water and ran dripping to the phone.

"Hello."

"Oh Dave…thank God you're there. This is Doreen Tate calling…I think Trixie has just had a stroke."

"What makes you think that, Doreen?"

"She can't stand up. When I first got home, she staggered when she came to me. I took her to her basket thinking she'd hurt her leg and I'd get you to look at her tomorrow, but when Ken got home she tried to greet him and had to pull herself along with her front legs. She drags the back ones."

"You better bring her right in. I'll be waiting."

I hopped back in the tub and quickly finished washing my hair. While I dried off and threw on clean clothes, my mind was whirling about hind-leg weakness in dogs.

Rushing downstairs, I searched the record cabinet for Trixie's medical chart. I reached the Ts and quickly read through the dozen notations on the card. The little white poodle had been presented for regular vaccinations. On her last visit I had clipped her nails and plucked hair from her ears. The only history of pathology was a mildly inflamed ear that I had treated with a topical preparation called Panolog. There were certainly no clues in her history as to the cause of her present malady.

I stared at the file card as if it held some strangely encoded message. A middle-ear infection could cause Trixie to lose coordination, but the Tates would surely have noticed something coming on.

22

The dog was ten years old; a stroke would not be impossible. If that were the case, I'd expect some localizing signs—a drooping face, lameness affecting one side more than the other, depression. No, it had to be a spinal lesion of some sort—a prolapsed disc or a tumour. But a tumour would have shown a more gradual onset…had to be a prolapsed disc. But Trixie was not an ounce overweight, and Doreen never mentioned pain.

The door opened and my client stepped inside. "Thanks for seeing her, Dave. She has us worried sick." The slight dark-haired woman was in her early forties. The owner of the local Century 21 real estate franchise, Doreen was a going concern. Her husband was a local roofing contractor. "Ken's bringing her now. I just wanted to make sure you were here already."

She stepped aside as a lithe, wiry man rushed in with the dog. I escorted him to the exam table and watched as he carefully deposited her on the stainless steel surface. His weathered, deeply tanned face was grim as he stepped back to allow me access to his pet.

"Has she yelped in pain at any time when you handled her?"

"She hasn't made a peep," Ken replied. "Doreen thought at first her right hind leg was sore…but it looks to me like she's paralyzed."

I knelt beside the table and ran my hands over the poodle's body. She was immaculate, with a big pompom on the end of her tail and a curly little mass of hair on the top of her head. She smelled faintly of perfume, as if she'd been recently groomed.

"When was she last bathed?"

"This Wednesday," Doreen responded. "Why do you ask?"

"Just wanted to rule out some sort of reaction to a pesticide if you had used a flea shampoo recently."

"No, and I've been using the same conditioning shampoo for years. Trixie's never had a problem with fleas."

"Is there any chance she could have gotten into poison? Would she have access to anything rotten—like compost?"

23

"No," Doreen said firmly. "She was in the house all afternoon while I was at work."

"Could she get at any plants?"

"Yeah, but she's never shown any interest in them in the past."

Trixie remained as Ken had positioned her, with her hind legs scrunched slightly under her. There was something about the position that looked abnormal—uncomfortable.

"How're you doing, girl?"

The dog's tail wiggled ever so slightly as I lifted her head and peered into her worried eyes.

I lubricated a thermometer and slid it into her rectum, paying careful attention to the tone of the anal sphincter. It didn't appear to be flaccid, as I would have expected with a spinal paralysis. Running my hand over her back, I massaged along the muscles of her spine to focus on her hind legs. The muscles of her quadriceps were totally without tone, and she made no attempt to move her limbs as I flexed them and squeezed her toes. I removed a needle from the cold sterilization tray and began poking on either side of her flank.

"Her feeling is gone, isn't it?" Doreen watched mournfully as her pet tried to pull herself forward after the most aggressive of my jabs.

I nodded vacantly but found myself wondering. The dog had a very worried expression. Was she not feeling the prick of the needle, or feeling it but not able to do anything about it? She was aware enough to know that something was going on.

I squeezed the poodle's toes deeply one more time. After pro-longed compression she squirmed and struggled with her front legs to pull away from me. I lifted her, extending her back legs behind her. Both limbs were the same length; the manipulation met with no resistance. It definitely wasn't causing her pain. I left her legs behind her in a frog position when I returned her to the table. They remained exactly as I had placed them. I positioned my fingers directly over the spine and applied pressure on the surrounding musculature of Trixie's neck. Watching for a response, I progressed down her spine, manipulating one vertebra at a time until I reached her pelvis.

My patient's mistress watched me intently. "She sure doesn't seem to mind your doing that."

"No, she doesn't."

Doreen fidgeted, glancing first at her husband, then at me. "I'm sorry, but I'm having a nicotine fit—I've got to have a smoke." Digging in her purse for her cigarettes, she retreated to the door with Ken following closely at her heels.

"What's with you, Trixie?" I asked my patient as she gazed sorrowfully in the direction of her retreating family.

What was going on? Although it was clear that the dog couldn't move her hind legs normally, things were not adding up. I had never seen a dog with a prolapsed disc that wasn't in pain. Although a tumour could certainly produce paralysis, it wouldn't have come on this quickly. Trixie was a grade-A, number-one lap-dog. I would bet that she was rarely out of the Tates' sight at home. I was sure Doreen or Ken would have noticed something before now if it was coming on slowly.

I wracked my brain. What kind of toxins could cause this sort of reaction? I really didn't know enough about houseplants. I seemed to recall that the delphinium was toxic, but I had never actually heard of anyone diagnosing a case of it as a poison.

I carried the dog to the middle of the room and put her down. "Come on, girl…Come here!"

Trixie looked uncertainly toward the exit.

"That's a girl…go find Mom."

Just then the door opened and the Tates returned from their smoke break. Trixie pivoted. Struggling up on her front legs, she dragged her back end toward her owners for a couple of seconds before crumpling in a heap.

"That's okay, girl." I picked up the frantic dog and returned her to the exam table. "You're sure she couldn't have gotten into something rotten, Doreen? A mild case of botulism can look similar to this."

Doreen turned to her husband. "Ken, you went out with her this morning. Could she have found something then? I'm sure she didn't get anything from the house…She was in the living room the whole time we were away."

Ken shook his head adamantly. I got the feeling he thought I was wasting precious time. "Would an X-ray help?"

"If I was concerned about a spinal lesion, it certainly would. We may have to consider several options if I strike out here. I'd still like to rule out a few more things."

I rolled Trixie over on her side and began a systematic examination of her underbelly.

Doreen glanced uncertainly at Ken, then asked, "What are you looking for?"

"It's pretty late in the year, but we have to rule out a tick. Most tick infestations in our area happen in the early spring. I haven't seen one past April before."

"A wood tick? So you don't think she's had a stroke?" Ken asked.

"No, I don't. She's too bright." I continued my search.

"Is that the same tick that causes Rocky Mountain spotted fever?" he asked.

"Same critter, but a very different disease. Ticks can be carriers of a number of infectious diseases in both humans and animals, but when we see paralysis, it's the result of a toxin, not an infection." I turned to Doreen. "It should be comparatively easy to find a varmint on her—she's got a nice short coat. Ticks almost always climb as far up as they can go before they attach. That usually means the groin, the top of the back, or the head."

Doreen began running her hands over Trixie's back.

"When I was in grade school in Casino, one of my friends ended up with a strange progressive paralysis. She was in the Trail hospital for days and getting worse by the moment when one of the nurses found a tick while she was washing her hair."

"I've never heard of ticks causing paralysis," Ken said brusquely.

"They don't talk much about this condition at college either because it's so regional, but I've seen a couple of cases since I've been here."

I rolled the dog onto her tummy and ran my fingers over her torso. It was when I got to the top of her head that I felt it—a lump at the base of her ear that was hidden by the long tassels of her topknot. I smiled the moment I parted her locks and spotted the crusty black concretion of critter droppings.

"Look at this." The Tates bent close to stare at the grey-brown blood-filled wood tick that was a quarter of an inch in diameter. I parted the hair further and worked my way down to the level of Trixie's skin. "See where the little sucker is attached?"

"Oh, gross!" Doreen groaned. "Poor Trixie." She knelt beside her pet and gently stroked her muzzle.

"I'll be darned," Ken drawled. "I thought you were spinning your wheels."

I grabbed a pair of forceps and applied them to the base of the tick.

"Is that an old wives' tale that you can burn their butt with a hot needle?" Doreen asked.

"I've tried it before but never had much success in getting them to let go." I partially closed the jaws beneath the creature and gently teased it free from its mooring. Holding it up, I studied it intently to make sure the head was still intact. "Bet you didn't know that ticks are members of the spider family. They're arachnids."

"Really? They don't look anything like spiders."

"They don't, but somehow they seem about as cuddly. See the big hunk of skin that pulled away with it?"

They moved in for a better view. Doreen screwed up her face and looked away. "Oh, Trixie, you poor girl."

"Look at the legs moving," Ken prompted.

"Oh, gross!" Doreen moaned again.

I grabbed a swab, doused it in alcohol, and scrubbed away at the raw, inflamed area on the poodle's head where the tick had attached itself. Next, I shaved some hair from the surrounding area.

"What happens to poor Trixie now?" Doreen was still staring at the swollen blob I had left on the table.

"If she's like every other case I've seen, she'll be right back to normal by this time tomorrow."

"Oh, I hope you're right!" Doreen beamed. "I had visions of her not coming home from here."

I took the tick into the lab and placed its engorged body upside down on a microscope slide.

"Come have a look."

Doreen peeked hesitantly through the eyepiece. "Oh my God, look at those legs going, and those ugly pincers. Is that its mouth? And is that white stuff part of Trixie's skin?"

"Yes, that's how Trixie got in trouble. The tick cut her skin with its lancets, then secreted saliva to keep her blood from clotting. Trixie absorbed some of that into her bloodstream, and the toxin caused her to lose control over her muscles. It would do the same thing to a horse or a cow."

"I've never heard of that," Doreen said. "Is it common?"

"Common, no, but it happens." I edged her away from the place at the microscope, grabbed the tick with the forceps, and flipped it over. "You talked about how ugly it was. Just come and see this." I flipped the microscope head to a higher power and moved the carriage up and down until the protective structure on the tick's back was in perfect focus.

"What is that? I've never seen anything like it," Doreen marvelled. "Look at the intricacy of those patterns...They're absolutely gorgeous."

"Isn't it amazing that a varmint perceived as so hideous can be so beautiful? That shield on her back identifies her as *Dermacentor andersoni*. This species is only found in a narrow strip through the Rocky Mountains—from Fernie to Grand Forks in our area. They show up in northern Idaho and Washington, too."

"You called it a *she*," Doreen noted with a hint of irritation. "How do you know it's not a *he*?"

"Only the females cause paralysis. I guess because they need the blood to be able to make eggs."

After a long session of staring through the microscope at Trixie's tormentor, we moved to the office where the Tates settled their account. They headed home, ecstatic that their beloved pet would soon be back to normal.

I returned to the lab and seated myself at the microscope. The distended creature was trying desperately to move her body with legs that could barely reach the slide.

I smiled ruefully. Right at the moment, she and I had a lot in common. We had both taken on more than we seemed capable of digesting.

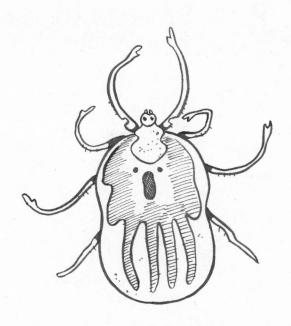

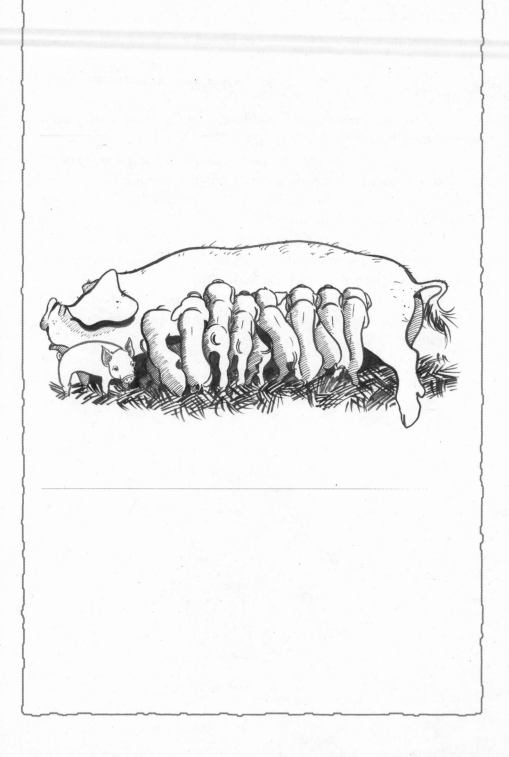

Old Bats

"Don't forget you have a meeting tonight with Jack!"

Doris pulled the door closed behind her. Out of desperation, I continued to stare through the eyepiece of the microscope. This was the second fecal flotation I had checked from Hank today—there just had to be something out of the ordinary.

Jim Forner had left only a few minutes before Doris. The appointment with him had been one of the most strained ten minutes of my veterinary career. How do you explain to a good client that you've exhausted all the diagnostic options at your disposal and are still unable to find a single thing wrong with his pet? Most clients would be delighted to know their animal had been found sound and healthy. But they didn't have to go home to a house that reeked from a farting dog and try to motivate him to get out of his basket and go for a walk with the kids.

What was I overlooking? Even after spending a half-hour on the phone with the pathologist who had interpreted the blood results, I was no wiser. He insisted that every parameter we had examined was well within normal range. I was still tempted to try the dog on thyroid medication. Maybe Hank was one of those rare cases that wasn't able to convert T4 hormone, the circulating form, into T3 hormone, the active form.

But if that were the case, how could I explain the two-week

period when the dog magically got better? I couldn't make any sense of that. Jim swore that for the entire time they camped at Kootenay Lake, Hank had been a different dog. We had put him on a special digestive diet two days before they left, and Jim was certain we'd finally found the key. But the day after they returned home, Hank was right back to his pathetic norm. Could there be something in the environment of the Forner home that was affecting the dog adversely?

I pulled the slide from the microscope stage and fired it into the wastebasket. There sure as hell were no parasites. I sighed deeply and shifted in my chair. Lug stirred from the floor at my feet and placed his muzzle in my lap.

"You're ready to get out of here, aren't you, fellow?"

He wagged in anticipation.

"You can come today."

For the last few weeks, he couldn't understand why I was forcing him to stay home while I worked on the house. I was sure he thought I was punishing him. Last night he hadn't even been at the door to greet me on my return.

He just couldn't seem to behave himself at the Ahlefelds'. I had tried repeatedly to take him to the house as I worked, but on every occasion the same thing happened. Ben's old collie would begin circling the truck, wagging his tail and barking in his shrill voice, and Lug would prance up and down and dig at my windows to get at him. I couldn't handle the constant din, and I certainly didn't appreciate getting into my new truck to find slobber over everything and fresh scratches on my doors.

He slowly wagged his tail and stared up in expectation. He could sense the day was over and was hoping for a trip to the farm.

"Okay! Today you can come."

He twirled excitedly and galloped toward the door. At the front counter, I resignedly scratched a notation of the negative fecal on the dog's card and threw it into the to-file basket—one more thing that wasn't wrong with Hank.

I felt unexpectedly lighthearted as I approached the rock cut near the Ahlefeld property. Father had joined me three weeks ago in the dismantling of the old house. He had been living on Kootenay Lake in the little community of Riondel since his retirement and, thankfully, he was getting bored with fishing. Last night we had dislodged and lowered the last of the rafters. In anticipation of actually moving the logs, I had booked an appointment with Scott's crane for one o'clock on Saturday. That meant we had two days to mark all the logs and finish removing the remainder of the flooring and joists from the second floor.

I had gotten an early call to treat a milk fever at Tsolum Farms and by the time I returned to my apartment at eight, Father had already left for the job. I couldn't see him as I pulled up to the house. I parked next to the stack of salvaged lumber, held Lug in the truck, and closed the door. "Lie down on the floor, Lug!" I tried to sound stern. "Behave yourself! I don't want to hear a peep out of you."

Although the logs looked like little more than a stack of tinker toys from a distance, they still seemed formidable when I was standing beside them. There was a loud screech as spikes relinquished their hold on the larch plate that had once been part of the bathroom wall, and a loud crash as a stud hit the floor. I stepped gingerly through the back door.

"Well, how's it going?"

Father groaned and stripped off the blue bandana that covered his mouth and nose. "I'm finally free of most of the bat shit." He pushed his green and white John Deere cap to the back of his balding forehead and smiled grimly. "Looking pretty good, isn't it?"

Good was not exactly the word most people would use to describe an entanglement of wires and cast-iron pipes amid a jumble of rough-sawn two-by-fours, but yeah, it did look good. Dad had gotten a lot done today. He had finished stripping the flooring from the second level and was working on the remainder of the supporting uprights.

I scuffed at the debris on the floor and shook my head in amazement. Bat droppings were everywhere. When we'd finished pulling down the ceiling of the upper floor, we had shovelled piles of the revolting stuff over the side. Now there was even more. The evening we finished stripping the shingles from the roof and began removing the boards, the poor creatures had swooped around us overhead, distraught that we were destroying the home that had served their ancestors for generations. Their feces covered everything, and no matter what you looked at—two-by-fours, logs, wires, pipes—turds clung to them all. Every crack in every log was filled with bat dung.

"I wonder if we'll ever get rid of that horrible smell?" I asked, tasting the acrid flavour at the back of my throat with each breath I drew.

Pop threw his crowbar in the corner and shook his head. "That's sure something else, ain't it?" He wrinkled his shiny brow and wiped his face with the bandana. "I've been coughing up that black crap all day. There doesn't seem to be an end to it—every wall's full of it."

"Well, let's go for supper…Jack'll be heading to the farm around seven, and I'm anxious to see what he thinks of that site on the hill."

Over the last couple of weeks, I had solidified a lot of details about the design of the house. Closing my eyes, I'd walk from one room to the next, take the stairs to the upper and lower levels, and open and close doors. Poor Father had been dumbfounded when I explained to him that the wing on the house would be built of stone.

"Stone?" he had asked in his usual gruff tone. "What in hell do you know about building with stone?"

When I produced a book on how to create a stone house using a technique called slipforming, he stared at the cover for an uncomfortable moment and set it aside without saying a word.

34

"I want to build it over here on the edge of the gully."

Jack followed me from the grassy clearing where we had parked under a magnificent pine tree to the edge of a tree-covered slope that tapered to the stream below.

"I was thinking that if I built on the slope, then a guy could walk out of the basement rooms onto the ground floor. You've seen how tall and awkward the house is now. I think adding a wing will take away from that a bit...and if I go down, I can increase the square footage by a third and get room for a couple more bedrooms."

"You'll be moving a lot of dirt," Jack mused, drawing on his cigarette.

"Yeah, I guess I will."

"What are you planning to do with the area down there?"

"I'm not sure I understand."

"Well, if we dig out all this area..." Jack motioned by lifting his arms in the direction of the creek. "...you'll need something to keep the dirt back—a retaining wall or something."

I closed my eyes, trying to picture what he was talking about. I imagined walking through the living room and kitchen and down the stairs. When I opened the door from the basement and went outside, I found myself in a courtyard with a fountain trickling water down a bed of rocks to the stream below.

"That's where the courtyard'll be...and the entrance to the root cellar." I opened my eyes.

"The courtyard?" Father asked, staring at Jack in bewilderment. "What the hell's a courtyard?"

"Sort of a secluded little area with a fountain and flowers and stuff...where you can get away from things," I stammered. "I'll make the retaining walls out of stone, too."

"Stone?" Jack looked at me with a blank expression.

"Yeah, there's nothing else that goes with logs other than stone."

Jack glanced at Father, then turned to me. "Have you any idea how hard it is to get someone to do that kind of stonework around here? There are only two guys and they're both very busy and very expensive."

Father smiled his agreement, happy to hear someone talking sense to me.

"I'll do it myself, using a slipform."

"A slipform?" Jack looked again at Father.

Father shrugged and shook his head. There was no need to ask for an explanation of what he was thinking.

"Yeah, it's a technique I read about where you raise a wall two or three feet at a time. Using a ten-inch form, you place rocks one on top of another and pour concrete behind them. When the concrete starts to set up a bit, you strip the outside form and chip away the area between the rocks while the cement's still green."

"What do you chip it with?"

"The book said a welding hammer," I answered timidly.

The look that Jack and Father exchanged this time said it all. Father appeared ready to voice his opinion, but before either could comment further, I pulled out my notepad and showed them the sketch of my floor plan.

"I'd like it to be facing this way," I said, motioning with my arms. "And I want the front door to open somewhere around these trees." I pointed to a pair of sheltering fir trees behind us.

"So your log house is 24 by 36." Jack lit another cigarette and pointed to the rectangular box representing the log portion of the house. "That means we'll need a bearing wall in the middle of your basement to carry the weight of the logs. I haven't got a clue how big a footing we'll need to carry that much weight, but the building inspector should be able to tell me."

He doodled around the outside of my sketch with his pencil. "If you're talking a ten-inch concrete wall here..." He indicated the outline of the addition. "...we'd need an even heavier footing here." He saw the notation I had made at an outside wall of the log house. "And what's this?"

"That's the fireplace. I want a big stone fireplace to offset the logs and tie in with the outside of the house."

"And here?" He pointed to the notation on the second floor.

"That's a fireplace, too."

"In the bedroom?" Father's voice was incredulous.

"Yup."

Jack smiled at Dad. "We're talking a real bachelor's pad here."

"I'm not sure I'll live long enough to see it finished," Father grumbled.

Jack produced some one-by-four stakes and a ball of baler twine from the back of his truck, and we were soon jockeying back and forth on the hillside trying to find the least disruptive location for the house. Jack and Father argued the value of building in the open where there was no danger of trees blowing down and no needles to litter the eavestroughs, but I would hear none of it. In my mind's eye, the structure was surrounded and protected by trees. My entire focus was to save as many of them as possible.

It was getting dark by the time we had things laid out. We had repositioned the stakes a dozen times trying to save a mature larch, but finally I admitted that it had to go. I walked within the confines of the stakes, trying to visualize the view from each window. It was hard to believe that within a week's time we would no longer be focusing on tearing down, but on building. I couldn't imagine it.

When I went back to the truck, Father and Jack were still arguing about building the walls with stone as I was proposing.

"It'll look pretty spiffy, Marsh. Dave's got a point when he argues it's hard to add onto a log house and make it blend in." Jack waved the book I had given him in the air. "And with all that concrete and steel it sure won't be going anywhere."

Dad shook his head emphatically. "Yeah, but it seems to me the kid needs to simplify things—all this extra stuff is just complicating the issue. He doesn't have time to scratch his arse now with all the running around he does with work, and I know how hard it is to build your own house when you can't afford to do it properly. I was still adding on to my place in Casino when we sold it."

I had heard enough. "I'm going over to check the cows!" I headed down the slope toward the creek with Lug close on my heels.

I wasn't interested in listening to Dad's ideas of what I was doing wrong. Although he was handy at a lot of things, he was more concerned with function than appearance. So long as a roof kept the rain out, he could care less what it looked like. He had already been bugging me about putting tin on my roof like he had on his. He argued that the snow always slid off so you didn't have to worry about it. In spite of his insistence, there was no way there'd be anything other than cedar shakes on my place.

As we walked through the trees in search of the cattle, a squirrel bolted across our path. Lug took after it but it scampered up a big bull pine before he could get anywhere near it. Chattering profusely, the squirrel glared down at us. Lug dismissed it, then charged on toward the corrals.

Several cows were standing at the feed trough cleaning up the remaining stocks from the hay I had fed the night before. The calves were lying together under the canopy of an old poplar at the edge of the draw. I did a quick head count before I turned toward the hay shed. It was the end of July and it hadn't rained in more than a month; the pasture was struggling to keep up and I was forced to supplement the herd's intake. I had broken a couple of bales into the trough and was kicking the hay flakes to spread them out when I was interrupted.

"Perri! Perri...Can you take a look at a gilt for me?"

There was my nemesis and neighbour, Verna Levett, standing next to her milk house with her hands on her hips. We hadn't had an altercation in six months, but the last time she'd spoken to me was when she held Lug hostage after she caught him breeding her German shepherd bitch. Although at the time she had threatened a paternity suit, I had never heard any more about it.

"Sure, Verna…what seems to be her problem?"

"She farrowed last night about four in the bloody morning…had nine babies without a bit of problem. I got 'em all up and on the nipple before I went to bed. The piglets weren't looking too hot this morning. Now her udder's harder than a friggin' rock and the piglets aren't getting a bloody thing out of her."

"Let me get my truck and I'll be over in a few minutes."

Jack was pulling onto the highway when I got back. Father was sitting in my truck with his arm out the open window, thumbing idly through the book on slipforming.

"Still think it's a waste of time?" I asked.

He tossed the book on the dash. "Just think you're biting off a pretty big wad is all."

I opened the driver's door and Lug hopped onto the seat between us.

"We have to stop at Verna's on the way home," I said uneasily.

"Verna! What do you want with that old bat? Hasn't she caused you enough grief already?"

"She's got problems with a young sow that's farrowed, and she actually asked for help."

"That doesn't sound like her," Father muttered dryly.

"If she's ready to bury the hatchet in the backyard rather than in my skull, I think I'll take the offer."

"Humph," was his only reply.

Verna was waiting at the barn door when I pulled up beside the milk house. She watched in silence as Father and I approached.

"She's in here," she said tersely.

The barn was uncomfortably warm and the air was heavy with the smell of hogs. Stepping around a wheelbarrow filled with soiled straw and manure, I followed Verna down a long aisle to a farrowing crate about a third of the way down the barn. Lying on the concrete floor enclosed within the metal apparatus was the gilt.

"Couldn't get her to eat a bloody thing," Verna said dejectedly. "And those poor little buggers haven't sucked all afternoon." She pointed to a mound of dejected-looking piglets that lay huddled beneath a heat lamp in the corner.

I knelt next to the creature to examine her. She grunted softly as my hand roved across the coarse hairs of her side to the velvety skin of her udder. Rubbing a circular pattern on her belly, I shifted from one nipple to the next in search of milk. I palpated the last two glands deeply and squeezed out a few drops of pearly white milk.

"The bitch is dry as a bone," Verna observed. "Them poor little buggers have given up on 'er."

Fishing out a thermometer, I spat on it and slowly rotated it into the mother's rectum. "Have you farrowed any of her sisters yet?" I asked.

"I have a couple more coming soon, but she was the first." Verna gave me a worried look. "Why do you ask?"

"Some bloodlines can be a bit more high-strung and have a problem letting down their milk."

I lifted the sow's upper leg, gently palpated her rear end, and removed the thermometer. There was no evidence of a vaginal discharge, and I didn't notice any unusual odour. "Have you seen any discharge since she pigged?"

Verna shook her head.

I glanced at the thermometer: 39.8.

"What's it say?"

"It's up a bit but nothing to get upset about."

"Well, what the hell's going on with her then?"

"There's a nebulous condition referred to as mastitis metritis agalactia syndrome where the sow has a mild fever and something going on with both the udder and the uterus. We'll get her started on a product called Azimycin that acts as an antibiotic and an anti-inflammatory. We'll also give her a hormone called oxytocin to see if she'll let her milk down."

Verna watched me skeptically as I retreated down the aisle. I loaded my syringes at the truck and returned to the barn. Father and Verna were talking amicably about the price of hogs and the amount of work it took to run an operation this size.

"I'm getting too old for this bullshit!" Verna sounded tired. "It's not bad when everything goes good, but when you stay up all bloody night to make sure you don't lose any babies and then something like this happens, you ask yourself why you bothered."

I shuffled to the far end of the farrowing crate and drove a needle into the gilt's hind leg. Verna grumbled on as I slowly injected the milky-looking solution.

"I've got half a mind to selling this place when the price of weaner pigs is high. There's got to be some fool out there who thinks he can make his fortune."

"See if you can get those guys to suck now, Verna." I knelt beside the young mother and rubbed vigorously at her ear with an alcohol swab.

"What the hell for?" my neighbour grouched.

Driving a 25-gauge needle into the ear vein, I pulled back on the plunger and drew a stream of blood into the clear solution. After injecting the hormone, I compressed the vein with my thumb and pulled out the needle. Almost immediately the sow grunted softly as if talking to her piglets. I grabbed a nipple and sprayed a stream of milk across Verna's boot.

"Well, I'll be damned!" she said, stooping down to scoop up the piglets.

Within a few minutes, the gilt's udder was covered with a swarming mass of pink bodies. Little jaws were pumping madly at her teats and tiny hooves were kneading in every direction. The air was filled with slurping sounds as we walked down the aisle to the door. Verna was all smiles.

I decided to push my luck. "How did you make out with Lug's puppies?"

"Not bad." The woman grinned slyly. "She had ten and I sold 'em for seventy-five bucks apiece...Did better with them than I do with a litter of piglets."

Sweetums

Doris leaned backward to avoid a cloud of erupting steam and gingerly opened the autoclave door. She rattled the stainless steel tray free of the chamber and bustled toward the surgery with a burden of linen-wrapped packages.

"Looks like I'm going to get to the bowling alley on time for a change. Good thing, too. The girls are giving me a hard time about always being late."

I sat at the counter and closed my eyes, trying to visualize what I had done at Hansons during their herd health session last week.

"Have you caught up on those bills yet?" Doris nagged. "Marg's about ready to skin the pair of us. It's the end of the month. You know how she is about getting the statements out on time."

Doris paused in front of me long enough to make eye contact. "Dave, how's she supposed to do that when she has to pry out of you at the end of the month what you did on calls at the beginning? You know how upset she can get." She raised her voice to be certain I was listening. "This office is just too small to be around when you get her worked up!"

I squirmed uncomfortably as she glared at me, struggling to remember how many bottles of penicillin I had left with Morris Hanson. Although I was trying not to think about it, I was all too familiar with Marg's behaviour when things didn't go according to her liking. The fact that her once red hair was now snow-white seemed to have done little to quell the high-spirited fires that burned within the woman. Only last week, she had tuned me up royally. As was her habit when the office was busy, she had turned her hearing aids off to avoid the constant din of barking dogs, yowling cats, and the ringing of the telephone. I had been in the lab peering into the microscope to read some fecal samples when she asked me about an order I had placed with a supply company called Clark Cody. I answered her, so I was surprised when the big black ledger book she laboured over began thumping her desk. Although I was intent on studying a slide, I was subliminally aware that she was communicating with me. I mumbled a further reply into my armpit. It was when the doors of the filing cabinet started banging ferociously that I abandoned my search for tapeworm eggs and headed for her desk. I got there in time to duck the ledger book that flew across the room. My misguided attempts to pacify my bookkeeper fell on non-functioning hearing aids as she threw on her coat and stomped out the door.

I shivered at the memory and went back to the Hanson bill. Certain that I had used two bottles of Intracin and treated a cow with cystic ovaries, I hurriedly scratched down the medications, totalled the bill, and grabbed another from the top of the pile.

"Well…wish me luck," Doris said as she headed for the door. "I'm feeling hot tonight."

The telephone rang. Adjusting her silk scarf, Doris rolled her eyes. "I sometimes think there's a conspiracy…that someone's watching us from across the street." She retraced her steps to the phone. "Hello. Creston Veterinary Clinic." I watched her face and sighed when she finally spoke. "Is he bleeding badly? I see…I see." She paused. My heart sank when I realized we wouldn't be finishing any time soon. "It certainly sounds like something that needs to be looked after right away." She hung up the phone and headed for the back room, peeling her jacket off as she went. "Dora's going to kill me."

"What's coming in? Maybe you can give Margaret Berg a call and see if she can come in a few minutes early. She was going to be here at six anyway to help Marg with the bills. I hate to see you get in trouble with your teammates."

Giving me a smug little smile, Doris picked up the phone. Margaret apparently agreed the moment she was asked to come in, and Doris quickly threw on her jacket and headed out again. The door was just closing when she hollered over her shoulder. "Oh, by the way, Margaret said for you not to be eating peanut butter sandwiches and ruining your appetite! She's got supper brewing in the Crock-Pot."

I smiled as I got back to my bills. Margaret was not only competent with animals; she was also a great cook, and one of her wholesome creations would be a pleasant alternative to my usual fare.

Margaret lived on a small farm in West Creston next to the Wildlife Interpretation Centre. Her job with me at the clinic helped her support a menagerie of critters including a Jersey cow, a fat black Lab, several broken-down old horses, a flock of chickens, a herd of rabbits, and a multitude of feral cats.

I was halfway through the stack of bills on the counter when the front door opened and a middle-aged couple entered. A tall blonde woman clutching a blanket-enshrouded bundle to her breast was followed by a jovial-looking fellow I took to be her husband. Removing his cap, he exposed a shining pate surrounded by a fringe of grey-brown hair.

As his wife nestled on a bench in the waiting room and watched over the swaddled treasure in her arms, the man stepped forward to introduce himself. "I'm Drake…This is my wife, Orma. We arrived here last night from Alberta." He shook his head in a disgruntled fashion. "It seems that my brother's dog took exception to our little pet."

Orma peeled back the blanket, presenting me with a glimpse of my patient. "This is Sweetums," she said reverently. Drake cringed as she divulged the pet's name; he feigned interest in the fox-and-hound painting on the opposite wall of the office. "He's so scared right now," Orma offered. "He's usually good at travelling and not much upsets him, but no one's ever hurt him like this before."

Looking up at me from the recesses of the blanket was a little brown bunny with stubby ears. Orma stroked the creature gently on the brow.

"Is it normal for him to be breathing so fast?" she asked mournfully. "He squealed terribly when the dog got him. I hope he's going to be all right. I've had him since he was a baby…bottle-fed him until he was able to eat solid food. He's almost seven now." Orma sighed and glanced worriedly at her husband. "He's the best pet we've ever had."

I checked the bloody area at the base of the rabbit's neck and gently lifted a flap of skin to expose bare flesh to the middle of his back.

"Oh my," Orma moaned. "It's worse than I thought. We should have been more careful. We let Sweetums out on the bed and didn't see Mike's Jack Russell until it was too late. Before we knew what was happening, he had Sweetums in his mouth. If Drake hadn't grabbed the dog when he did, it would have been all over."

Her husband took a deep breath and gave me a stern look. "Who'd ever believe anyone could get so attached to a rabbit? Orma will hardly leave the house without him."

Kneeling beside the distraught woman, I carefully rolled back the animal's lip. Although I had raised rabbits as a youngster myself, my sessions of handling rats during lab sessions at vet college had given me a very healthy respect for the ability of four long incisor teeth to draw blood from an exposed tender fingertip. Sweetums' sides continued to pump like a bellows as I cautiously examined his gums. The membranes were pale with a blue-white hue.

"He appears to be in shock," I said. "Has he lost much blood?"

Orma watched her husband while she answered. "Only what's on the blanket here…It seemed to quit bleeding quite quickly, didn't it, Drake?"

He nodded at me as I retreated to the surgery. I hurriedly jammed the sabre-tip of an administration set into the reception port of a bag of intravenous fluids and hung it on the stand.

"Could you bring Sweetums in here, please, Orma."

By the time she had settled the bunny on the surgery table, I had soaked a gauze in alcohol and was stripping back the cellophane from a 26-gauge needle.

"We're going to give him intravenous fluids to treat his shock before we try and do anything with his wounds. Could you hold your finger here, Drake?" I indicated the base of the rabbit's ear.

I scrubbed vigorously back and forth over the vein that ran parallel to the ear margin. A tiny blue ribbon manifested under my persistence. Orma looked away and wrinkled her nose at the strong smell of the alcohol.

I connected the intravenous apparatus to the end of the long flexible tube and waited until the fluids pushed the air through the canal and began dripping from the tip of the catheter. Folding the ear down slightly, I drove the fine stiletto through the skin and manipulated it down the vein for the full length of the needle. I turned on the valve and watched with satisfaction as the fluids dripped through the chamber, then grabbed a roll of tape and secured the wings of the butterfly catheter to the rabbit's ear. I had just finished when I heard Margaret enter.

"Do you need me in there right away, Dave?"

I rushed to meet my assistant, determined to prepare her for our unusual patient. As good as she had become at her job, I was still leery of her expressing her views freely with my clients. She was a rough-and-tumble farm girl first and was forever dropping bombs about people spending too much money on disposable pets. A few days earlier, while a woman was writing a cheque for several hundred dollars for the repair of a diaphragmatic hernia in her six-month-old kitten, Margaret declared it was a shame to spend so much money fixing up little Charlie when there were so many notices on our bulletin board for kittens that people were giving away.

Margaret bustled past me holding a Crock-Pot in her great padded oven mitts. "I had this stew on the go at home…Marg Rogers was going to stop over and join me for a bite to eat before we worked on the bills. I called her and told her to meet me here instead…We can all eat together when we get done."

Before I could explain anything, she plugged the pot into the wall receptacle and headed back out the door. "Just let me get everything ready," she said.

In a minute she returned with a big tray covered with tea towels. My stomach rumbled as the back room filled with the smell of stew and fresh-from-the-oven baking powder biscuits. I waited until she had everything settled to her liking, knowing full well she wouldn't pay me any heed until she was ready to listen.

"Margaret, you have to be very careful what you say when you're dealing with these clients. Our patient is their pet rabbit…I know you raise rabbits for slaughter, but I don't want you to even think of telling them you'll give them a new one."

She squirmed under my continuing stare.

"I know what you think about cats, and I know that, to you, rabbits are food, but these people love their bunny dearly and they want me to fix him."

"But, Dave, I've got dozens! I butchered ten this afternoon. Their carcasses are still soaking in cold water…" Her voice trailed off as I grabbed her forearm and continued to stare her down.

"These people have a bunny for a pet! He's our patient and we're going to do our damnedest to make sure he's still around when we're finished with him. I don't want to hear any comments about how you could easily replace him."

"Well…it just seems so unnecessary when I've got so many at home."

"None of them are Sweetums. Margaret…please…do this for me."

I rushed back to the surgery. Fluids were still drip, drip, dripping through the chamber, and the little guy was breathing noticeably slower.

"He's shivering terribly," Orma observed. "Is that bad?"

I smiled reassuringly. "No, that's great. When an animal goes into shock, its circulation cuts back to everything but the core of its body. When we give fluids, more blood flows to the peripheral tissues, and the body starts trying to return to normal. Shivering is a mechanism for generating heat."

"Oh, I'm glad I asked," she said. "I thought it might be something worse."

I knelt beside the surgery table to check Sweetums' gums. They were looking pink. "His circulation's already improving," I told her cheerfully.

Margaret carried the stool I used for surgery to my client. "You have a seat and relax," she said sweetly.

She went about her duties in silence, getting things ready for surgery while we waited for the fluids to work their magic. I returned to my bills, determined to get them finished before Marg Rogers arrived.

"How in the world did you end up with a rabbit for a house pet?" came the question I was dreading.

I cleared my throat and shot my assistant an accusatory look.

"Drake was working outside with the front-end loader and unearthed his nest," said Orma, launching into the story she'd probably related a hundred times before. "He was a week or so old and was starting to get some fuzz. He was the only one alive from the whole litter…We certainly never expected to keep him as a pet initially. We kept bottle feeding him to see if we could save him, and then we got hooked. Once he started eating on his own he was so cute." She glanced at the man of the house before she went on. "He had such a personality he won us both over."

Drake wilted when Margaret looked in his direction. "I guess it's just different for me," she muttered, doggedly avoiding my glare. "You see, I'm a farm girl and raise rabbits myself."

"I am, too," Orma replied enthusiastically. "We farm three sections."

I got up from my seat and retreated to the lab. "Margaret, can you give me a hand with this fecal?" I called. My tone left little doubt that I wanted their conversation to come to an abrupt end.

"Do you have a sample you want me to prepare?" she asked, sheepishly poking her head around the corner.

"No...I just wanted to get you out of there before you offered to knock the lady's bunny on the head and give her a new one."

"But, Dave, I—"

"I know, Margaret...I know. You have three litters of the cutest bunnies you've ever seen at home. But remember, none of them are Sweetums!"

Margaret opened her mouth to reply but changed her mind as I raised my eyebrows and towered over her with my hands on my hips. She nodded, then retreated to the front desk where she began addressing envelopes for mailing.

Sweetums' colour improved remarkably over the next hour, and his breathing slowed to almost normal. With Orma still hovering at my elbow, I adjusted the oxygen and nitrous oxide flow on the anesthetic machine and slipped a mask over the rabbit's nose. He squirmed slightly as I turned the dial to increase the flow of halothane. After holding his breath for a short while, my lagomorph patient began breathing rhythmically. Within a few minutes, he sagged onto his side and I had Margaret take over my position. Orma pushed her chair back to get out of the way and watch the proceedings from a distance. Her husband moved to her side and took her hand.

I lathered my hands at the sink, then examined the wound. Although the skin over the middle third of the rabbit's back had been separated from the muscle as efficiently as if he'd been skinned with a knife, there was no evidence of damage to the underlying tissue. I poked and prodded, making sure there was no injury to the skeletal structure.

"Hold this up here for me, will you, Margaret?" I lifted the skin flap by grasping the hair along the margin of the wound. "Time to put Sweetums back together."

I picked as much hair from the wound as I could see, then soaped the wound margins with surgical scrub and shaved them clean with a razor blade. Once I had bared an inch of skin, I fired up the clippers. The bunny's soft fluffy brown hair formed a pile on the table.

"I wonder what colour his hair will come back in," Drake mused. "He turns snow-white in the winter, you know, but if we keep the house too warm, he starts turning brown."

"That's interesting," I replied. "I wouldn't have thought of that, but he is a wild rabbit and would turn white in the winter. A similar thing can happen with Siamese cats. If you shave their hair or cover a body part with a bandage, the hair often comes in darker. It apparently has something to do with the temperature of the skin." I brushed away a few tufts of hair from the edge of the wound and shut off the clippers. "Could you give him a good scrub, please, Margaret."

She filled her bowl with water and began scrubbing as if she were working on a prize show animal. I was thanking the Lord she didn't mention she had already yanked the skin from a dozen other bunnies that were every bit as sweet as our patient.

Within forty-five minutes, Sweetums was back in his mother's arms, swaddled in blankets. A series of stitches adorned the wound edges and plastic tubes poked through the skin at various intervals for drainage. I advised Drake and Orma that they were welcome to stay with Sweetums as long as they wished, but that it was safe for them to leave at any time. I thought it best that he stay with us overnight as he was still groggy, and the intravenous fluids had not finished running.

Margaret and I got to work on the bills while our clients kept watch over their rabbit. By the time our bookkeeper arrived, we had a stack of sealed envelopes and all I had left to do was write up a bill for Sweetums. The smell of Margaret's stew was driving me insane with hunger, but it somehow seemed inappropriate to eat while we still had clients in the clinic.

I was in the back room thumbing through a textbook to determine which antibiotic I'd best start Sweetums on when I heard Drake and Orma leave. I went to the kennel room and found Margaret bedding down our patient. He was sitting up on his haunches. He looked rather dejected with the apparatus still taped to his ear, but he was wide awake and his colour was good. I adjusted the flow of the intravenous and closed the kennel door.

"Well, let's eat!" I pronounced enthusiastically. "I hated to suggest it with our clients still here."

"Oh, I asked them to join us," Margaret asserted. "But maybe I shouldn't have mentioned what we were having."

I closed my eyes and drew in a deep breath. "What is it…Margaret?"

"Baking powder biscuits and rabbit stew."

Lashes to Die for

"Darn it, Doris," I grumbled, "I had plans tonight."

Doris glowered at me as she hung up the phone. "Don't blame me! I did, too."

I was hot and tired. It was almost four, and all that remained on the appointment book was a Lab to vaccinate and a kitten that was scratching at its ears.

"What did she say?" I asked flatly.

"Only that her nanny couldn't deliver and she'd get here as quickly as she could. She was getting her sister to come out from Kitchener to help her load the goat."

"Where's she coming from?"

"Yahk."

I gave Doris an exasperated look. First of all the sister had to get to Yahk, which was on the road to Cranbrook, and then they had to drive all the way back to town. This was shaping up to be one of "those" days. I filled my lungs with air and focused on releasing it ever so slowly. Oh well...plans had changed. There was no sense in making things worse than they already were. I sat at the counter in the lab completing the morning's client records.

It was hard to keep my nose to the grindstone at the office when there was so much going on with the house. I'd just have to wait to see what progress my builders had made today. From the

moment the stately larch came crashing to the ground, each day at the farm brought about more dramatic changes. Where the tree once stood gaped a massive hole. It was there that Father and Jack were laying out the footings for the house.

Watching the big yellow backhoe carve away at the hillside, scooping out one bucketful of blue Lister clay after the other, had been a near-spiritual experience. I smiled as I picked up the odd little clay pot from the counter and rolled it over to inspect the dedication one more time: "Wrought from the clay of Dr. Dave's basement—as obstinate and hard to work with as the laird."

I ran my fingers over the rough texture of the inscription. Ruth and Gordon Veitch had shown up for a few minutes while the machine was working, and Ruth had dug some clay. That evening she struggled to produce this unique vessel from material that refused to hold its form. I kept telling her she should focus less attention on her job as a real estate salesperson, and more time on her potting and painting. Like Gordon, she was truly multi-talented.

Although things were definitely progressing on the farm, not everything had gone smoothly. Jack and Father had been ready to string me up when I decided on a last-minute change that cost us several days' delay. They had already pounded in most of the stakes for the footings when I decided to add a foot and a half of stonework to the height of the basement wall. It made sense to me. How to blend the log and stone portions of the building so the addition didn't appear to be tacked on was constantly on my mind. I'd had my arm up a cow's rear end at the Adams' dairy when I was struck with the insight that the logs simply had to sit on a ledge of stone! I had rushed through the remainder of my palpations in order to get news of the change to Jack.

"What do you mean, we need to go a foot and a half deeper?" He had a bewildered expression as he lowered his hammer.

"I know it sounds crazy, but it just has to be."

It took me over an hour to convince the pair I was serious—

that it was the way to blend the logs with the stonework. Besides the cosmetic benefit, there was also one very practical one. I was determined not to have to duck my six-foot-eleven frame to get through any door in my house! With an eight-foot basement there was no way to accommodate the seven-foot-six doors I had decided on and still provide sufficient strength to support the weight of the logs overhead. An additional eighteen inches of concrete would solve that problem.

Every time Jack asked, "Do you realize how much extra work that'll be?" I nodded.

"Why can't we just make it out of concrete?" Father insisted.

"Because I don't want to see concrete...When I look at my house, I want to see both logs and stone."

Finally, they accepted what they considered yet another of my eccentric schemes.

We had to wait two days before the backhoe operator could return to complete the excavation. Every time I thought about whether or not I had made the right decision, I felt a moment of weakness. After all, what did I really know about working with stone? And Father was right that doing things the way I wanted would take a lot of time or a lot of money. Right now, I had no idea where either one of those assets was going to come from.

I gave the old black Lab a pat and lowered him to the floor. Tugging at the leash, the dog dragged his owner toward the exit.

"Oh come on, Charger," I called after him, "it couldn't have been that bad!"

"The needle was no big deal, but you know how much he hates getting his nails trimmed." Louise called over her shoulder, "I'll get him to the car and come back to settle the bill!"

I smiled at my next client, who sat patiently in the waiting room. "Okay, Ginger. Let's have a peek at that new kitty of yours."

The stately grey-haired woman rose gracefully from the bench and carried her cardboard box to the exam table.

"There was no way I was going to get another cat after old Marmalade passed on, but now look at what showed up on my doorstep." She unfolded the flaps of the box and withdrew a bedraggled orange kitten. Holding the creature at arm's length, she shook her head and smiled. "I have no idea where she came from…When I was having my morning coffee a couple days ago, there she was, hunched up outside the sliding doors of the patio. Of course, I had a few cans of cat food left over…" She shrugged as she handed me the kitten. "She's even got the same marking as Marmalade."

"So she's been scratching at her ears?"

Ginger nodded. "She digs at them constantly."

I set the pot-bellied little feline on the tabletop and ran my hands over her several times. As I parted the hair to search for fleas, she arched her back and emitted a rattling purr.

"Aren't you the friendly one."

Ginger frowned. "I'm sure someone dropped her on my deck. She's obviously been handled a lot. I keep wondering if she belonged to someone who knew me."

I smiled. I wouldn't doubt that in the least. But as distasteful as I found the practice of dumping kittens on other people's doorsteps, I couldn't think of a better place for some well-meaning person to choose to leave this one. It was more than six months since I had put old Marmalade to sleep. I was never fond of performing the task of euthanasia, but this one had been doubly hard, knowing that Ginger's husband, Bob, had been buried a few weeks before. An ailing cat and a husband with cancer were more than any woman should be asked to bear.

The moment I touched the kitten's head and folded back her ear, she crouched and began scratching madly. Meowing plaintively, she continued her attack until I picked her up and cuddled her.

"Poor thing," Ginger groaned. "She can't seem to leave those ears alone."

I grabbed a cotton-tipped swab and swiped a huge gob of black crusty debris from inside the kitten's ear. Handing her to Ginger, I retreated to the back room. I rolled the material back and forth over a glass slide and popped it onto the stage of the microscope. It was as I expected.

"Come have a peek, Ginger."

She gave me the kitten, then slipped into the chair I had vacated.

"What am I supposed to be seeing?" she asked as she bent over the scope and peered through the eyepiece. "Oh my God!" she exclaimed. "What are they?" She leaned back and moved in close to examine the muck on the slide before peering again through the microscope.

"They're ear mites."

"I've never seen anything like this before…There must be hundreds of them wiggling around under there. Look at all those ugly legs! And there are some eggs…there's one just hatching…there are two of them breeding! You poor kitty."

We zipped the kitten into a restraining bag and took her to the sink. By the time we had finished syringing both ears, the entire sink bottom was covered with black debris. After demonstrating to Ginger how to apply and massage in the eardrops, I returned the kitten to her.

It was gratifying to watch the two of them together now. Although Ginger may have been disgruntled when she found the kitten on her doorstep, I could tell from the look on her face that she was secretly glad of its company.

While waiting for the goat to arrive, I sat in the lab flipping through the book on slipforming, studying different examples of stone buildings that the writer had erected. If I could in some small way approximate what this guy had created, I'd be more than happy with my decision. I read carefully through his instructions, paying particular attention to how he had done his corners—how he had placed his rocks. One over two…two over one. It sounded simple enough.

The author made the point that one could never have enough stones handy to make the job flow smoothly—that there was always a need for the peculiarly shaped rock that would interlock perfectly with the ones above or below. Stone gathering—one more job I'd need to get at.

I glanced at my watch; it was 6:25 and still sweltering back here in the lab. The air conditioner kept the front half of the building almost liveable, but helped little in this cubicle. I had been sitting for more than an hour and still no word from the goat lady. I peeked again through the microscope. Legs still flailed in all directions as the mites worked their way through the black gunk on the slide. What was God thinking when he created these creatures? Surely he wasn't enamoured of the ugly things…I wouldn't think he enjoyed watching a kitten claw at its face until it was raw and bleeding.

I thought idly about a sect of Buddhists who went to the extreme of wearing masks over their faces as part of their resolve not to kill a living thing. What would they have done today? Would they have left the kitten to suffer as generations of these hideous vermin replicated and perpetuated an environment in which they could thrive? Was I a murderer for bringing about their destruction? There was no doubt I had displaced an entire population of the critters. Those that were not wandering aimlessly across this slide were either drowning in the trap under the sink or about to die an oily death in the drops I sent home with Ginger.

I heard the front door open and a quavering voice, "Hello…"

"Be right with you."

Doris and I arrived at the front counter at the same time. She had left a gown folded and half wrapped on the surgery table.

"Sorry to keep you waiting," the goat lady said tentatively, "but we had a devil of a time getting her in the car."

"In the car?" I asked incredulously.

The well-rounded woman wrinkled her brow in exasperation. Peering at me through black horn-rimmed glasses that seemed too big for the delicate nose that supported them, she smiled nervously and ran her fingers through long, matted hair.

"Yeah," she sighed, picking a piece of straw from the shoulder of her jacket and dropping it on the floor. "My brother-in-law was supposed to come and get her with his pickup, but we finally got tired of waiting on him and stuffed her in my car. I'm sure he's still sitting in the bar…I wasn't about to wait all night for him to show up."

"How long has the doe been trying to kid?" I asked, slipping into my coveralls.

"She pushed out a bubble right after lunch, but hasn't done much of anything since then."

"Is she still straining?"

"She pushes once in a while, but there's nothing sticking out except that long pink string."

I filled my stainless-steel bucket with warm water, stuffed a container of surgical scrub in my back pocket, and followed my client onto the street. Parked on the yellow line next to the cross-walk was a pale blue Volkswagen bug. I stared at the woman in disbelief as she opened the passenger door of the squat vehicle and struggled to pull the seat forward.

"She never had any difficulty last time," the goat lady said. "I just went out in the morning to find two babies following along behind her."

She stood back and looked at me expectantly. I took my cue from her and knelt to peer into her cluttered car. A flake of hay rested in the back window; candy wrappers and sunflower-seed shells littered the floor. Standing on the seat was a fawn-coloured doe with pointed upright ears that projected straight at me. The animal sniffed the air and thrust her nose in my direction.

"Is she a Toggenburg?" I asked.

My client gave me a blank look. "Not sure what her last name is...I just call her Pansy because she keeps raiding my flower garden."

I smiled. "Actually, Toggenburgs are a Swiss breed of goat."

"Oh," she responded absently. "I have no idea what kind of goat she is, but she milks good."

"I see."

The nanny's expressive brown eyes widened when I extended my hand to her. She twirled on the seat, balancing uncertainly as the springs gave way beneath her. Hunching her back, she first strained as if trying to expel the string of membranes that hung from her, then sent a stream of urine down the back of the seat.

"I guess we'll have to get her into the clinic...I'm sure not going to be able to do much with her out here."

I carried my bucket back into the office and found a thick rubber-backed bath mat in the kennel room. Placing it on the exam table, I returned to the Volkswagen to find my client nestled on the back seat holding the leather collar around Pansy's neck and doing her best to console the worried beast.

"How did you get her in here?" I asked.

"I got in the back here with her and pulled while my sister pushed."

"Well, I guess we'll reverse the process to get her out."

The doe rolled her eyes and resisted as I applied traction to her collar, but with the owner pushing from behind, the animal soon scrambled over the folded seat and onto the sidewalk.

"I have to tell you," I chuckled, "this is the first time I've had someone bring me a farm animal in the back of a Volkswagen."

The woman slowly extracted her plump body from the back seat. Adjusting her glasses, she picked a goat hair from her lip and responded dryly, "You can thank my brother-in-law for that."

I encircled Pansy with my arms, pulled her to my chest, and lifted. She released a plaintive blat, reefed her head over my shoulder, and scissored her legs back and forth in an effort to break free.

When she finally quit thrashing, I made a beeline for the clinic. My client reached the door a step in front of me and flung it open.

"Doris...Doris! I'm going to need you!"

The moment I entered the room there was a plop, plop, plopping as a multitude of brown smelly turds hit the floor and followed me across the worn carpet as if they were marbles.

Doris rushed from the surgery. "Oh my word," she gasped, picking her way through the rolling obstacle course.

I placed the goat on the table and held her firmly until she could gain her footing.

"Just hold her steady, Doris." I gave my reluctant helper the doe's collar and planted my hip against the table for stability.

Holding the bucket under Pansy's rear end, I scrubbed her vagina and slathered her with surgical soap. I cupped my gloved hand to reduce its diameter and pushed carefully through the vaginal lips. Pansy bleated woefully as my hand approached her cervix. I moved slowly, trying to do as much manipulation as possible with the tips of my fingers. I prided myself on my obstetrical abilities but knew my limitations. Where my thirty-seven-inch arms and big hands gave me a distinct advantage over smaller veterinarians for managing difficult presentations in cattle, they were a true hindrance in small animals like this one.

Moments after the doe gave a second mournful blat, her owner rushed around the corner. Jamming her glasses back on her face, she nestled next to Pansy, pulling her against her chest. "Sorry to abandon you," she gasped, "but I thought I better get my car off the street."

Following the ribbon of membranes, I found my hand making a distinct detour to the right. Where the womb would have normally opened up, I could get no more than two fingers through.

"Oh no!" I groaned. "She's got a torsion of the uterus."

"A what?" My client stared uncertainly in my direction through debris-speckled lenses.

"Her uterus has twisted so there's no room for the baby to

come through." I rinsed my hand and pulled my arm out of my shirtsleeve. "Like this." By twisting the cloth of my sleeve 180 degrees I demonstrated that there was no way to push my hand back through.

"Oh..." The gravity of the situation settled like a wet sheet over the goat lady's face.

"In cattle we can sometimes turn the calf or roll the cow to correct the twist, but with Pansy I don't think it would make any difference. Her cervix feels like it's completely closed down, and I'd never be able to get my hand into her."

"What does that mean?"

"The only option is to do a Caesarian."

"That would be expensive," she stated matter-of-factly.

She contemplated her feet for almost a minute in silence. Her eyes reddened; a tear broke over the edge of her left eyelid and trickled down her cheek. Doris glanced uncomfortably in my direction as the woman dried her face with her sleeve and resolutely raised her chin.

"Can I make payments?" she asked. "My car insurance is due this month, and yesterday my daughter lost her glasses."

I felt that familiar sinking feeling—the one I got whenever I knew I'd probably be performing a procedure for free—then nodded without further consideration.

With the goat still standing on the table, I shaved over the base of her tail and washed the area with surgical scrub. After introducing a needle through the last sacral inter-vertebral space, I slowly injected lidocaine. As Pansy's hind legs began to weaken, I pulled her tightly to my chest, lifted her up, and deposited her on her right side. The goat stared suspiciously at her hind end, thrashed for a moment, then lay still.

While the two women held Pansy's head, I shaved her left side. She made a few paddling motions with her hind legs, but by the time I was finished clipping, they were paralyzed. To make sure the procedure was pain-free, I injected over a few more nerve routes to further numb her left side. The whole time I worked, Pansy's owner focused intently on stroking the animal's forehead, taking great pains not to notice the needles.

After vacuuming the loose hair from her side, I carried the doe to the surgery table. My client followed in lockstep as if her palm were glued to the critter's brow, cooing constantly about what a good girl Pansy was. The poor woman was sweating profusely. Her cheeks were red and glistening; a steady rivulet of perspiration trickled down her slender nose and dripped onto the table. With increasing frequency, she alternated her attention between stroking the goat and shoving her glasses back onto her face.

"Are you all right?" I asked.

The woman peered at me through lenses so plastered with sweat and grime that I wondered if she could even see me. She nodded.

While I scrubbed up, Doris finished preparing Pansy and then tied me into my gown. I donned my gloves, placed my drapes, and made an incision through the skin of the animal's left flank. With scissors, I severed the oblique muscles of her abdomen and the transparent layer of the peritoneum. After I pushed the rumen forward, I ran my hand over the glistening pink surface of the uterus, doing my best to explore its contents. To my surprise, there was only one fetus—a big one. I had been expecting twins. I reached to the far side of the abdomen, grasped the baby's hocks, and lifted them through the incision.

"Oh, he's a live wire!" Doris noted gleefully as the baby kicked and the uterus bulged. Her eyes bugged with anticipation when I picked up the scalpel and incised the uterus.

The baby's hind feet popped through the incision and I grabbed hold of them. "It's a boy," I announced as a pair of testicles came into view.

Placing one hand over the newborn buck's rump, I applied traction with the other. His long legs, loins and abdomen slid under my hand to give way to the chest and shoulders. Finally, I lifted him free of his mother. The baby shook his head; his eyes popped open. I cleaned mucus from his nostrils and he snorted; immediately his chest began to heave. I passed him to Doris, clamped his umbilicus, and cut the cord.

"Look at those eyes!" Doris squealed with delight. "The little devil has lashes to die for." Grabbing a towel, she wrapped him up and cuddled him like a newborn infant. As I sutured up the mother, Doris continued to fuss over the baby. She acted like a doting grandmother, drying him off and cheering when he took his first steps in the waiting room. She beamed when she held him to his mother's udder for his first drink of milk.

It was dark by the time I carried Pansy back to the car. Doris was glowing as she buzzed around the office cleaning up straw and goat turds. There was something about a birthing that lent wings to the spirit and gave even the most mundane of chores significance. Even though we'd been cranky at the thought of having to work late, neither of us would have missed this experience for the world.

The moment I was back in the office, I hollered up the stairs for Lug and headed for the truck. I couldn't wait till morning to see what had happened at the farm. I was giving birth to something there, too, and like an expectant father, I didn't want to miss a thing.

Enough to Choke a Horse

I had nicely started with a herd health appointment at the Kemles' dairy in Lister when Phil's wife Donna poked her head around the corner of the milking parlour and hollered at him.

"Get Dave to call the office...He has an emergency!"

I finished palpating the cow I was working on and pulled off my manure-plastered glove. "She's pregnant," I announced.

Phil made a note in the book while I headed to the phone.

Margaret answered. "I'm sorry to interrupt, Dave, but I thought it couldn't wait. Hans Reimer just called in a panic. Apparently, his mare's in a bad way. He begged me to get you there right away."

"What's the matter with her?"

"He wasn't sure, but he kept saying she'll be gone if you don't get there soon."

"What's his number?"

"He was apparently home alone today, so I'm sure he rushed back out to the horse as soon as he hung up."

I excused myself from the Kemles, promising to return as quickly as I could. I hated interrupting or cancelling a herd health appointment. Getting ready for one of these sessions was a lot of work. First Phil had to spend hours flipping through records figuring out which cows needed to be examined for pregnancy and which were having reproductive problems. Then he had to sort all the cows. Wasting his time was bad enough, but delaying the release of his cows was even worse—every moment a cow stood in a concrete holding area was time she wasn't eating or resting in a stall.

Fortunately, I was only a few minutes from the Reimer farm and was soon pulling into the drive. The moment I veered off the main road, I could see Hans with his horse on the front lawn. I groaned when I saw the animal. It was his Belgian mare, Heidi, and she was down. I had stomach-tubed the beast on a few previous occasions to deworm her and had developed a decided disliking for her. The fat critter was Hans's pride and joy, and he spoiled her without limit.

A pair of barking dogs trundled from the porch as I drew near. One was a fat German shepherd, the other a dachshund so rotund that her belly appeared to be dragging on the ground. I slowed to a crawl as I drew near the house, fearing that I'd pop one of them beneath the wheels of my truck.

"What's the problem, Hans?" I hollered over the barking.

"Roland! Olga!" he bellowed. "Go lay down and shut up!"

The robust man was sweating profusely even though the morning was overcast and rather chilly. There was no mistaking the look of apprehension on his face.

"Heidi's in a bad way," he puffed in his thick German accent. "I've been trying to keep her up but it's hopeless."

The huge mare was breathing heavily, panting as if she had been worked too hard. She was soaking wet; her normally sorrel hair coat was now a rich chocolate brown. Sweat dripped from beneath the clumped hair of her throat latch like rain dripping from an eave. As Hans spoke, she lunged to her feet, almost bowling him over. Sticking her neck out straight, she coughed, then swallowed violently. Green slush gushed from her nose. She shook her head like a spoiled child and swallowed again. More dirty green fluid trickled from her nostrils.

"Easy, Heidi…there's my girl. The doctor's here now…we'll get you fixed up." Hans looked hopefully at me as he ran his hand over the horse's trembling neck. "She was fine when I fed them all this morning, but when I came out a half-hour ago she was all sweated up. She stands for a bit then just throws herself."

As if on cue, the immense animal charged forward, knocking Hans to the ground and sandwiching me violently against the door of my truck. Air gushed from my lungs as my body was compressed; there was a sickening crunch as metal gave way behind me. Hans lumbered to his feet and took off in pursuit of his mare; I caught my breath and stared in disgust at my newly dented door. The moment my client approached the horse, her legs crumpled and she dropped to the ground.

"What could be the matter with her?" Hans moaned. "I've never seen her act like this."

I approached the animal cautiously and inserted a thermometer as she lay on her brisket, groaning loudly with each expiration. I listened to her left flank, trying to focus on something other than the sounds of her breathing. There was a reassuring tinkling all along her flank. I thumped along her left side with my index finger, searching for the high-pitched ring of compressed gas that might indicate a torsion or a grossly distended stomach. Nothing.

I thought back to one of Larry Kramer's lectures on equine colic and gastric distension. His forceful words echoed in my mind. "Horses do not vomit! If a horse vomits in an episode of colic, it's game over because the stomach has already ruptured."

I checked the thermometer—right on normal. Surely, if her stomach had distended to the point of bursting, her temperature would already be sky-high. Couldn't be distension…besides, that green crap had only poured from her nose when she tried to swallow. I cautiously knelt next to the mare's head, ran my finger in her nostril, and sniffed. The smell of fresh mown hay was unmistakeable.

"What did you feed her this morning, Hans?"

69

"She got her usual ration of grain, and I started her on some alfalfa pellets I picked up from the pea shed yesterday. The pasture's been getting down, and I thought a couple coffee cans of that would keep her from getting poor." He searched my face worriedly. "Why do you ask?"

"Because it looks to me like she's choked...got something stuck halfway down her esophagus. From what I've heard, alfalfa pellets can often be a culprit."

Hans removed his cap and wiped his shiny forehead with a handkerchief. "Is that really serious?"

"It sure can be. You can see the distress she's in. You know what it feels like when you swallow something that's too big and it just doesn't want to move down. It hurts like heck."

"What do you suggest?"

We both scrambled to our feet as the mare stood and stumbled forward.

"You keep her walking to keep her mind off her problem while I get things ready."

Hans reefed on the lead shank in an effort to keep the horse moving, but even with his three-hundred-plus pounds of body weight as persuasion, Heidi pretty much determined their pace.

I drew up Dipyrone and Banamine in separate syringes and stuffed them in a pocket of my coveralls. My plan was to resolve the spasm in the smooth muscles of the esophagus and get rid of some of the associated pain. As an afterthought, I prepared a syringe with some tranquillizer.

Hans was halfway down the drive heading away from the house. He and the mare were taking alternate turns dragging one another in a three-steps-forward, two-steps-back fashion.

"Let's see if we can hold her still for a moment," I said when I caught up with him.

I jammed my fingertips into the horse's jugular furrow to block the vein, flipping back and forth over the resultant bulge. As blood recoiled through the rope-like vessel, I drove a needle into the vein and drew back on the syringe. Blood shot into the clear liquid, and I was about to inject when my patient reared. Her front foot struck me in the chest and sent me rolling across the ground. Fortunately, the beast dragged her owner in the opposite direction, because for the second time in a matter of minutes, I had the wind knocked out of me and was in no hurry to get up. When I could breathe again, I returned to the truck for my twitch.

"I'm sorry about that," Hans apologized. "This just isn't like her."

The mare's eyes were filled with malice as I approached her, and I had no doubt that she'd gladly plant another blow on me if I gave her the opportunity. She reared again, dragging Hans along as if his weight were insignificant.

"Be nice, Heidi…be nice," the hefty man pleaded.

As the horse hit the ground, I grabbed her muzzle and squeezed with all my might. She stood trembling as I slipped the chain of the twitch over her lip and tightened it upward. I braced myself for an explosion as the animal stared at me with all the antagonism she could muster.

"Oh, I hate that thing," Hans whined, eyeing the twitch with a pained expression.

"So do I, but I'd like to live a little longer." I extracted the syringes from my pocket. "You hold this now." I cranked the twitch upward several times to get Heidi's attention and applied a bit more tension. Hans reluctantly grabbed the wooden handle without taking his eyes from the chain that bit into the animal's lip. "Keep it tight," I directed.

I repeated my earlier performance with the injection site and shot the medication into the jugular vein.

"Can I let her go now?" Hans asked as the horse began to relax and her hostile expression gradually faded.

"No," I growled. "Just keep it tight."

I palpated her neck in search of a bulge over the course of the esophagus. When I found none, I grabbed my stomach tube resignedly. This mare was a pain to tube at the best of times, and my ribs were aching terribly from our earlier encounter. I stood to her left and slowly introduced the tip of the tube into her right nostril. She glared straight at me as I directed the tube through her nasal cavity to the back of her throat. I rotated the tip of the tube upward, and when she swallowed, pushed it further. Green slimy fluid filled the tube as I advanced. I was sure the tip of the tube had to be somewhere in Heidi's chest when it ran into an obstacle.

I was jockeying the tube back and forth wondering how much pressure to apply when all hell broke loose. The mare reared again, flinging her head to the side. Her feet parted the air in front of me, and the twitch whistled past my ear to strike the ground twenty feet down the driveway. I held my end of the stomach tube as my patient retreated in the direction of the house.

"What do we do now?" Hans asked dejectedly. Heidi was standing with her head down. "It's so hard seeing her just staring at the grass. She's usually mowing the moment she gets out here."

I nodded to acknowledge I believed him. Considering the substantial ridge of fat on the animal's neck and my inability to feel her ribs, it was obvious she was a big fan of eating.

"I know it's hard, but now we'll have to wait."

"Wait?"

"I'm afraid so…You saw how she acted the moment the tube came in contact with the blockage. Right now the muscles of her esophagus are all in spasm, literally locking the stuff in place. The medication should help relax them so they can move things along."

"Have you seen anything like this before?"

"This is the first time I've seen a horse choked. I've seen it several times with cattle—usually when they've swallowed something like an apple or a potato whole. It's more of an emergency with them because they can't burp off the gases produced in the rumen…They can die of bloat."

Hans shook his head woefully. "It's going to be tough just standing here watching her."

"It is, but she seems more comfortable now."

It was almost noon by the time I finished at the Kemles'. I was tired and aching all over from my confrontation with the mare. I gently probed my left side, wondering if her blow had cracked some ribs. It certainly felt like it—every time I drew a breath it was as if someone were jabbing a knife into my chest.

Strange how adversity always seemed to fire up my worry machine. All I could think of was what life would be like in six months' time when all my clients knew about Cory and Marcie's new practice. Would everyone flock to them? On the drive to town I convinced myself that Hans would have called Cory if he'd been aware they were open for business. After all, my ex-partner had post-graduate training in the equine field and had most likely seen cases like this before.

I passed Goat River Road and clicked on the signal light to turn up Archibald Hill toward the office. I was already starting into the turn when I changed my mind and continued on Highway 21. Dr. Marling's veterinary clinic was located at the bottom of town on the bench overlooking the Creston flats. I'd just drive by and see how busy he was this morning.

All the while I lectured myself. It didn't really matter how busy Keith and Cory and Marcie were. I had more on my plate than I could handle, and the appointment book was full for the rest of the day. But...how could there possibly be enough business to go around for all of us to survive in a small town like Creston? The very thought of my better clients deciding to switch to the new vets made my blood run cold.

I was roaring into panic mode when the vision of Swami Radha popped into my mind. There my friend sat under her canopy at the ashram sipping a cup of tea. Her intense eyes peered right into my soul as she questioned me. *Does the fact that people choose another veterinarian detract from who you are? Does it mean that you are less of a man?*

"Of course not!" I literally shouted the answer. I just had to keep on plugging and doing my best. If people decided to shop around or choose another vet, it didn't mean I was doing something wrong or that I wasn't good enough.

I reached the bottom of Canyon Street and signalled to turn right. There were three cars at the Kootenay Animal Clinic besides Keith's. I slowed to a crawl and craned my neck in an effort to take in the activity through the little office window. I could see several clients in the waiting area, and Keith was talking to someone standing at the door. It opened and a man came out. I groaned when I recognized him. Dragging his fat old cocker down the clinic steps was Jim Forner. He had finally given up on me. I was overcome with a feeling of guilt and stepped on the gas before he could identify me. It had been weeks since I'd heard from him, and I hadn't given another thought to his dog during that whole time. The poor man had decided to go to someone who cared.

I wondered if Keith had found something wrong with Hank right away. Oh man, within a couple of weeks it'd be all over town how Jim had wasted months looking for answers from me, while Marling had come up with a diagnosis on the first visit.

I spent the rest of the day in a fog. Although it was busy all afternoon, I stewed about the future. Every second that I wasn't on the phone or dealing with a client, I was worrying about how to handle Hans's mare or the unfortunate situation with Jim Forner. I had called Hans several times without catching him in the house.

Just before leaving the office I phoned again and his wife answered. Heidi was still standing out on the lawn with her head hanging and crap running from her nose. Mrs. Reimer was worried about Hans. She hadn't been able to get him to eat a thing since she got home, and she was sure if something didn't happen soon, the pair of them would both die of starvation. I made arrangements to show up before dark to try one more time to tube the beast. There'd be no way that either Hans or myself would be able to sleep with the mare in this condition.

I grabbed my text on equine medicine and thumbed to the section on choke—the author recommended gentle irrigation when dealing with refractory blockages with material like beet pulp. I stared at the page trying to visualize that obnoxious mare holding still with water and alfalfa gushing from her nose.

I was in a funk as I drove to my farm; Lug seemed to sense my despair. As we passed the Creston Golf Course, he sidled over to me and put his head in my lap, his all-knowing eyes searching my face until we made the final turn onto Canyon-Lister Road. The moment we changed direction, he bounced up, looked out the window, and whimpered quietly. As I turned into the yard at the farm, he twirled on the seat and howled excitedly.

"Yeah, I know you want out. Go see where Grandpa is."

As soon as I opened the door, he scrambled over me and ran to the building site in search of Father. I swallowed a deep breath of fresh Lister air and surveyed the job. Things had progressed out here, but not anywhere near as quickly as I'd have liked. We had poured the basement walls and stripped the forms. Yesterday, Father, Jack, and his helper had managed to pour the floor. "The project" was finally beginning to resemble a house.

I walked to the gaping hole on the edge of the draw and peered tentatively over the side into the basement. There was Father carrying two-by-fours and setting them out for the next morning's work. He and Jack had spent the day laying out the templates for interior walls because the two-by-twelves for the floor joists hadn't arrived on time. They were supposed to be here tomorrow along with the plywood.

"Well, how'd it go today?"

"You and that damned extra foot and a half...Every two-by-four has to be cut. Would have been a lot simpler with an eight-foot basement."

I had heard about that addition so many times now that it wasn't worthy of a comment. Father appeared as tired as I felt.

"Why don't you knock it off for now. It's been a long day."

He wearily made his way up the bank to stand beside me. I studied the stonework that we'd done on the weekend. When I examined it from here, I was totally satisfied. When I focused on one stone at a time, there was hardly a one I wouldn't change. One over two, two over one still rang in my mind. For the most part, I had managed to do a decent job.

"Do you think it'll look okay once we get the logs on it?" I asked, fishing for Father's approval.

"Yeah, it looks okay." He gazed around him, then shook his head. "I don't know how we're ever going to get this finished, though…It's a lot of buggering around."

I silently agreed. It was a lot of buggering around. By the time we had finished the pour on Saturday, I was exhausted and worried that I'd made a mess of things. It wasn't until we stripped the forms the next morning and began pecking away at the green concrete with welding hammers that I began to relax. After we had removed the excess material from the face of the rocks for about ten feet, I knew I was on the right track. I'd just have to do better on the other walls.

"I'll go over and get something rustled up for supper," Father offered. "Have you eaten yet?"

When I shook my head, he rambled off across the gully. He had been having so much trouble sleeping in town with the heat and the noise of the traffic that he had set his camper up on blocks at the farm in a grove of pines. I envied him his opportunity to sleep here where it always cooled off in the evenings. I had yet to spend an entire night on my property for fear of missing an emergency call.

I positioned the sawhorses and glared at the stack of logs at the edge of the clearing. Cleaning them up was proving to be a tedious job. For the last few nights, I had worked into the wee hours with the aid of a trouble light. It was a gratifying experience to attack the century-old blackened surface of a log with a disk grinder and find clean wood somewhere underneath. I did the finishing work with a vibrator sander, being careful not to remove all the irregularities. The logs had initially been crafted with a broadaxe. I had never even seen one of the tools before and was certain there wouldn't be a handful of people left in the world who knew how to use one. I was determined to leave evidence that one had been wielded in the construction of my house.

I looked for the shortest, most slender fir log in the pile and stared at it with determination. It still hurt to breathe, and I knew my ribs were going to complain.

Closing my eyes, I hefted the weight; my side screamed in protest as I straightened. I was telling myself I shouldn't be lifting when I took the first hesitant step. By the time I dropped one end on the sawhorse, I was having trouble breathing. I probed my side gently with my fingertips, sure that something must be grinding around in there.

I held my breath, stooped, and grabbed the other end. Ignoring the searing pain in my side, I heaved it up and dropped it with a clunk on the sawhorse. It was several minutes before I could motivate myself to start the grinder. The log had landed with the black side up. That meant I would start on the tough exterior first. With a screwdriver I picked a collection of dirt and bat shit from the deep cracks running the length of the log. Attaching a new piece of sandpaper to the disk pad of the grinder, I plugged it in and flipped the switch. The motor whined and dust flew as I ground away at the surface of the old wood.

With each stroke, black grunge peeled away to reveal more of the original character of the log. I marvelled as the golden tones and intricate patterns of the grain came to the light of day. It gave me pleasure to see how nail holes blended with knots and the marks from the bite of the broadaxe to add character rather than distract from the beauty of the wood.

I had the first side sanded and was rolling the log when I heard Father bellow. "Supper's ready!"

I felt logy and downhearted as I headed to the Reimers' after our simple meal of beef patties and boiled potatoes. I knew Father wanted to come with me, but I didn't want him there for this case—I couldn't bear the thought of losing face in front of him. I had shut Lug in the camper and snuck away while Dad was washing dishes.

The whole time I had been sanding, visions of impending disaster flashed through my head. One moment I was locked up in a kennel with Hank, the farting dog; the next, I was being trounced by Heidi's pie-sized hooves.

It was eight o'clock. That meant I had almost two hours of light to resolve the horse's problem. I drove like a geriatric school bus driver through the back roads of Lister, taking a longer route than I normally would and pausing for a minute or two at each stop sign. By the time I turned onto the road to the Reimer farm I was a nervous wreck.

Although the thought of putting my life on the line with Heidi scared me, I feared even more not being able to resolve her case. I knew I wouldn't sleep tonight if I didn't at least try to pass a tube and dislodge the mass. I'd rather face personal injury than damage my fledgling reputation.

From the moment the Reimer house came into view, I had my neck cranked in search of Hans and Heidi. I was praying I'd turn down the drive and find the horse with her head down, greedily consuming grass. I found them at the entrance to the barn. Heidi's head was down, but she wasn't eating grass. She appeared totally dejected—and so did Hans. The horse was a mess: sweat had dried to mat the hair of her neck and side, particles of alfalfa clung to the fine hairs of her muzzle, and pale green fluid dripped from one of her nostrils.

"I see we're still in trouble."

"Yeah," Hans mumbled. "She isn't throwing herself any-more...she just stands there like this." Refusing to look me in the eye, he stared listlessly at the ground beneath his horse's feet. "Are you okay?" he asked.

"A bit sore, but I'll make it."

"What now?"

"I guess we better try and tube her again. Hopefully, that mess has softened up, and the esophageal muscles have had a chance to relax."

"Where do you want to do it?" By the tone of his voice, Hans wasn't looking forward to this procedure any more than I was.

I knew from previous experience that his barn was certainly not set up for this sort of activity. How I'd love to have a facility like the one they had at the college in Saskatoon, where stainless-steel stocks set in concrete would keep this equine lummox from grinding me to a pulp.

"Let's take her over by the house," I suggested. "I'll need some water anyway."

By the time Hans had convinced his reluctant steed to cover the short distance from the barn to the house, his reluctant vet had gotten Mrs. Reimer to give him some warm water. I resolutely coiled my tube and slipped it into the bucket. In desperation, I surveyed the yard in search of a structure that was an appropriate height to work behind—something that could shield me from fly-ing hooves and the better part of a ton of cascading horse flesh. That's when I spotted the maple tree near the garden. The stout trunk came to a Y about three feet off the ground. There were a few branches that would get in the way, but a saw would fix that soon enough.

I held Heidi while Hans retrieved some tools from a little shed behind the house. When he returned with pruning shears and a saw, I began hacking. By the time I was satisfied, a considerable pile of branches had accumulated at my feet. Picking up every last clipping, I packed them to the end of the garden and threw them next to the compost pile. I was doing a fine job of wasting as much time as possible. Finally, I indicated to Hans that we could proceed. He smiled limply.

"Let's get her over here as close to the trunk as we can." I helped him lead the horse to the tree several times from both directions, trying to get her to cooperate and stick her head through the Y. She'd have none of it.

"That'll have to do," I said as Hans pushed her sideways so her muzzle was at the same height as the Y in the tree.

We passed the rope over the tree trunk and my muted assistant took a couple of wraps around a branch. With the horse secured, I applied the twitch. Heidi pulled back for a moment, struggled against the taut rope, then stood rigidly. I ran around the tree and reached awkwardly over the divide between us. Hans's darling glared at me as I once more introduced the tube into her right nostril. I passed it through her nasal passage, flipped it over, and maneuvered it back and forth until she swallowed. Puffing on the tube, I slowly advanced to the obstruction and pushed on it firmly, determined to apply a steady pressure.

Heidi reefed back, pulling with all the strength she could muster against a tree that refused to go with her. The halter groaned with the strain; I kept the pressure on, all the while feeling that something was about to give.

"Whoa, Heidi...whoa," Hans pleaded, as she leaned back on the twitch.

Without a hint of warning, my tenacious patient charged forward. I was bowled over backwards as her head and neck rocketed over the fork of the tree. The twitch rattled to the ground next to me as she came to an abrupt stop with her chest jammed against the trunk. I had been unprepared for the mare's charge and had maintained a steady pressure on the tube.

With trepidation, I picked myself up. Heidi was now in the position I had initially hoped for, with her neck fully extended through the yoke of the tree on my side, her chest against the trunk on the other side. She stood trembling as I timidly advanced the tube.

"Did it break loose?" Hans asked in disbelief.

I said nothing as I puffed on the tube and directed it another foot or two down her gullet. In a moment of panic, I wondered if I had torn through the devitalized wall of the esophagus. Surely it wouldn't move this freely if I was forcing it through structures in the critter's chest cavity. I blew into the tube, discharging mucus and debris, then brought it to my nose. The air that gushed back smelled like fermented hay. I withdrew the tube slowly, looking for evidence of blood. It was clean.

"Let's see if she'll drink," I suggested, a glimmer of hope in my sights. "She must be getting pretty thirsty."

Hans backed the critter away from the tree, and I offered her the remains of the water in my stainless steel bucket. It disappeared rapidly as she literally inhaled the contents. Hans beamed and dropped the lead shank to the ground; Heidi immediately lowered her head to attack the grass at her feet.

"Isn't that a beautiful sight?" the man bellowed. Giving me a resounding thump on the back, he trotted off toward the house. "Mother! Mother! Come see!"

I breathed a sigh of relief as I finished stowing my equipment in the truck. I felt at that moment as if one tremendous burden had been lifted from my shoulders.

Hans was standing on his front porch devouring the remains of a corned beef sandwich. Roland and Olga sat at his feet expectantly waiting for tidbits. Mrs. Reimer smiled from the kitchen doorway. The only time I saw Heidi lift her head from the lawn was for the few minutes it took for her to down a five-gallon bucket of water.

"Isn't that a beautiful sight, Dave?" Hans commented with his mouth full. It must have been the tenth time he'd repeated that question in the last five minutes. "It's not very often you get the right combination of beauty and brains in one of God's creatures," he affirmed. "I tell you, that one has it all."

I winced involuntarily as I glanced at the massive dent in my truck door. I rubbed my throbbing chest and cautiously drew in another breath. I was sore, but happy. Seeing Heidi with her head down voraciously devouring grass was indeed a beautiful sight.

Hans's wife brought him another overstuffed sandwich and he took a large bite. He smiled broadly. "It just doesn't get any better than that."

A Definition of Dung

"It's Tom on the phone again!"

"Already?"

Doris rolled her eyes at me and I hurriedly removed the thermometer from the immaculately groomed poodle. It was only ten after eight, and it was the second time Tom had called this morning.

"It's right on normal. Tell him he can come and get Belinda...and thank him for the flowers."

Margaret carried the dog back to her kennel while I sprayed the table with disinfectant.

Doris's voice floated from the front. "Tom says he bought those bloody flowers for the love of his life, and you better make sure they're where Belinda can see them!"

I laughed out loud. Tom was my tempestuous hairdresser. He and his partner Norm ran a local hair-styling shop called the Manell House of Beauty. They were the only openly gay people living within a hundred-mile radius.

Belinda was a delightful creature. A four-year-old toy poodle, she was the mother of six and the undisputed madam of the House of Beauty. She officially greeted every client who stepped through the salon doors, but graced the laps of only the most privileged. Today her hair coat was her normal apricot colour and her nails

were clear gloss, but that changed according to the boys' whims. Just before Christmas last year, I had purchased one of her puppies as a birthday gift for my sister Kay. Since then, it had been contingent upon me to provide regular bulletins on how Tom and Norm's "granddaughter" was making out way over in the metropolis of Trail.

Yesterday, while I was still removing the drapes from the dog's tummy after performing her ovariohysterectomy, the local florist arrived with a bouquet. We were surprised when we discovered that the delivery was not in error—that it was in fact for our patient. The deliveryman informed us that the red roses were to be placed in front of Belinda's kennel so she'd see them the moment she woke up.

I had my cap and mask on in preparation for a cat spay when Tom arrived to pick up his charge. The moment I heard his tenor voice in the reception area, I went to the kennel room and opened the door to Belinda's cage. She galloped from the room, and before I turned the corner I could hear her yipping excitedly to Tom in the waiting area. I followed with the vase of flowers and the wicker basket Tom had insisted she spend the night in.

"Oh, for me?" Tom teased. "You shouldn't have…You know how jealous Norman can get."

I handed him the bed and offered him the flowers. He took the basket and motioned toward the roses. "You keep those. You need something to jazz up this old pit."

"Leave them with me at the counter," Doris suggested. "It's been a while since anyone brought me flowers."

"I can imagine," Tom quipped. "And working for this cheap old bugger, you sure as hell can't afford to buy your own."

Settling on the bench with Belinda on his lap, he dug through the fanny pack at his waist for his chequebook. He rapidly scratched his name on a cheque and handed it to Doris.

"You can fill out the rest for me, sweetie."

Doris smiled. "A blank cheque from you, Tom?"

"And put that old skinflint down for an appointment right now. Just look at him!" He grabbed the long hair sticking out from beneath my cap and yanked it mercilessly. "How am I supposed to be able to afford to take my poor pet to the vet when my customers wander around looking like that."

"I know," Doris agreed. "I've been bugging him for weeks."

"Tonight's men's night at the shop, and I should be able to squeeze him in." Tom grabbed a pen and made a notation on my daybook: *Haircut with Tom, 7:30 sharp.* He snapped the leash on Belinda's rhinestone-studded collar, grabbed her basket, and headed for the door. "Don't be late! And don't show up in your dirty coveralls smelling like you've been rolling around in cow shit."

I stood there with a silly smile on my face, knowing there was no sense in protesting with both Doris and Tom plotting against me. Today was certainly not the day I'd have chosen to waste time on a haircut. We were getting ready for the final pour on the stone wall that would face the courtyard, and I wanted to see how Father was progressing. I had helped lift the three-foot plywood forms into place the night before, but it was going to be quite a job bracing them properly. We were now working more than ten feet off the ground; it took a lot of ingenuity to support the structure well enough to keep it from bowing once the weight of the stones and concrete were pushing out against it.

At four o'clock I had finished vaccinating a puppy and was drawing up the medication to deworm her when Doris interrupted. It had been a leisurely afternoon of appointments, and I was ruminating on how running a practice with only small animals would be a breeze.

"It's Gary Koebel on the phone...He's having trouble with another sow."

I grabbed the phone. "Hi, Gary...How did you make out with that last prolapse sow?"

"I farrowed her out without any trouble and she gave me eight healthy piglets, but I've got two more—one that's pushing her vagina out again and one that's just puffy."

The man sounded weary. It wasn't surprising. When I sutured up that sow last week, I had left wondering how any one man could take so much punishment. He and his wife had worked like hounds for the last two years trying to get Birch Hill Farms functional. Now that his wife had left him, he was trying to manage with the help of his two pre-teen sons.

"Are the sows related?"

"The gilt that's swollen now would be a half-sister to the one you treated last time…but the sow that's prolapsed already is from a completely different bloodline."

"Okay…" I was trying to think of alternatives. "The stools are looking normal? There's no evidence of diarrhea or constipation…nothing that would get them straining?"

"Nope, I checked 'em both. Their crap was soft…and I haven't seen any of 'em push until after the pink ball sticks out."

There had to be some explanation for a sudden rash of prolapsing vaginas. This condition was accepted as hereditary in cattle where excessive laxness in the pelvic girdle seemed to predispose their vaginal floor to balloon. Most cases I had seen with pigs, though, had been fat older sows with tummies that bulged as a result of big litters of babies.

"There has to be something up with the ration, if you've got two more."

"I haven't changed much of anything in the last two months."

I hesitated. "I tell you what, Gary, I'll be there as soon as I get done my appointments at the office."

"I'll be out feeding. Come to the barns. The kids're staying over at a friend's place tonight, so there'll be no one at the house."

I peered out the side window as I drove past the Creston Golf Course trying to recognize a few of the duffers on the course. Some people in this world actually had life figured out—they knew what to do on a beautiful sunny afternoon. Why would anyone want to wrestle a sow in a stinky hog barn when he could be out chasing a golf ball, breathing fresh air, and feeling the sun on his face? I sighed. Maybe some day things would be different.

Lug whined with excitement when I turned right onto Airport Road. This route had become familiar to both of us now that Gordon and Ruth Veitch owned property out here. Gordon had finally started building the dream house he had been planning on paper since he started as a realtor eight years ago. Every house he viewed or sold that had "something special" had contributed to the design.

To insure that no one could invade his privacy, Gord had built in the middle of a forested property next to the surgeon from the Creston hospital. What a shock it had been to him when Dr. Nunn went into partnership with Gary Koebel and began erecting hog barns near the property line that separated their farms.

It was amazing how the high price of pork had motivated one producer after the other to take the plunge and enter into hog farming. When I first started my practice in the valley, there had only been three of any size—one run by my neighbour, Verna, and the other two by farmers who had immigrated to Canada from Denmark. Now facilities were popping up all over.

As I drove past the entrance to the airport a small plane buzzed overhead. I followed it out of the corner of my eye as it banked and made a final approach for landing. I lost sight of it when I began focusing on the turn to Birch Hill Farms—the road angled off halfway down a gentle slope, and I had missed it several times before when I hadn't been paying attention.

I slowed, turned onto the drive, and followed a long arc to the house. A horse watched me from the paddock where the Nunns had once grazed their sheep. I wondered if the Koebel boys ever had enough time to ride—they had so many chores to keep them occupied. I parked beside the rambling log house that Peter Nunn had built. It was the sort of place you'd see on an episode of

Bonanza—the isolated "Ponderosa" ranch in the outback of Nevada. I almost expected to find Hoss Cartwright tying his horse to the hitching rail out front.

Built in a lazy-L shape, the house was spread out and had a disrupted roofline. The garage and kitchen at one end of the L were covered by a peaked shake roof, as was the wing with the bedrooms and bathroom. Those two outer parts of the house were joined by a section that the Nunns had used for their living room. The roof in the middle extended in a long, gentle slope and was covered with sod.

Seeing that patch of grass reminded me of the time I had climbed a ladder to treat a ewe on the roof. Peter had somehow gotten her up there and tethered her to a vent pipe so she could trim down a proliferation of grass. He called me when he found her chewing madly and pressing her head against the brick chimney. The moment I heard the incessant grinding of her molar teeth I suspected heavy-metal poisoning. Discovering that she was blind and had a totally static rumen added further weight to my hunch. The clincher came when I found several flashings on the roof that were made of lead.

I stared melancholically at the place for several minutes after shutting off the truck. Lug looked expectantly in my direction wondering if I was going to let him out. I held his head and patted him as I sat there. Peter had built this place while working full-time as Creston's only surgeon…If he could create his own home, then so could I.

Balancing the instrument tray and stainless steel bucket on top of my surgery box, I walked past the garden toward the barn. I moved slowly, being careful not to tip the tray and spill the disinfectant. When the Nunns were here, this entire area was sheep pasture. Now, the open stretches on either side of the well-packed thoroughfare were cordoned off with strands of electric wire to contain groups of sows while better facilities were being constructed.

A dozen sows crowded around a trough in the open area adjacent to the barn. Two animals at the end pushed one another back and forth for access to the feed. Suddenly, the bigger one squealed and grabbed the smaller animal by the ear. The entire group dispersed in pandemonium as the wounded pig screamed and scrambled the length of the trough over the backs of the others. The din intensified as I approached the barn. Oinks and squeals from feeding pigs echoed over the droning of fans. I skirted a stack of two-by-sixes and set my box on a partial lift of plywood.

"Gary!" I hollered. "Where you at?"

"I'm over here," came a muffled voice, "in the farrowing barn."

I stepped through the open door into the concrete-block building. The air was stifling, heavy with moisture and the sickeningly sweet smell of hogs and their offal. I waited while my eyes adjusted to the diminished light. Searching up and down the aisles, I finally saw my client leaning against a farrowing crate at the far end of the third row.

There were thirty metal crates in this part of the barn arranged in three rows of ten. This was where sows were confined to deliver their piglets and feed them until they reached six weeks of age. Although a sow could stand in her crate and move backwards and forwards a few feet, she was unable to turn around. In theory, it didn't give her opportunity to trample her babies.

"She's over there." Gary pointed to a crate in the middle of the second row.

I made my way down the aisle past hundreds of piglets in various stages of growth and activity. Some were newborns; others were approaching weaning. A few were actively sucking—jostling back and forth with their littermates for possession of a teat—but most were stretched out on their sides sleeping. The atmosphere here was repressive.

"It's still way too hot and humid in here," I noted.

"I know," Gary replied wearily. "We've even got fans forcing air in the back door. I'm at my wit's end trying to deal with it."

I glanced at the ceiling, just a few feet over my head. The once-white paint was now grey; mould was growing everywhere.

"You've got to do something about the ventilation. I don't know how you can stand to work in here all day."

I steeled myself for his response. Last time, we had quite a go-round when I told him he should tear out the entire ceiling and get some air moving. I knew how diligently he and his crew had worked during construction to seal everything off to prevent winter drafts in his piggery. Plastic vapour barrier had been taped and bonded so there'd be no unauthorized movement of air. I could understand that it was hard for him to rip it all out now, but something had to give. In order to continue operating in this facility, he'd either have to dramatically cut back on the number of pigs under this roof, or find a way to get new air in and the stale air out.

"These critters are producing more moisture in here than a good-sized hot tub would. You keep this density and don't change anything by winter, and it'll be dripping like a rain forest."

The man stood gazing dispassionately in my general direction. This wasn't like him; last time we had been nose to nose in a heated debate.

I focused my attention on my patient. Noting her long white body and huge floppy ears, I presumed she was primarily of Landrace breeding—a line of pigs first developed in Denmark. She was reclining on her right side. Bulging from her rear end were two pink blobs—the smaller one protruding from her rectum, the larger from her vagina. The sow seemed to have developed a pattern: she'd take two or three breaths, then hold her breath and strain as if trying to expel something. Each time she pushed, the lower mass increased in size. When she relaxed and breathed normally again, it diminished.

I knelt behind her crate. Running my hand over her belly, I squeezed her teats then palpated over her ribs. Her udder was developing nicely, but there was no evidence of milk production yet. She was in ideal shape for farrowing, certainly not over-fat. At

91

the tip of the big pink blob was a rosette of swollen tissue. I gently prodded it with my fingertips; the membranes on the surface were cold and squishy, but underneath there was a firm band of tissue. The cervix was not softening.

"She's still a few days from farrowing." I looked at Gary for some indication that he'd heard me, but he said nothing.

I left the barn and retrieved my equipment. I drew up some lidocaine in a syringe, stuffed it and a spool of umbilical tape into one of my pockets, then threw a bottle of soap in my bucket and grabbed the instrument tray. As I filled the bucket with warm water, I studied my client curiously. The Gary I knew was a perpetual-motion machine. This Gary hadn't moved from his mooring since my arrival—he was leaning on the same crate as if shackled to it.

"How did you make out on the last load of feeders?"

"Not bad," he replied blandly. "But as always, the bank's eagerly waiting for the cheque to arrive."

I scrubbed up the sow's back end, then lay down on the concrete as close as I could get to her. Doing a spinal on a pig was not as simple as doing one on a cow, and I wanted to be perfectly perpendicular to her when I was placing the needle. That way, I'd be more likely to enter the spinal canal on the first attempt. Manipulating the tail up and down, I slipped the needle behind the last sacral vertebra and injected my anesthetic. Within a minute the tail hung limp and the sow stopped straining. I removed the needle and returned to my knees, peering over top of the metal crate in Gary's direction. I couldn't believe that he hadn't moved since my arrival. He was usually at my elbow watching my every move and anticipating my needs.

"Are you all right, man?" I finally asked.

"Not feeling very good..." His response was so muted that I could hardly hear him.

"I can see that."

I scrubbed the sow's perineum and gently massaged the

swollen tissues of her rectum. Applying a steady pressure, I pushed the mass back into her body and inserted my fingers as far as I could to make sure it was totally everted. After I rinsed my hands, I drew up a foot of the umbilical tape, cut it off, and threaded the eye of a four-inch-long needle that was shaped like a lazy S. I drove the needle through the soft skin beneath the sow's anus and worked it around the orifice until it popped through the skin at the top. I pulled the needle through, then reversed the procedure so the sow's rectum was completely encircled by the loop. With the two strings dangling side by side below her bum, I tightened the string and adjusted the tension. I knotted it, cut it, and began working on the vagina.

The delicate lining of the structure oozed fluid from the jelly-like surface as I massaged it. The moment I forced my fist gently into her pelvic cavity, a gush of urine erupted from the vaginal floor, ran over the surface of my arm, and dripped from my elbow. I maintained a steady pressure until the flow from the trapped bladder stopped, then slowly extracted my hand.

I threaded my needle and drove it into the tough skin adjacent to the vagina. After I tied this knot off, I placed five more loop ties. Repeating the procedure on the other side, I ended up with six loops through which I laced umbilical tape. When it was done, cotton crisscrossed the vagina in a shoelace-like fashion to prevent it from protruding again. Finally, I injected the sow with antibiotics to prevent an infection and went over to talk to Gary.

"The other one's right here." His voice was monotonic as he waved his hand at the crate next to him. "So far she's only swollen up, but if she's like the others, she'll start pushing by tomorrow." He leaned against the farrowing crate as if it were the only thing keeping him erect. His skin was sallow.

"Jeez, Gary, you look terrible…Did you tie one on last night?"

"I wish," he muttered. "You know, I work like hell around here, and I can't seem to do any more than keep up. I've got concrete to pour, critters to feed, kids to look after, and now I'm about ready to take your advice and start tearing apart the only thing that's halfway finished. I got mould growing everywhere. I just can't win."

I prodded the swollen tissues around the gilt's rectum. The mucous membranes looked as if they'd been scalded. This was certainly not a normal progression of the pregnancy, and I could see why the animal would be irritated enough to start pushing.

"Have you added any wheat to your ration?"

"Nope...why?"

"Well, I pawed through my notes from medicine lectures before I left the office, and the professor mentioned that rations heavy in wheat can predispose sows to prolapse."

"My ration's mostly barley with a bit of corn, protein supplement, and minerals."

"The other thing he mentioned as a predisposing factor was mycotoxins in the feed."

"Mycotoxins?"

"By-products from mould."

Gary stared at me blankly.

"Penicillin's a form of mycotoxin—one that's been found useful for killing bacteria. There are a lot of others that don't have beneficial effects. Could be we're dealing with one of them." I waited for a response. When he continued to stare, I addressed him directly. "Have you seen any mould in the feed?"

"Yeah..." He shook his head apathetically. "There seems to be mould everywhere here...there was some growing inside the hopper when I shovelled feed into the mixer-mill. I figured it'd be so diluted it wouldn't cause a problem."

He wavered, lost his footing, and almost fell down. I jumped up and grabbed his arm to steady him. He looked out across the room as if I wasn't even there.

"What's going on, Gary?"

His entire body was trembling as he tried to stay erect. "I feel terrible," he muttered.

"I can see that…Do you think you can make it to the door for some fresh air?"

He nodded feebly. I stooped slightly so he could put his arm over my shoulder and began shuffling toward the door.

"I feel so cold," he mumbled.

"Cold?"

"So cold…A couple hours ago while I was feeding the outside sows, I puked my guts out. I was hot and sweaty then. Now, I'm just cold."

I got him outside as far as the lift of plywood and supported him until he sat down.

"I'm sore all over. My back's killin' me…My knee's so painful and swollen I can hardly bend it."

"When did you notice that rash?" I pointed to the red blebs on the backs of both hands. He turned his hands over; the palms were horribly discoloured.

"Started coming up this morning, but it's really gotten worse since I started feeding…It's itchy as hell, too."

"Is that the only place you have it?"

He pulled lamely at the heel of one boot with the toe of the other. "My feet're itchy, too."

I pulled his boot the rest of the way off and lowered his woollen sock. Tiny pink bumps speckled his ankles, the tops of his feet, and his toes. I checked the bottom of his foot and quickly replaced the sock. The skin of the entire sole was the same brick-red colour as the palms of his hands. I reached into the surgery box and pulled out a thermometer.

"Slip this into your mouth." He looked at me suspiciously and hesitated. "It's a new one straight from the shelf. It's never been used…honest."

He reluctantly opened his mouth and let me direct the thermometer under his tongue. Closing his eyes, he lowered his head. "I've got a pounding headache."

I hadn't the foggiest idea what he was suffering from, but

whatever it was, it looked infectious. I wondered vaguely if he had managed to contract erysipelas, a disease seen commonly in swine. I remembered reading that the streptococcal organism could cause disease in people as well. If that's what it was, and it killed humans as fast as it killed pigs, it was time to get Gary out of here.

I rotated the thermometer in the sunlight so I could see the mercury level—39.8 Celsius, 104 Fahrenheit.

"Is it up?" For the first time, Gary appeared concerned.

"Yes…I'm going to bring the truck around to pick up my stuff. Will you be all right here till I get back?"

He nodded, then lowered his head until his chin rested on his chest. I walked hastily up the path to the house. As soon as I was out of Gary's sight I broke into a run. I shoved Lug over and fired up the truck. By the time I reached the access road to the barn, Gary was stretched out full length on the bed of plywood. I pulled up beside him and quickly loaded my equipment.

"Come on, Gary," I prompted. "Let's get you checked out." I helped him to sit up.

"Checked out? What do you mean?"

"I'm taking you to town…to the hospital."

"Are you kidding! I can't go to the hospital. You see all the work I've got to do around here. Who'll look after the kids?"

"We'll have to work something out. You're going to the hospital with me…You won't be much good to the kids or the farm if you end up on a slab in the morgue."

"I can't go like this," he groaned. "I'm all shitty."

"Didn't your mother tell you to always start the day with clean underwear because you never knew when you'd end up in the hospital?"

"What about the other gilt?"

"She's in better shape than you are right now. Get in the truck…I'll come out and check on her in the morning."

It was after seven by the time I left the emergency room. There was no doubt that Gary was staying for the night. As I left, nurses were stripping him of his dirty clothing. He had called a friend who agreed to finish his chores and let the kids' sleepover family know where he was.

I was on my way down the hospital hill toward the office when I remembered my appointment at the house of Manell. Intending to stick my head in the door and cancel, I pulled up out front and hurried along the wooden board walkway. I stood back as another men's-night customer departed, then called for Tom.

He appeared with a broom in his hand. "Well, what're you waiting for, hot stuff! I got this seat all warmed up for ya."

"I only stopped by to tell you I couldn't make it tonight. I just got finished with a call at a hog barn and I'm all stinky."

"What do you mean you can't make it? You're here, aren't you? You make it sound like your being stinky is something new…Get your ass in here."

I reluctantly shed my dungy boots and coveralls and left them sitting outside the door. Tom shook his head as he watched me.

"You sure as hell don't have to worry about anyone stealing those shitty things."

I timidly walked across the tiled floor to where Tom stood in front of the sink. Although I had long since lost the ability to detect any odours on my clothing, I knew from the reaction of the nurses at the hospital just how bad I must smell.

"Oh my God! You weren't kidding." Tom grabbed dramatically at his nose.

"I'll come back next week," I offered.

"You're a month late already!" Tom scolded. "Maybe you should go in the back and take off all those stinky clothes." He smiled mischievously. "You can jump in my tub and I'll come and give you a bath with Belinda's shampoo. It says right on it that it's a veterinary product—that must mean it'll be good for soaping up veterinarians."

Usually, I could go along with Tom's antics, but I wasn't really in a joking mood. I turned to head for the door.

"Oh, sit down," he said with his characteristic frown.

I slumped into the chair, closed my eyes, and leaned my head on the rest. My mind was jumping back and forth from worrying about Gary to wondering how Father was making out with the forms for the courtyard wall. I opened my eyes when I heard a guffaw from the owner of a local ready-mix company, who was getting a cut in Norm's chair. There stood Tom with a clothespin on his nose.

"Sit up, little man, and let's get this over with." He threw a cape over my clothing and tied it tightly around my neck. "Maybe if we tape the bottom closed, it'll cut out some of the stench."

I leaned back with my head in the sink and struggled to ignore his continuing banter. By the time he was done, I had shut out my anxious thoughts by focusing intently on his massaging fingertips and the warmth of the cascading water. He had to poke me in the side to get me to sit up.

"Earth to Dr. Perrin," he said sarcastically.

"Sorry, but I guess I had you tuned out."

"You sound like Norman...I can talk all day to him and he doesn't remember a damn thing I say."

Tom ushered me to his chair and lowered it the moment I sat down. "They don't make these things for working on giraffes." He removed the peg from his nose and began putting clips in my hair. He had just started snipping when he stopped. "Oh damn, I forgot about the godfather."

He ran to the side door of his house and hollered, "You okay out there?" He returned and carried on snipping. "I had to check on Father Buseppi. He showed up for supper and he's still here soaking in my hot tub. You may as well move in with us, too, Dave. All the other freeloaders in Creston are here."

He continued his snipping until the bottoms of my ears were in view. "You sure you don't want it short like mine? It's the *in* thing, you know." I shook my head and he continued cutting and talking.

He was almost finished when he ran to the door and yelled again. "You still okay?" He walked in a wide arc around me, viewing me from different angles. "He's out there soaking with his bottle of wine and a pack of smokes. Have you ever known a Catholic priest that didn't have good taste in wine? It'd be my luck for him to die of a heart attack. We'd have a hell of a time explaining to the ambulance attendants what a fat old priest was doing naked in our hot tub. The whole works of 'em are Catholic and they'd probably burn us at the stake."

He pulled a bottle from under the counter and poured a healthy glob into his hand. He rubbed his hands together, then massaged the potion into my scalp. I held my breath as I caught wind of the perfume—it was Tom's rosewater.

"Not that shit again!"

Tom wrinkled his nose and raised his eyebrows. "Vets certainly have a different definition of 'shit' than hairdressers."

He undid the tie behind my neck and whipped the cape away. I stood up and checked my reflection in the mirror.

"Well, what do you think?" he asked cheerfully.

"It looks okay."

"Okay! I turn a sow's ear into a silk purse and all you can say is it looks okay?" Tom appeared genuinely hurt.

"How's Belinda doing?"

"Sure, change the subject," he grouched. He opened the door adjoining their apartment. "Come on, sweetie."

The pretty poodle trotted up to me and sniffed appreciatively.

"At least someone likes the smell of you."

I sat in one of the waiting room chairs as Tom flitted around sweeping up the hair he had lopped off. Belinda bounced over and put her front legs on mine to indicate she wanted up.

"You watch out for him, Belinda, he's a bad bugger. Don't you remember what he did to you?"

I picked her up and rolled her onto her side so I could massage her bare tummy. Her incision was hardly visible, and there was no indication of swelling. I noticed with interest that her nails were now a flaming red, the pompoms above her feet hot pink.

Tom stopped his sweeping and extended his hand in an exaggerated limp-wristed fashion. "I had to do something to pick up her spirits after the mess you made of her."

I paid my bill and rushed to the truck. I couldn't wait to get home for a bath. Although I could no longer detect the sweet smell of the pigs, the stench of the concoction Tom had plastered on me was making me ill.

Intoxicating Affair

I had given up hope of getting organized this morning. Every time I thought I might get on track, some new catastrophe presented itself. They should have offered a course at vet college called Calamity 101 that could have, in some small way, prepared me for life as a solo practitioner.

After I'd checked the day page the night before, I thought today would be a breeze—a vaccination at nine, a dog with a lame hind leg at ten, and then a trip to Wynndel for a horse castration—a nice quiet day to end the week.

Because we only worked half a day on Saturdays, that meant I'd be able to spend the rest of the time at the farm. I had been impatiently waiting for this day. We were finally ready for the resurrection of the log portion of the house, and I was so anxious to see the walls go back up.

Unfortunately, it was now almost ten o'clock and I had yet to get to my first appointment. It wasn't because June Miller was late. She had been sitting patiently with her poodle-cross Mookie for close to an hour now. It wasn't because I had slept in either—my day had started at quarter to six when Vanessa Simpson called. She had let her dogs out for a run while she hopped into the shower. When she went out to feed the horses, she received a disconcerting welcome. Both dogs came wagging their tails to greet her,

riddled with quills—they had tangled with a porcupine. The German shepherd was bad enough, his snout white with the sharp projectiles, but the boxer had them everywhere—his mouth, his legs, his thighs. It had been impossible to find a place to touch him without getting jabbed myself.

By the time we had removed the quills from both dogs and they were recovering in their kennels, Ross Fletcher had arrived with a horse that had been kicked by his stall mate. The gelding was still dripping blood from a gash at the point of his hock. The wound looked simple enough to handle, but the horse wasn't. He was a green-broke Arab whose training to date consisted of having a saddle blanket tossed onto his back half a dozen times. Even with heavy tranquillization, he created quite a rodeo before I could get his wound frozen and sutured.

I ran upstairs to change my pants as Doris brought Mookie into the exam room and checked his temperature. She had called the lady with the ten o'clock appointment while I was working on the horse. Her dog was actually putting his foot to the floor this morning, and she chose to wait until Monday to decide if she would bring him in.

I felt terrible about keeping poor Mrs. Miller waiting, but she knew all too well what my off-hour activities were like. She and her husband Bill ran Creston Taxi and acted as an answering service for us when the office was closed.

I whipped off my jeans and threw them into the bathtub, at the same time running cold water over the bloody spot on my knee. It seemed as if everything I owned was stained with either blood or manure.

Hurriedly hopping into clean jeans, I descended the stairs still threading my belt. I eavesdropped on Mrs. Miller's conversation with Doris as I cinched up my buckle.

"Mookie just doesn't have the energy he used to have," she went on. "But then, neither do I."

Doris chuckled. "I know what you mean."

I threw on my last clean smock and turned the corner into the exam room still knotting the ties behind my back.

"Good morning, June...I'm sorry to keep you waiting like this."

As I spoke, one of my quill patients protested his confinement with a mournful howl and the rattle of his kennel door.

"I can see you're busy," she went on. "I kind of wondered if it wouldn't be this way after passing on the message about the horse getting kicked."

"It's certainly been one of those days," I admitted. "And those two critters that are howling in the back came in with quills before I turned the answering service over to you this morning."

"I sometimes wonder how you keep up with all the calls you get. Bill always breathes a sigh of relief when the wee-hour calls are for you, but then it's amazing what time people call us for a taxi."

"So Mookie is slowing down?" I interjected.

Mrs. Miller gave the poodle-cross a look of concern as I stroked his head. The moment I touched him, he nervously stuck out his long pink tongue and attempted to climb into his mistress's arms. He shivered mightily. This was not his favourite place, and sitting in my waiting room for nearly an hour listening to the objections of recovering patients had done nothing to relax him.

June smiled and gently extracted Mookie's feet from inside her jacket. "Yes, he's a bit more sluggish on our walks, and when he gets really excited he has a nervous cough."

I nodded and turned the plump little dog to face me. He licked his lips and almost rotated his eyes back in their sockets in search of his benefactor.

"It's okay, Mookie, we're not going to hurt you."

I continued to pet him, then stopped and rolled back his lid to examine his eyes. His colour was good—there was no evidence of an engorgement of vessels. I flipped over his ears one at a time and sniffed each in turn. Both were clean and free of odour. I peeled up his lip and examined his teeth; they were sparkling white and his gums were a healthy pink.

"I see that you're keeping up with his brushing."

June smiled and rolled her eyes. "He still hates it and runs when he sees the toothbrush, but that beef-flavoured paste you gave me last time really seems to make a difference. I have to say, though, that I find the smell revolting…I can't brush my own teeth for hours after."

I chuckled. I knew what she meant and couldn't imagine tasting it myself. Releasing Mookie's head, I allowed him to turn and thrust his overshot little jaw into June's jacket. As he shivered on, I ran my hands over his body in search of abnormal lumps or bumps. Everything felt normal.

Doris removed the thermometer she had been incubating and rotated it in the light to read it. "It's 38.5," she said matter-of-factly.

I reached for my stethoscope and slipped the tips into my ears. Taking a deep breath, I listened over the dog's left side. Instead of the normal lub-dub, lub-dub, lub-dub, all I could hear was whoosh…whoosh…whoosh. The clicking of the valves between the atrium and the ventricle had been replaced by the sound of turbulent blood flow. I moved the head of my stethoscope to different positions on the chest and listened intently. I couldn't hear the vibration with the stethoscope head lifted from the dog's side, nor could I feel the vibration grossly with my hand when I held it in gentle apposition to his side. But the abnormal sounds were loud and present with each contraction of the heart.

I picked up his card and scanned the notations. There was no mention of a murmur, and on his physical exam fourteen months earlier I had commented that his heart sounds were normal.

June peered at me with concern. "Is there a problem?"

"He has a murmur."

"Is it bad?"

"We grade them on a scale of one to six. I'd place him somewhere between a three and a four."

"Oh my, I was afraid of that. He's been acting just like my husband…Bill's been having a lot of problems with his heart lately, too." She watched her dog sadly. "What causes something like that?"

"When we're dealing with a small dog like Mookie, three times out of four it'll be the result of degenerative valve disease. For some reason, nodules form along the edge of the valves that regulate flow of blood." I folded my hands flat, one on top of the other, and separated them to show a hole in the middle. "When that happens, the bumps get in the way so the valves can't fit together smoothly. Then, every time the heart contracts, blood leaks back and creates the turbulence I can hear. Most often the mitral valve is affected on the left side of the heart, but the tricuspid valves can also be compromised. Occasionally, a bacterial infection develops on one of the valves. But that's usually in dogs with bad teeth and gums…Mookie's teeth look great."

June shook her head slowly. "I hope so with all that brushing."

"We see murmurs like this most commonly in the smaller breeds, and it's mentioned in the literature that males have a higher incidence than females."

"Why is he coughing? Do you think it's because of his heart?"

"It sure could be…if you think about the heart as if it's two pumps working together in series." I drew a diagram on a piece of paper towel depicting two pumps sending blood in circles. I pointed to the right pump, then followed the arc with the point of my pen. "The right heart pumps blood through the lungs and back to the left heart, which pumps the blood out to the rest of the body. If one pump starts working less efficiently, then a pressure gradient builds between the two, and it's like turning on a drip irrigation system. If the mitral valve is affected and the left heart fails, then pressure builds up in the lungs and fluid creeps out into the air sacs. If the tricuspid valve is affected and the right heart fails, then we start to see fluid buildup in the tummy."

"That's why they have Bill on water tablets?"

"Yes. I don't think that's necessary with Mookie yet, and it may not be for some time. I'd suggest we get a blood sample. We'll check his white count to rule out an infectious process and his enzymes to rule out other systemic problems. We should have another look at him in a couple of months to see how things are going."

"Is it likely that he'll just keel over one morning with a heart attack?"

"That's certainly not common in dogs—most live for years with proper care. Getting some weight off him, though, would go a long way toward reducing the amount of work his heart has to do."

June nodded. "We all have that problem, and you know how he likes to eat."

It was after eleven by the time I had vaccinated Mookie and finished collecting his blood samples. I stood in the waiting room going through my mental checklist to make sure I had everything necessary for the trip to Wynndel to castrate Bill Merkley's colt. I didn't want to forget anything; this was the second time he'd booked the procedure. I had cancelled the previous appointment three weeks ago when I found out that the horse hadn't been vaccinated for tetanus. The silty bottomlands of the Creston Valley were an ideal source of *Clostridium tetani*, and whenever possible, I wanted my patients vaccinated three to four weeks before doing elective surgery.

Doris interrupted my process. Throwing a plastic bag with a tetanus booster and a bottle of ice into my surgery kit, she pushed me out the door. "You're late. I phoned Agnes to tell her you were on your way, and she says Bill's been outside on the lawn with his horse for a half hour already."

I rushed to the truck with Lug at my heels. I was tired of running, disgruntled with always being late. Just once, I'd like to be on time.

I began to relax as I drove down the hill toward Highway 3. Gazing across this beautiful valley always had a calming effect on me. To the north, a black cloud hung over Kootenay Lake. I was praying that we didn't get a big dump of rain in the middle of the surgery. Late-August thunderstorms could be impressive affairs in our little valley, and I couldn't very well abandon the operation halfway through.

As I admired the mosaic of colours before me—the varying browns of the plowed fields, the warm golds of turning crops of grain, and the cool greens of the pastures—I found myself wondering why the mountains looked so blue. When I really focused I could see green in the trees, but if I were capturing them with paint, there was no doubt they'd be blue.

Lug perked up as we approached Ahlefelds' farm. Certain I was going to stop, he whined and performed his well-practised twirl. I craned my neck to see what Ben had done with the site of the old house. It was as if it had never been there. The entire area had been filled, levelled, and was already turning green with the grass he had planted.

I veered onto the Lower Wynndel Road. On both sides, cattle grazed the lush pasture grass that grew so well on the loam that had been deposited by the waters of the Kootenay River. In the distance were crops of barley, wheat, and oats, all rapidly approaching maturity.

I slowed as I approached the rolling mountain that hosted the community of Wynndel. Houses encircled the girth of the hill but the rounded peak was still covered with trees. As the buildings and stacks of sawmill lumber came into view, I turned across the flats and onto a dirt driveway. The lane was lined on either side by tall, overhanging pear trees that were laden with ripening fruit. Lug whined and turned to watch a calf gallop along in the pasture next to us. He seemed disappointed when I rounded a weathered wood-clapped barn and parked in front of the house.

"Glad to see you were able to make it!" A stocky man lay

stretched out on the lawn with his head propped against the trunk of a cherry tree. In his hand he clutched the end of a heavy cotton rope that looped to a tall lanky colt grazing beside him.

"Sorry to keep you waiting, but it's been one of those days."

"Not a problem, I'm just looking to get this over with…Champ here didn't mind the wait a bit. I don't think he's looking forward to this as much as I am."

I grabbed my bucket from the back of the truck and headed for the house. It was a cute cottage that I guessed had been put up as a homestead by someone returning from one of the wars. Although the pale green paint on the wood siding was fading, it somehow seemed fitting and gave the place a homey feel. I knocked on the wooden screen door and waited for Bill's wife to answer.

"Well, you made it, Dave. How are you doing today? Doris tells me you've been running around like a chicken with your head cut off."

"Doing fine, Agnes. Thanks for asking." I handed her my bucket. "If we can have this about two-thirds full of warm water."

"Sure thing."

The sprightly woman grabbed the bucket and disappeared around the corner. She talked on from the kitchen. "Bill's anxious to get this over with. It's hard keeping the animal locked up in a little corral all the time. The colt's mother was in season here last week and Bill was fit to be tied with all the whinnying and carry-ing on. He's about had enough of broken fences."

Retreating to the truck, I set the bucket on the tailgate and sorted through my materials. I drew up the Rompun I'd use as a tranquillizer and stuffed it into my coverall pocket, then set out the lidocaine, needles, and syringes.

Bill got to his feet and brought the colt's head up from the grass as I walked over to them. He looked at me curiously.

"I hear tell you don't knock them right down when you cut them."

109

"I do them standing if I can. My size is a bit of a handicap for the technique, but I still prefer to just drive away after I'm finished without having to worry about the horse's recovery. They'd usually eat through the whole procedure if we'd let them."

Bill smiled. "You can give me a foot 'r so of that height of yours if it'll get you closer to your work."

We both laughed. I repeatedly wiped the hair over the horse's jugular vein with an alcohol-soaked swab. When I could see the vessel, I drove the needle through the skin and into the vein. The colt jerked his head upright and stood with wild eyes as I injected the Rompun. I withdrew the needle. Bill scratched the horse's fore-lock and rubbed his ears.

"Bring him a little closer to the truck, if you will, Bill. I'll set all my instruments on the tailgate where they can't get trampled."

My client led his now staggering horse around a cherry tree to an open patch of grass by the truck.

"He's drunk already," Bill observed.

"We'll give him a few minutes more to settle down before I do anything. Let him pick away at the grass for a bit longer."

When Bill let the lead rope dangle, Champ just stood there, head down. With his lower lip hanging, his eyes closed, and his ears drooping, he did look for all the world as if he could be inebriated.

I filled a couple of 35-millilitre syringes with lidocaine and slipped them into my back pocket. Rolling up my coverall sleeves, I positioned myself to the left of the horse and splashed water between his hind legs. The colt lifted the hind leg nearest me to push me away, then put it back down as if it would take too much effort. I squeezed my bottle of soap and sent a jet of the reddish-brown fluid all over his groin. Leaning close to the horse's body, I pushed my head into his side and stretched forward to wash him.

After working the soap on his penis, thighs, and scrotum into a rich brown lather, I rinsed him down with handfuls of water and started all over again. I examined the scrotum and immediately found the right testicle. Only after persistently palpating the left inguinal ring could I feel the other one. It was only half the size of the right and held deep within the ring.

"Well, they're both down."

"Good," Bill growled. "I've had about enough of a stud colt around here. Like I told you on the phone, I was afraid he only had one."

"It's not uncommon for a yearling to have one that's a bit smaller or that doesn't drop as quick."

"You'd never know he wasn't well-endowed the way he carries on when his mom's in heat. I was none too happy when you didn't want to do him last month, and I had to go through another heat with all that whinnying and carrying on."

I squirted on more soap and began scrubbing again. "I can understand that he's been a real pain, but I don't think you'd want him to get tetanus. I saw one at your neighbour's a couple of months ago—it wasn't a pretty sight."

"You're right...I wouldn't."

The foal lifted his foot as I directed a needle through his scrotum and began administering lidocaine. After injecting both sides, I massaged the area, doing my best to disperse the local anesthetic. I withdrew my second syringe and knelt next to him. Palpating deeply, I located the left testicle and struggled to hold on to it. I leaned into the colt's side, pressing my cheek firmly against his rib cage. When working with a big critter that had a will of his own, I always tried to be as close as possible in order to feel his reaction and move in harmony with him. I directed the needle into the cord, then deposited lidocaine into the testicle itself. The horse tensed but stood with his feet planted. When a testicle was as small as this one, it was important to be able to paralyze the muscle to the cord, so the horse could no longer pull it back up into his body.

"There's a boy, Champ..." Bill soothed. "Pretty soon you'll be able to run with your mom again."

111

He chattered on to his horse as I concentrated on freezing the other testicle. It never seemed to fail that when I was scrubbed and ready for surgery I developed an itch that I couldn't scratch. For some reason today, though, all the areas that had been exposed to Champ's hair were itching terribly. It was strange, because horse-hair didn't usually bother me. I ignored the sensation and focused on directing the needle into the cord that represented the cremaster muscle and spermatic duct. Content that I had accomplished my task, I grabbed my bottle of soap and began my final scrub.

"He's ready to go," I pronounced, getting off my knees.

This itching was really driving me mad. I rubbed my neck against the box of the truck trying to remove some of the hairs that were tickling me. When it didn't give me relief, I shrugged my shoulder up high enough to scratch my neck some more.

I tore the tape on the instrument pack and folded back the linen wrap to expose the scalpel handle, forceps, and emasculator. I opened a scalpel blade and dropped it onto the sterile field, then peeled back the wrap from a pair of surgery gloves.

The whole time I was scrubbing my hands and arms for surgery, I was experiencing a crawling sensation over my entire body. I began to wonder if my allergies were reviving. I sure hoped not— one of my classmates had developed allergies his first year out and had to quit practice. I had been seriously allergic to horses when I was younger but had overcome it by persistently disregarding its existence.

I was having a hard time ignoring the sensation now as I pulled on my surgery gloves. I picked up the scalpel handle, attached the blade, and assumed my position. I knelt next to the horse, grasped the scrotum, and incised over both testicles. Determined to get the most difficult one first, I pressed my face into Champ's side and probed for the left testicle. Each time I almost grasped it, it seemed to flit away as if guided by some intelligent force. I got even more intimate with my patient, planting my chest against him and manipulating with both hands. Finally, I cornered the little marble and dragged it back from its hiding place in the inguinal ring. I held it in place with my left hand and stripped it from the surrounding fascia with my right.

"Whew, I'm glad I've got that one."

Bill peered over my shoulder at the small blob of tissue that dangled from the incision site. "Is that all it is? No wonder I couldn't find it."

"The other one's a normal size."

"So would he have been able to breed like that? He got out a couple of times and I was worried he'd get after the neighbour's mares. He sure had a healthy interest in his mother."

I considered Bill's use of the word "healthy" but decided not to go there. "If he were Northern Dancer and you wanted to get a bunch of foals out of him, you can be sure he wouldn't have settled a one…but the way things go, if he'd gotten at the neighbour's mare, you could bet on her getting pregnant."

"Yeah, isn't that about the way of things?"

I grasped the larger testicle and dissected it free. Both were now dangling from their appropriate incisions. When I returned to the truck for my emasculators, I was overcome with an overpowering urge to scratch. I leaned against the box of the truck and pushed myself against it, rubbing up and down with my gloved hands in the air, determined to dislodge the hairs that were obviously the source of my discomfort.

"Looks like you got the seven-year itch," Bill noted.

"Yeah," I groaned. "I feel crawly."

I opened the emasculators and returned to Champ's side. Grasping the marble-sized testicle, I pulled down and slipped the jaws of the stainless steel instrument over the cord. It closed, the testicle dropped, and Champ was half a gelding.

"Tell me when three minutes is up, will you, Bill. I like to let this instrument crimp the cord long enough to be sure we won't have a bleeder."

I rubbed myself back and forth on the animal's side, determined to rid myself of the relentless itching sensation on my neck and back. I knelt there absently holding the emasculator, waiting for the minutes to pass. I stared at my gloves in dismay. Was that dirt on them? I was sure I had scrubbed the horse well. I flushed, thinking I must have missed something. I certainly didn't need these wounds turning into an infected mess. I carefully examined the back of my glove—the pieces of dirt were moving. In a moment of realization I bent down to peer at my arm. Tiny flecks covered everything—my gloves, my arms, my coveralls. I jumped back from Champ as if he were the carrier of a deadly virus.

Bill gave me a troubled glance. "What's wrong?"

"Champ's got lice."

"Lice?"

"Yeah…he's got lice and so have I."

I glared at the moving specks on my arms as I waited for the 180 seconds to expire. I had no idea how long three minutes could take to pass—all I wanted was to dig my nails into my arms and scratch. I closed my eyes and focused on the flow of air in and out of my nostrils.

"Time's up."

I pulled down on the other testicle and repositioned the emasculator. This cord was three times the size, but the testicle proved much easier to grasp. I compressed the handles. Champ lifted his leg as they closed with a sickening crunch; the testicle dropped to the ground.

"That's it?" Bill asked.

"He's a gelding…Give me three more minutes."

In those next three minutes, I tried to escape to every exotic place my mind had ever wandered to. No matter how hard I tried, I couldn't leave behind the reality that despicable critters were exploring more of my body with each passing second, and there was nothing I could do to stop them. When Bill finally told me that time was up, I whipped off the emasculators, tore off my gloves, and headed for the truck.

114

I had never felt so unclean—defiled. I doused myself in soap and scratched at my arms with my fingernails, desperate to scrape as many of them free as possible. When they clung tightly to the hairs of my arm, I grabbed clump after clump and yanked the hair out by the roots.

I peered in the side mirror. The despicable parasites were everywhere, on my neck, my face, my hair, my clothing. I ran to the back of the truck and grabbed a can of rotenone. Dumping some of the white powder into my hand I ground the foul-smelling material onto my skin and into my hair. Maybe it was time to listen to Doris and lop these locks off completely. By the time I returned to Bill and Champ, I was white with the chalky material and reeking like mothballs. My arms, my hair, my clothes—everything was coated with the repulsive powder.

Bill was parting the hair on his animal's neck and staring in disgust at the vermin that had claimed his horse as their domain. I dumped powder along Champ's neck and back, and rubbed aggressively to get it deep into the hair.

"These guys are the wide-headed type—that means they're crawling rather than sucking lice. If we get enough of this powder on him, they're bound to come in contact with it and die off."

I continued to attack the critters until the can was completely empty. It was as if the parasites had declared war on me, and I couldn't quit doing battle with them until the last one was dead. The air was thick with the stench of rotenone by the time I called it quits. Champ had pretty much metabolized the tranquillizer and was munching grass, seemingly unconcerned that he was now a foul-smelling gelding.

I hurriedly packed up my instruments and jumped in the truck. Lug thrust his nose toward me, anxious for a greeting.

"Stay over there, Lug! Get away from me!" I pushed him to the far side, determined to keep him from contact with both me and my clothing.

Convinced that I was angry with him, he crouched low and

looked at me in confusion. I pushed him away again as I turned around and headed down the driveway.

"Stay over there!" He gave me the saddest look, and I could see he was wondering what he could possibly have done to make me reject him like this. "Oh, hell...come here, ya big boob." He turned toward me with his tail wagging uncertainly and rested his head in my lap. "You're going to regret this," I warned him as I turned onto the highway. He looked up at me, still confused by my outburst, sighed deeply, then closed his eyes.

I was relieved that none of the members of the local RCMP detachment were out using their radar this afternoon, because I wasted no time getting back to the office. I rushed into the clinic and locked the door behind me. As Doris had already left for the day, I ripped off my clothes and threw them directly into the washing machine. Tiptoeing around the corner of the waiting room, I peeked at the street to be certain no one would catch me streaking. I crept to the cabinet and grabbed a bottle of flea shampoo. With Lug at my heels, I raced upstairs and started running the bath.

I peered into the mirror. Stationary flecks freckled my face and neck. I felt a vague tickling sensation on my forearm and angrily picked off a crawling louse. Vengefully squishing it between my thumbnails, I chucked it into the toilet bowl and made my way to the tub.

I noted the instructions on the bottle of flea shampoo. *Shake bottle well before using.* I gave it a good shake. *Wear rubber gloves*...I took a deep breath and read on. *Wet animal and apply shampoo full strength working it thoroughly into the coat. Allow to remain for 3 to 10 minutes, permitting the insecticide to kill fleas.*

Kneeling in the warm water, I wet down my body and soaked my hair. I threw a towel on the floor and began slathering myself with the viscous yellow liquid. Disregarding the disgusting smell, I doused my hair with handful after handful of the pesticide. I was only going through this indignation once!

"Lug! Lug, come here."

My faithful friend slunk toward me as if he were about to be beaten. The only times he got called into the bathroom were on occasions when he had gotten muddy or rolled in cow manure at the farm. He knew what was about to happen.

"I warned you, old buddy…I tried to keep you away from me, but you wouldn't listen."

I lifted his front feet into the tub, then followed with his hind legs. He stood with a hangdog look while I wet him down and applied the shampoo. When he was thoroughly covered in suds, I grabbed him by the collar and trotted him through the kitchen to the stairwell. As soon as I closed the door he shook himself, splattering the porch and the window.

I returned to the bath and rinsed myself off. My arms were still covered with flecks that wanted to stick to the skin. Satisfied that none were still moving, I got out and towelled myself down.

"How could we possibly have lost the tags from three logs from the same side of the house?" I moaned. "If they were all from different sides, we'd be able to figure it by the process of elimination…but this…"

Father shrugged his shoulders and pushed the weathered green cap farther back on his glistening forehead. "I told you we should have nailed them on right away."

I glared at the butt of the log where the tag should have been. When I applied the sticky plastic marker tapes, I was certain they'd be the perfect answer, especially as there was one on either end. Father had suggested we put a tack in each, just in case they got jostled in transit, but I didn't think it was necessary. A little nail hole in the extremity of each log didn't seem like such a big deal now. How in the devil was I supposed to reassemble this puzzle without knowing each log's number? It wasn't as if the pieces were tinker-toy size and we could try them one at a time until one looked like it was sitting in its original seat.

We had finished the final pour of the wall on the courtyard side of the house, and I was thrilled with how it had turned out. Although the stones were still grubby from where they'd been embedded in concrete, I was sure they would regain their former character once I got to them with a sandblaster. I was feeling good about my ability to make the stonework attractive. Maybe I'd finally be able to get Father to admit that all this work was worthwhile.

With the stone platform now in place, I had been enthusiastically anticipating the resurrection of the building. I had realized from the outset that I was going to have to be innovative when it came to laying the first round of logs. The house had initially been built on large cornerstones that had settled over the last century. The result was that the bottom log on the north side of the house had rotted where it came into contact with the ground. I'd somehow have to replace that one.

Even if this hadn't been the case, I would have had to come up with a new way of setting them on the foundation. Most modern log builders started with a half-log on parallel walls as a base for the structure, then notched the next logs into them. I had decided to do the same thing and fashion them myself.

It was harder than I thought to come up with dry logs of a size big enough to satisfy the need. After walking my own property, I went to visit Jim Powell, who ran a small mill in Arrow Creek. He had four suitable fir trees he had stacked several years earlier and never got around to cutting. I got him to square them up on his mill and deliver them to the building site. I had been whacking away at two of them on the south side of the house for days trying to make them appear part of the original structure. I was thankful that both logs didn't have to run the full length of the house, because they were cut for the front door on one side and the passageway into the kitchen on the other. We dragged the thirty-foot bottom log over with the tractor, and each time I made minor adjustments I would lift it and reposition it for fit. I was finally

118

almost satisfied with their joints and rejoiced when the next round of logs fit exactly as they should.

I was beginning work on a new base log for the side nearest the courtyard when Gordon Veitch paid a visit. He wagged his head and wandered around the building site making suggestions. "You just have to put a balcony on the second floor overlooking the courtyard—that's where you'll want that morning cup of coffee. It'll be the place you'll write the book you're always talking about."

Father rolled his eyes. "Damn it, Veitch…Get out of here with your suggestions. He's got enough crazy ideas of his own!"

Father's admonition came too late. From that moment on, the only question in my mind was how big the balcony should be. It was after Gordon left that I started scheming. I had added a foot and a half to the height of the house with the rock ledge, so the logs now started above the level of the first floor. If we were going to cut a hole in the wall for the balcony anyway, I could probably take the log from the top and move it down to replace the rotten one. That way I'd only have to change the notches a bit and the log would look the same as the rest.

We spent more than an hour searching through the piles of sanded logs that we had scattered around the yard.

"It has to be one of the ones that lost its tag," Father said.

"Seems that way," I agreed.

We went back and forth comparing the possible candidates.

"It's this one," Father declared confidently. "The top logs had these notches all the way along them for the floor joists."

"Well, if this is it, then we only have two left to figure out."

We hooked the log in the middle with a chain and Father lifted it with the front-end loader of the tractor. After dropping it and readjusting the chain so it was balanced, I held onto one end as he maneuvered toward the house through the maze in the yard. Because of the gaping excavation for the courtyard, we could only get close enough for a third of the log to rest on the floor. For the remainder of the distance I had to drag it with brute strength. I almost had the log in place when I heard my call signs over the radiophone. I ran to the truck. It was the answering service. Jim Forner had left a message that he wanted me to get back to him immediately. I called the operator and gave her the number, then waited impatiently for her to make the connection. I hadn't heard from Jim since I'd seen him leaving Dr. Marling's office over a month ago.

"Hello."

I depressed the button and spoke into the hand-piece. "Jim...this is Dave Perrin calling on a radiophone."

"Yes, Dave..."

There was a long silence and I waited for him to talk.

"I...I want you to come and put Hank to sleep."

I waited for him to go on before pushing the button and interrupting him, but there was only silence.

"Could you repeat please, Jim...I'm not sure I caught that right."

"You did...I'm asking you to come and put Hank out of his misery. He's staggering all over the backyard and can hardly stand up. This is a good time to get it over with because Lisa and the kids are up the lake with the in-laws."

I took a deep breath and depressed the send button again. "Has Hank been going downhill since I saw him last? Has he taken a sudden turn for the worse?"

"Nah...it's been the same old thing. He's on again...he's off again. For a few days in a row he almost looks like he's going to rally. Down the lake he goes for walks with the kids—even chases after a ball. We get him back home here and he's flat out, and half the time he won't even get out of his bed." I waited in silence, trying to think of something else to ask him. "I've never seen him like he is today, though...He's staggering all over, even falls on his side. When I was out there with him a few minutes ago, he couldn't even make it across the yard to the house."

"I'll come right away and have a look at him."

120

"Dave, I appreciate that you've tried your best with this damn dog, but I've had enough. I want you to understand before you come over…you're not coming to examine the dog. You're coming to put him to sleep. I'll have the hole dug before you get here."

Father stood beside the truck door studying my face. "Looks like we're done here for a bit. I'll go make supper. Do you expect you'll be back?"

I nodded. "It doesn't sound like this'll take long. Could you keep an eye on Lug for me?"

Father grabbed him by the collar. Lug whined and strained against his fetter in an attempt to follow me, but I backed onto the road and left without looking back at him. I didn't want even him to witness this crushing defeat.

I had everything I needed so headed directly to Jim's home. All the way to town I berated myself. I had screwed up this case from the very beginning and now I was going to bump the poor critter without the slightest clue of what ailed him. I wasn't grieving for Hank—the truth of the matter was I didn't like the dog much myself. I was grieving my failure to come up with a diagnosis. I had failed plain and simple. What had I missed?

I veered off Highway 3 onto Canyon Street and halfway up the hill turned onto 6th Avenue. I drove two blocks then parked in front of a tan and white bungalow that overlooked the Creston flatland. I grabbed my kit bag and climbed the stairs up the hill beside the house. Jim was in the garden busily digging a hole for Hank.

"Sorry to screw up your day off like this, Dave…I've just reached the end of my rope."

I nodded and walked over to Hank. He was stretched out on his belly with his legs stretched behind him like a frog.

"Hey there, old man…What's up with you?" I ruffled the hair on the top of his head, then stood back and called him. "Come on, Hank…come here, boy."

The dog opened his eyes and peered apathetically in my direc-

121

tion. He belched and closed his eyes as I knelt beside him. The moment I got a whiff of his breath, I leaned forward for a closer inspection.

"Jim, Hank's drunk!"

"What do you mean, drunk?"

"Exactly that...Hank is rolling-down drunk."

Jim put down his shovel and walked briskly toward me. "Where would he get into booze?" He knelt on the ground beside me and stuck his nose next to Hank's. The dog stared off into the distance, ignoring both of us. He hiccupped, then yawned. "Damn...you're right. He does smell like booze."

"Where could he have gotten into it?"

Jim glanced toward the house next door. "I don't know for sure, but I think I'd better have a chat with Clancy."

He crossed the lawn and knocked on the door of the adjacent bungalow. He waited impatiently with his hands on his hips, then rapped a second time. After several minutes the door opened. A wiry man no more than five feet tall was still doing up the buttons on his shirt.

"Hello there, Jimmie!" he gushed in a cockney accent. "What can I do for ye today?"

"Clancy, Hank's wasted...Would you know how he got into the booze?"

"Well," the little man answered, "we did get into a few pints this mornin'."

"A few pints?" Jim asked incredulously.

The man nodded matter-of-factly.

"He's so hammered he can't even make it across the backyard!" Jim bellowed.

Clancy looked down at his feet sheepishly. "I guess I got a bit carried away this mornin'. Hank does have a taste for Guinness."

"A taste!" Jim yelled. "Do you mean this is a regular thing?"

Clancy nodded solemnly. "He stops by pretty regular—whenever you put him out by hisself, he gives a scratch on my door. We share a pint or so and a few pieces of Polish sausage. Polish sausage is his favourite, ye know. He'll take that over plain garlic sausage every time."

Jim flushed. "Do you see that hole I'm digging in the backyard, Clancy?"

"Yes, Jimmie."

"Well, that hole's for Hank!"

Clancy's jaw dropped; his eyes filled with horror. "What do ye mean, Jimmie?"

"That's the bloody vet standing over there!" He pointed at me. "He's here to give Hank a needle and put him to sleep!"

A look of absolute horror settled on Clancy's face. He flushed and put his hand onto Jim's arm. "You can't do that, Jimmie! Hank's me buddy."

"That damn dog has been driving me nuts ever since we got him! No wonder he's always lying around the house fartin' all the time if you're filling him up with beer and Polish sausage." Jim turned to me in despair and shrugged. "What do I do now?"

Hank struggled to his feet and took a hesitant step toward the house. He knew he was being talked about. He yawned and gazed in our direction as if wondering what all the fuss was about.

I smiled and shook my head indecisively. I was faced with yet another deficiency in my veterinary education. Maybe they should have taught us AA's twelve-step program for dogs.

As the Stomach Turns

"How in heck do you expect to get it up there without hiring the crane?"

Father and I had been arguing back and forth for more than an hour about lifting the next log onto the north side of the house. Everything about that wall had been difficult: taking into account the excavation for the courtyard, we were working more than twenty feet off the ground. Placing the other logs on that side had been scary enough. After the first three, they were mostly short spans between windows that we had to support with two-by-four strapping from the outside. Now that we were nine logs high, without having a full-length span to tie things together, the entire wall was unstable. Placing this log would be challenging.

It was the last of those that had lost the number stickers, but I was sure it was the right one. I had measured the size of the notch half a dozen times, and the spike holes on the corners looked as if they should match perfectly. I hefted the butt end and dragged it a few feet. Even though it was larch and heavier than a cedar or fir of the same size, I could still handle it.

"I'm just going to get it inside the house and see if we can't think of a way to get it up there."

Father shook his head in disgust. "One word from me and you do as you damned well please."

His words stopped me for a moment, and I almost said something I knew I'd regret. I lifted my tongue to the roof of my mouth and took a deep breath. During my stay at the ashram, Swami Radha had suggested that I place a stone or cherry pit under my tongue when working with my father. I wasn't to speak until I had taken the time to move it. Those precious seconds, she said, would help me to temper my response.

Focusing all of my attention on the log, I wrapped my arms around it and braced myself as if in a tug-of-war competition. I leaned into it, dragging it one step at a time across the living room floor. Father shuffled ahead of me, moving a sawhorse to set it on so I could periodically stop for a breather.

"Now what?" he asked when I reached the far wall.

I glanced up to where the thickest end had to sit—a little over eight feet from the floor we were standing on. I dragged my aluminum ladder to the corner and leaned it against the wall. The entire structure pushed out when I tested the first rung.

Father looked worried. He pointed out the window. "That's a long bloody way down."

I grabbed a sixteen-foot two-by-four, spiked it to the top log, then pounded several nails through the plywood flooring into a floor joist. I pushed on the ladder and tentatively stood on the rung. It seemed solid enough. I lifted the log to what should have been the third rung; the ladder was missing the bottom one after a previous mishap when a log from the middle of this same wall had crashed down on it. I stood on a chair and raised the log another rung.

"This is plain crazy!" Father said vehemently.

I rested for a moment, then ran to the truck for my lariat. Fastening it around the butt, I threw the free end over the top log on the west wall and handed the rope to him.

"I knew you were gonna get me into this fool scheme one way or another," he groused.

I stood on the next rung, pushed the log back a foot, then

lifted it onto the next step. Laboriously, we advanced one step at a time until I finally heaved the end onto the west wall. I stared down into the courtyard that seemed a hundred feet below me and sighed with relief. Father stood back with a grim look on his face. I climbed down and dragged the ladder over to the east wall. Father secured the lariat to keep the butt end from falling, and I struggled up the ladder once again. We were one step from the top when Jack's vehicle pulled up.

"My god, man!" he hollered. "Those aluminum ladders aren't designed for that kind of weight."

"I've been trying to tell him that," Father bellyached. "But he's as pigheaded as his mother when he makes up his mind to do something…It must be that Russian blood."

I hefted the log the final step and coaxed it far enough to rest it on the top log of the east wall.

"Russian, hell!" Jack hooted. "That's a 'Yukerainian' crane if I've ever seen one."

Straddling the wall, I rolled the log to align the notch, pushed it to the edge, and dropped it into place. It landed with a resounding thud and the entire wall shook.

"Oh man, I better hit the road before someone from the compensation board catches me here," said Jack. "I have enough trouble with those buggers as it is. They see what you're up to, and they'll never let me work again."

"We'll be ready for you to start on Monday!" I called after him.

Following a few minor adjustments, we dropped the other end into its notch and nailed it in place. There were only two more rounds of logs to put up before we could start on the wing that would house the kitchen and the ground-floor bathroom.

Because it was going to be built of concrete and stone using the slipform technique, there'd be lots of framing to keep Jack busy. Summer was rapidly coming to an end, so I decided to have him put up the two-by-four walls that would be used as the inside forms and frame the second floor. With fall on the way, the long dry spell we had enjoyed for construction would likely end; the house would soon be in need of a roof.

We managed to suspend the next log for the south side of the house from a chain and lift it with the front-end loader of the tractor. Within half an hour, it was seated and spiked into place. We repeated the procedure for the east side, and things went every bit as smoothly. That left the last full-length log on the west side to deal with. I wasn't looking forward to handling it; the thirty-foot fir was so heavy I could hardly lift it. Using a chain and the front-end loader, we moved the log so one end rested on the plywood floor of the yet-to-be-constructed wing. Using fence posts as rollers, we pushed the huge timber into place across the plywood decking.

"What now?" Father asked. I could tell he was dreading my answer.

"The Yukerainian crane?"

"Are you crazy? It was bad enough climbing up that rickety ladder with a twenty-two-foot log…This one's thirty."

"Have you got any other brilliant ideas? We can't drive the tractor onto this floor." I studied the situation for a few minutes. "We can reach over with the front-end loader to lift this side." I pointed to the south end of the log.

"But that leaves you with the thick end to shinny up that bloody ladder," Father pointed out.

I went to the other end of the log and heaved. I could do it. Hooking the chain onto the small end, we lifted it into place. With pressure still on the chain, Father shut the tractor down, leaving the hydraulics of the bucket to hold the log in place.

"At least that end isn't going anywhere," I said, trying to pluck up my courage.

Father scowled. "Don't be too sure of that."

Looping the lariat around the butt of the log, I threw it over the top of the wall and gave the end to Father.

He glared at me. "I just want to get this straight…If that ladder collapses and the log squashes the shit out of you, will it be my fault for not holding the rope properly?"

Transferring my imaginary cherry pit from under my tongue, I forced myself to ignore his comment. I moved the chair into place and lifted the log onto it. There was no doubt that with the bottom rung of the ladder missing, it had far less structural strength than would be desired. I grunted and lifted the timber as high as I could manage. "Can you hold it there?"

"I hope so," Father said, taking a wrap around one of the bottom logs.

As he strained to keep the log in place, I managed to get my foot onto the bottom rung. Heaving for all I was worth, I dragged it up to waist level.

"Have you got it?"

"Yeah," he grunted.

The ladder wobbled and creaked as I slowly made my way up, but it held together. I'm not sure which of us was more relieved when I gave the final heave and the log clunked into place.

"Well," I said exultantly, "that's the last one before we put on the second floor! Getting the other ones in place should be a breeze when we have a floor to stand on."

Even though he was exhausted, Father was able to grin at me. "Give me a call when Jack has the floor down…I'm going to fire up my boat and go fishin'." With those words, he patted Lug on the head and made for his car.

I sat on top of the wall and watched his blue Toyota disappear down the road. I stared at the fine Lister dust for several minutes after the sound of his vehicle had faded. Although there had been a few minor disagreements during the two months we had been working together, we had gotten along pretty well.

My relationship with my father had always been difficult for both of us. I looked up to him and respected him, but there was part of me that feared him and hated being judged by him. Neither of us would have defined our relationship to date as close, and I instinctively realized he was trying to change that—trying to build the friendship we never really had when I was younger.

I felt lucky to have grown up in the tiny mountain community of Casino, but life there had not been without trials—a lot of them resulting from my poor self-esteem. I saw myself as awkward, clumsy, and inferior to most of the other kids, even though I was always two heads taller than they were. When I struggled with arithmetic and bemoaned not making the baseball team, Father boasted of his own athletic abilities as a youth and affirmed that math had been his favourite subject. Whenever I heard him expound, I understood him to mean that I was a klutz—that I should try to be more like him. I knew I was a disappointment to him and that he was resentful I couldn't live up to his macho image.

I smiled grimly as I revisited one of the formative incidents in our relationship. I don't know why I allowed this memory to have so much power over me, but I just couldn't let go of it. Like a recurrent nightmare, it popped right back whenever anyone criticized me in the smallest way.

I was about twelve at the time and had invited an older friend to stay over for the weekend. Allen Conway was the nephew of my dad's friend Roy Johnson. Roy lived in Casino a quarter mile down the road from us. Although Father and he drove to work at the Cominco smelter together every day and helped each other on building projects, I always perceived a strong sense of competition between them.

Allen and I had been out in the pasture riding my horse, Beauty, when Father asked us if we wanted to go for a hike and pick some huckleberries. I couldn't remember his ever asking me to go with him before. Usually, when he went picking huckleberries, he'd go with his friend Mike Reiberger. We eagerly accepted his offer and were soon trekking through Blairs' field on our way to the mountain behind Art Schermelli's place. Mike and Dad had a special huckleberry patch they'd found on one of their hunting expeditions, and Allen and I were being let in on a closely guarded secret.

From the outset, our travelling order was well-defined. Father led the way carrying a galvanized water pail. Allen followed at his heels with a picking pail fashioned from a Squirrel peanut butter can and a piece of copper wire for a handle. I brought up the rear swinging a container fabricated from an old honey tin.

We came to Casino Creek just above the beaver pond. Father and Allen walked over a slippery-looking log and stood on the other side waiting for me. After searching desperately for an alternative crossing, I followed their tried-and-tested route. I was almost across when the toe of my sneaker caught a branch and I lost my balance. I made an awkward attempt to leap to the shore, but sprawled face down in two feet of water.

Father gave me a disgusted look as I struggled onto shore. I was struggling with tears and plastered with mud. As I bent to rinse out my honey bucket, he turned and walked away. Allen took a hesitant step in my direction, then wheeled and followed Father. I stumbled after them. Water squished between my toes with every step; the wet denim of my blue jeans chafed uncomfortably at my groin. Huffing and blowing, I slogged in the direction I had seen them disappear. Every step of the way was an effort. I tortured myself with the thought that Dad would be much happier with Allen as his son...I convinced myself that if Allen were his son, he'd probably even take him hunting when he went with Mike. As it was, I was only allowed to ride up later in the day to see if they needed my horse to pack out their booty.

By the time we got to the huckleberry patch, I was exhausted and not the least bit interested in picking the clusters of purple berries that hung heavily on every bush. I sat on a log sulking and swatting at a persistent deer fly that wouldn't leave me alone. It wasn't until Allen began picking on some bushes next to me that I became motivated to get going. He already had several inches of berries in the bottom of his peanut butter can, and I was damned if I was going to let him show me up at picking, too. With a sudden zeal, I began attacking the plump fruit. By the time we were ready to leave, my honey pail was heaped to overflowing. I kept checking out Allen's bucket, telling myself that mine was bigger than his. I gloated that he still had more than an inch to go to even reach the brim.

"Let's head back," Father said, crashing through the underbrush.

I resumed my position at the back of the pack as we headed down the mountain. Keeping up was as much of a struggle on the downhill slope as it had been on the uphill. Once in a while Dad would look over his shoulder and shake his head when he saw the ever widening gap between me and Allen. I tried to pick up my pace and was gaining on them when I slipped on a loose rock and stumbled. To avoid tumbling down the bank, I made a mad grab for a nearby tree. The jolt of my sudden landing caused the wires to tear loose from my honey can, and it rolled end over end down the mountain, leaving behind it a trail of berries.

Father's expression said he didn't expect anything different from his clumsy son. He turned his back on me and continued down the trail. Shortly after we got home, Allen went to spend the rest of the weekend with his uncle. Father and I never went berry picking together again.

It was Lug's barking that jarred me out of the unsettling memory.

"Hey, neighbour!"

I turned to see Bill Huscroft getting out of his pickup. I had been so lost in my thoughts that I hadn't even heard his vehicle.

"Hi, Bill," I answered vacantly.

"Dave, I'm afraid my old cow has a problem. She didn't calve with the rest of the herd in the spring and I thought she was dry. When we went to haul her out with a few others at the beginning of August, we ran her into the holding pen and noticed she was making udder."

Bill was a log scaler at the local mill and one of the descendants of the area's founding fathers. Although he was in his early fifties, he was still muscular, and at six-foot-six, he was a man that most people wouldn't care to mess with.

He sauntered across the yard and stood looking up to where I was perched on top of the wall. "I've watched her like a hawk all week, thinking she was gonna calve. This morning when I went to the corral to throw her some hay, I noticed crap on her tail and she sort of stinks."

"You sure she hasn't calved already somewhere out in the trees and you're seeing afterbirth?"

"I'm positive. I've had her in that little corral by the barn, and there's no way I wouldn't see a calf in there."

"Well then," I said, stepping onto the ladder, "maybe we better have a look at her."

I hopped in the truck with Lug and followed Bill to his corrals. Although we had driven half a mile around the block to get to them, I could see my building site plainly across the gully.

"She's been a good old cow," Bill said, pointing to the sleek Hereford that stood munching at the feed bunk, "but she looks to me like she's pushing her luck." He lifted his foot onto a corral rail and frowned. "I don't feel as much like fooling around with these critters as I used to. Had half a mind to sell 'em all last fall, but hay wasn't worth anything and we had to get rid of it somehow."

"Has she been eating well?"

"Yeah, she's been cleaning up all I give her."

He grabbed a well-used lariat from the top of a corral post and climbed up the rails. He widened the loop, adjusted the coils, and tossed for the animal's head. The loop settled around the deformed horn butts that curled down toward her face.

"Any port in a storm!" Bill hooted, quickly getting a wrap around the fence post.

The cow flipped her head, pulled back, then leaned resignedly against her tether.

"Have you got some water handy?" I asked.

"Not hot, but I can send the boys back to the house. They're over there fixin' fence." He pointed toward the gully.

"Cold'll do if that's close."

Bill took the bucket I handed him and headed for a hydrant at the edge of the corral. Filling the pail to the brim, he carried it back to the cow while I stripped off my shirt and pulled on a shoulder-length plastic glove. I couldn't find a pair of coveralls in the truck so would just have to do my best to avoid soiling my jeans. I lifted her tail and picked at the crusty material on her tail-head. Instantly, I got a whiff of her. Yes, indeed—she smelled rank.

"What do you think?" He wrinkled his nose and hesitantly took hold of the tassel of the cow's tail when I passed it to him.

"You're right...something's rotten."

I scrubbed her up, being careful to remove all the muck that had crusted on her. When I slipped my hand inside her, I immediately ran into a bulging membrane. Floating in fluid on the other side was the tip of a tail.

"She's a breech."

"You mean backwards?" Bill asked.

"The calf's backwards but its legs are pointing forward instead of coming first. Nothing was poking through the open cervix, so the poor old girl didn't realize she was ready to calve. I think the calf's been dead for days—there wasn't anything for her to push against."

I stood to the side and ruptured the membranes. A river of putrid, watery fluid erupted from the cow's back end, and the air was immediately filled with the smell of rotten flesh. At my intrusion, the cow gave an enormous push. With my arm in the centre of her passage, gas and fluid boiled out as if shot through a nozzle of a fire hose. Both Bill and I were showered in rotten embryonic fluid.

"Oh...sick," my neighbour groaned. Releasing the tail, he wiped madly at his face with his shirtsleeve. Within seconds he was doubled over in the corner of the corral, puking his guts out.

I inspected my bare arm for some small area clean enough to wipe my lips. My face was soaked with the noxious substance, and fluid trickled from my hair and down my cheeks. I found a spot on my shoulder and rubbed my face against it. I was overcome by the irrational desire to moisten my lips and had to struggle to keep them sealed tightly and my tongue in my mouth. Determined to get this job over with, I reached forward in search of the calf's right hock. I grasped it and pulled toward me, forcing the leg into a flexed position. All I needed to do to straighten this leg now was to grab the calf's foot and push its body forward with my other hand.

"Bill! Could you bring me the water?"

Bill screwed up his face, wiped his mouth on his shirtsleeve, and grabbed the bucket.

"Give me some soap, will you?"

He held the bucket in one hand and squirted a stream of the brownish liquid over my arm with the other.

"Can you hold her tail out of the way?"

He reluctantly selected a clean spot at the bottom of the cow's tail and stood back the full extent of his long arm. He watched my other arm disappear into the cow.

"How can you stand to get that crap on your skin?"

"These plastic gloves never fail to leak anyway. I doubt I could get filthier or stinkier than I am already—may as well get on with it."

I grasped the calf's hind foot. Planting one hand over the foot to protect the uterus, I pushed forward with the other. Just as I brought the foot out, the cow strained again, dumping a gallon of stinking fluid down the front of my jeans and onto my running shoes.

"I'm outta here!" gasped Bill. Covering his mouth, he headed for the far end of the corral. "Keith! Jimmy! You guys get your asses up here!"

Hearing Bill summon the boys in that booming voice of his brought back memories. One would almost think that he and my father had shared a vocal coach.

I struggled to get the calf's second leg straightened out, but every time I almost had the limb in flexion, the cow would strain or clamp down her tail and I'd be back to square one. I stood away and scanned the gully for a sign of the boys. Although I could hear their voices, I was still unable to see them. I smelled my hands. Detoxifying was not going to be a simple case of washing up and dabbing on a bit of extra deodorant. This smell would be following me for days. I looked down at my jeans and sneakers; they were covered with slime and hair. A long strand of pink flesh—part of the fetal membranes—was stuck to the side of my shoe. I closed my eyes and breathed in deeply, trying to shut out the putrid odour. I'd have to head straight home and chuck everything in the washing machine.

I repeatedly wiped my face on my shoulder, trying to remove the muck. The more I focused on keeping my mouth clamped shut to avoid tasting the revolting material, the more I had to struggle with the urge to lick my lips.

Bill sat on the top rail at the far end of the corral with his head in his hands. He still wasn't looking very chipper. He finally glanced in my direction and saw me standing there waiting.

"What's takin' you guys so long?" he bellowed.

"What do you want?" his son hollered in return.

"Dave needs you to help him with this cow!"

"Well, why don't you help him?"

"Never mind! Just get over here."

The oldest of Bill's three sons, Keith was blond, handsome, well-built, and only slightly shorter than his dad. He swaggered up from the gully where he'd been stretching wire, a pair of fencing pliers still in his hand.

"What's all the racket about?" He climbed over the fence at the bottom of the coulee.

"Hold that tail so Dave can get this over with!" Bill ordered.

Keith slowed as he got close enough to get a whiff of the situation. He noticed the leg that hung out of the cow's rear end, wrinkled his nose, and glared at his dad. "What stinks?"

"Just hold the bloody tail!" Bill barked.

As Keith grabbed hold of the cow's tassel and stood at arm's length, I resumed my task. I quickly located the hock and stretched deep to grasp the calf's other hind foot. When I applied traction on the foot, the hooves separated from the pedal bones. I reluctantly released my hold and brought the horny blanched caps out so they wouldn't be left behind in the uterus.

"Oh gross!" Keith groaned as I dropped them to the ground at my feet. He glared at his dad. "No wonder you didn't want to do this...Jimmy! Come hold the tail!" With that he was gone and over the fence.

I shot Bill a look of frustration in hopes that he'd come and help put an end to my nasty task.

"Jimmy! Jimmy!" he roared. "Come give Dave a hand!"

I closed my eyes and focused on my breathing. When I slowed it enough, I could almost forget that I was dragging in molecules of decaying flesh with each draught of air. It was agonizing to be stuck in this limbo knowing how close I was to finishing. All I needed was someone to get this tail out of the way so I could get both hands in there.

"What do you want me to do?"

I turned to see a thin, dark-haired lad about the same age as Keith walking up the hill toward me. Jimmy was a neighbour's boy Bill had hired to help manage the cattle. He communicated sullen resignation; one would have expected he had just heard a judge sentence him to the electric chair.

"Hold the tail to the side!" I said to the kid in exasperation.

I soaped up my arms again and once more chased the calf's foot to the depths of the cow's uterus. Grasping the foot with my left hand, I flexed it, then inserted my right arm to push the calf forward. As the leg began to straighten, the sharp little bones of the foot dug into my palm. I clenched my teeth and continued straining. With one more good push on the calf's butt, I was suddenly over the brim of the pelvis. I breathed a sigh of relief as the leg straightened and popped out beside the other one. I applied a chain to each foot, attached the hooks, and leaned back. The calf came easily until I made it past the hips. As soon as I met with resistance, I hooked up the calving jack. Over a period of ten minutes I extracted a carcass that was ballooned with gas and fluid to half again its normal size. I had to give Jimmy credit—he lasted to the bitter end.

Finally, I was able to wash up my equipment and attack my own body with a vengeance. Fine red hairs clung to me, coating my arms, abdomen, and chest. Tiny chunks of membrane adhered to my skin and clothing. Only after scrubbing several times and changing the water could I force myself to wash my face. Then, I scrubbed it over and over again, still tightening my jaw against the overwhelming desire to lick my lips.

The squishing of my sneakers on the way to the truck brought me back to my earlier memories from Casino. I smiled at Bill...He was planted on the top rail of the corral, directing Jimmy on how to dispose of the bloated carcass. Jimmy's stance suggested he wasn't necessarily in sync with his boss's wishes.

I found myself musing as I put away my implements. It was a good thing we weren't all cut from the same cloth. Most people would have reacted exactly like Bill and done anything to avoid what I had just gone through. I'd cheerfully endure the experience a hundred times over rather than revisit those seconds of humiliation as Father watched my berry bucket tumble end for end down the mountain.

I jumped into the truck and started it up. Before I could get out of the driveway, Lug was eagerly checking me out. Irritated by his amorous advances, I pushed him away. Within seconds, he was back licking my arm.

"Get over there! I'm not a bloody lollipop."

I squinted for the first glimpse of my building site. There were the logs silhouetted against the forest. The house was going to look pretty good tucked in among those trees.

On the way to town, Lug and I each continued to fight our own personal battles. He struggled with his dogged desire to attack my pant leg and taste what smelled so enticing. I drove with the windows open and my teeth clenched, thinking about the relationships between fathers and sons, still trying to avoid licking my lips.

Of Cows and Racehorses

"What do you think, Dave?"

Jack took a deep drag on his cigarette, exhaled a cloud of smoke over his kitchen table, and poked a finger at the papers in front of me. I had never seen him so excited.

"I don't know…It certainly sounds feasible on paper."

"I've been over it and over it and I'm sure I can swing it…All my life, I've dreamed of becoming a farmer."

"Well, I've read somewhere that more American farm loans have been paid off by raising hogs than by any other commodity. Maybe you can be a statistic here in Canada."

Jack nodded. "It's a long way from being a done deal, but Verna sounded interested. If she goes for our offer, she'll take over this place and we'll move over there." He paused, took a drink of his coffee, and looked almost dreamily at his wife, Sandra. "We'll have a pretty big mortgage but with the price of weaner pigs, we should be able to handle the payment without any trouble."

"Well, prices are pretty good right now. But remember they can go down as well as up, and the wave tends to be shorter for them than it is with most other commodities. It's much easier for small producers to get started into hogs than it is into cattle. It's amazing what a difference a few sows in every backyard can make— production throughout North America can change really quickly."

I took a sip of my coffee and studied the figures again. Nothing looked out of line. If Jack could keep his litter numbers anywhere near Verna's, and she really did have this many gilts and sows in her dry lot ready to farrow, then he should be able to make it with money in the bank.

"Provided you didn't introduce some unexpected disease problems, the most likely factors that could throw a monkey wrench in things would be an increase in the price of feed or a major decrease in the price of weaner pigs."

"I've been keeping track of the price of weaners for months now, thinking of getting a couple sows." Jack enthusiastically held up a copy of the *Western Producer* newspaper out of Saskatoon. "Verna got sixty-five bucks apiece for hers on the last load she hauled to Pincher Creek."

"I know they're good right now...Gary Koebel was telling me how well he made out with his last shipment."

"How's Gary doing now?" Sandy interjected.

"It looks to me that he's pretty much his old self. He was complaining about being a bit tired when I was over there the other day, but that's not surprising—he's right back to having ten projects on the go at the same time."

"What is ratbite fever, anyway?" she asked. "One of the cleaning ladies from the hospital was in for a perm, and she was telling me how sick he'd been."

Jack fidgeted with his coffee cup and got up from the table.

"It's pretty rare," I answered. "It'd have to be something pretty exotic to keep Gary in the hospital for six weeks. I'd never heard of it before. It's apparently a disease of rodents caused by a bacterium called *Streptobacillus moniliformis*. They think he must have gotten a cut infected with it when he was working around mouse droppings in the barn."

Jack grabbed the coffee pot and topped up everyone's cup. Sitting down again, he held the spoon over his coffee, poised the sugar dispenser, and let it pour. After tipping a fourth teaspoon into his cup, he curtailed the flow and passed the sugar to me. He stirred the black swill vigorously, then chucked the spoon on the table.

"You know, when we were fighting in Korea...dug into trenches on those godforsaken mountains, there was nothing we feared more than rats. The gooks couldn't hold a candle to them." He shivered involuntarily, ground his half-finished butt into the ashtray, and lit another with one of the three Bic lighters that seemed to have earned permanent-fixture status on his kitchen table. "Those bloody things were the size of house cats from feeding off all the dead bodies. Whenever a guy got bit by one of those buggers, that was it. He'd swell up and start shivering. The next thing we knew he was taken off the line and we never saw him again."

There was an uncomfortable silence as Jack stared into his cup. Sandy got up from the table and filled a plate with chocolate chip cookies from a cookie jar that was fashioned in the shape of a little boy's head.

"Just baked these this morning," she said cheerfully.

"Gary was telling me he's feeding most of his own weaners out now," said Jack. His face brightened visibly as he changed the subject. "I was looking at some plans from an outfit called Cargill. I think we could use their feeding system and set up to do the same thing—as soon as we get a few bucks ahead for all the concrete, that is."

"What do you think, Sandy?" I peered over my cup at Jack's better half.

"I don't know." She took a long drag on her cigarette. "It sounds pretty good...I'm not sure I'm ready to be a pig farmer, but I do know I'm ready to quit hairdressing. I've had enough of all those chemicals. Some days after doing perms for hours, I can hardly breathe—"

"It'll be good for us all to get over there," Jack interrupted, "the kids included. And if these figures are right, Sandy won't need to work." Reaching across the table, he grabbed his wife's hand and smiled. "You wait and see, baby...Stick with me and you'll be fartin' through silk."

I laughed and reached for my second cookie. I sure hoped he was right. Jack and his wife were hard-working people, but they were talking about putting everything on the line to fulfill a dream.

It was exciting to go to the farm every night and see all the changes to the house. Jack and his helper had framed the entire first floor for the wing, and the plates were ready to take the trusses for the upper floor. The site had been literally humming with activity this week. The stonemason, Bruno Laub, and his son Mark had been there, too, erecting the blocks and flues for the chimney and fireplaces. It seemed strange to drive up to the place and see a concrete monument extending high above the level of the logs. It reminded me of an epitaph to fallen soldiers— from the footing to the top of the chimney, it was thirty-eight feet high.

After Jack had finished decking the second floor, Father and I went back to work on the logs and finished placing the last of them. It was a breeze working on the few remaining rounds without fear of making a whole wall come tumbling down.

Scott's crane was coming tomorrow to put up the roof trusses. For the last three nights, I'd been working with Father reinforcing the old ones. It was amazing to think they had survived a hundred years and were still in almost as good shape as the day they were put up. All we had to do now was make sure they'd hang in for another hundred. This afternoon Jack had finished fabricating the last of the new trusses for the addition. What a difference it made to use new lumber; driving a nail into the old larch rafters was like pounding into concrete.

Tomorrow would be a big day. The structure would look so much different with a roof actually in place. I tried to imagine the roofline—somehow, I still had difficulty picturing how the two hipped structures would butt together.

After coffee with Jack and Sandy, I headed to the farm to see how Father was making out. Mom had come down from Riondel for the week, and it was obvious he was happy to be relieved of his mess duties.

Lug was putting on his usual show as I pulled into the little road where they were camped. Mother was outside their home-away-from-home busily raking. Since she had arrived, she'd accumulated piles of pine needles and sticks from an ever-increasing radius around the camper. The makeshift abode on stilts was now spotless, without a dirty dish or sock in sight. Mother took off her cotton glove to give Lug a pat as he bounded over and shoved his head between her knees.

"You're going to wear out that rake, Mom."

"I'm just trying to make things a little homier is all."

"I know, I know…You have it looking like a park already."

No matter where Mother was, she had to make things homey—orderly, with everything in its place.

She handed me a blue plastic bucket. "Could you fill that for me…I hate sticking my hand down in that hole. Keep thinking that something will grab me." I knelt beside the water box and filled the bucket for her. "We've been waiting supper on you. All I have to do is fire up the stove and start cooking. I've got the potatoes peeled and the pork chops thawed."

"Sounds good, Mom…I'm hungry."

"You better go and talk to your father. He went over to Verna's to get some milk this afternoon and apparently came across her boy lying hurt out in the yard. He didn't fill me in on all the details, but I could tell he was upset."

"What happened?"

"You better go talk to him…You know what he's like when he gets worked up about something. He never wants to talk about things that are bothering him."

A cool breeze was picking up so I pulled on my jacket and sauntered across the gully to where Father was working. The grass was blanched from the long dry spell and cropped close from the grazing of the cattle. The stubble crunched under my feet. The leaves of the birch and poplar trees were beginning to take on the orange and yellow hues of fall. Father was busy pounding on the plywood cleats that Jack had manufactured to add rigidity to the old larch trusses. When Lug greeted him, he threw aside his hammer.

"Damn, this old larch is like iron," he grumbled.

"What happened at Verna's today?"

Father suddenly looked sullen. "That poor bloody kid—" he started.

"What happened?"

"You know, Verna reminds me so much of my old man."

"What do you mean?"

"Well, you could never please him. Day in, day out, it was the same bloody thing. Pickin' rocks, plowin' with the team of horses…there was never any end to it."

I could see that something was really bothering Dad; whenever he was upset, he retreated to his boyhood in Saskatchewan.

"What happened over at Verna's?"

"Well, I was taking the empty milk jug back and going for another one when I heard a voice…I thought it was my hearing playing tricks on me. When I didn't see anything, I went in the milk house and got a new jar out of the fridge."

He picked up the hammer and pounded in a few more nails.

"So what happened, already?"

"When I came out, I thought I heard a voice again…I could barely hear him. It was Verna's youngest boy. He was leaning up against that old feeder by the corner of their barn. As calm as if he was sitting across the table from me, he said, 'Marsh, can you give me a hand?'" Father's voice was trembling; his eyes were red. "I set the jug of milk down and went over to see what was going on. I couldn't believe it…The poor little bugger was covered in muck

146

and sawdust from one end to the other, and the leg of his coveralls was half ripped off and soaked in blood." Father stopped for a moment and set down the hammer again. "It just isn't right the way she works those kids."

"What happened with him, Dad?"

"The boar got him. Apparently when he came home from school the fences were down and the pigs were out in the yard. Two boars were fighting and he took a shovel in to try and break them up. He said the last thing he remembered was giving the white boar a whack. He kept talking about that big mouth coming at him all filled with froth—like something out of a horror movie. The damn thing dumped him in a heap about twenty feet from where he first hit him."

He laid another plywood cleat onto the side of the rafter and began pounding. He swung the hammer as if he was taking his frustration out on the nails. "I've never seen anything like it, Dave. His knee was tore wide open and all covered with blood and sawdust. I could see the bone…It isn't right…"

He got up from the ground and grasped the side of the truss. I took hold of the other side and we carried it to the finished pile. Father grabbed another cleat and headed for the next truss. "These are the last of 'em," he said matter-of-factly, pointing at the two that remained.

"So what did you do?"

"I got him into the car and took him to the hospital. Poor kid couldn't walk on his right leg at all and had to hold onto me and hop to the car. He'd been trying to drag himself to the house, but those damned boars were still roaring around fightin' and he was terrified they'd be attracted to the blood and come back for him."

He looked at me with tears in his eyes. "It's not right…"

I nodded.

"The kid kept lookin' like he was going to pass out, but the whole way to town all he worried about was getting blood in my car."

It was after we had stacked the last of the trusses that he spoke again.

"Will something like that heal up, Dave? I mean, I could see right inside his knee, and everything was covered with sawdust. That boar must have rolled him around something awful before he got away."

"It doesn't sound good...I guess they'll have to clean things up the best they can and pump him full of antibiotics. I sure hope he'll be all right. It would be rough to have a permanent injury to your knee at fourteen."

"You know, Dave, your grandfather was just like Verna. It didn't matter how fast or how well I did something when I was a kid, I didn't do it right and I didn't do it fast enough."

I involuntarily closed my eyes and turned away. How many times had I said those exact words to myself, to Mom, to my sisters, Audrey and Kay? We all knew what it was like to feel we weren't meeting Father's expectations. I wondered if he had any idea how I was feeling right now? Did he realize how close the apple had fallen to the tree?

When Father resumed talking, his voice was muted. "You know, I never told you, but I left home two days after my fourteenth birthday. I couldn't take another minute of living with the old man on that windblown piece of dirt. He made me quit school, and from morning to night all I did was dig stumps and pick rocks. I pulled stoneboat after stoneboat of rocks off his precious bloody farm, and do you think there was ever a word of thanks in it? At least when I got a job in a fish camp up on Great Slave Lake, we got something to eat other than a crust of bread."

"Marsh! Dave! Supper's ready!"

I was subdued after I left the farm that night. We had eaten supper without speaking. Although Mother initially tried to make conversation, she knew her husband well and soon accepted the silence.

It was dusk as I proceeded north down Canyon-Lister Road, and I could see the lights of Creston in the distance. I was about to turn down 24th Street to go home when I decided to drive through Canyon to see if Eleanor Blair was around. Whenever I was in a pensive mood like this, talking with Eleanor always seemed the thing to do.

Most people knew her as the cat lady from Canyon. To them she was a charity case who lived in an old house that was coming down around her ears. I couldn't blame them for having those first impressions, because her house was literally falling apart, and she housed more cats in that ramshackle place than I had ever seen under a single roof.

I couldn't help but notice her eccentricities, but over the years of dealing with her I had come to see a lot more. She had talents galore—she was a good artist and clearly had the ability to write. It seemed, however, that daily happenings always interfered with her creativity. If she wasn't in a dither about a colicky horse or a cat that refused to feed its kittens, she was scheming about how she'd buy a pack of smokes when she only had enough money for a bag of cat food. Eleanor had a lot to teach me. Somehow all of my own character flaws seemed magnified in hers.

I pulled to the shoulder in front of her place and clicked off my lights. "No you don't," I said as I pushed Lug back in the truck. "You'd only get us both into trouble here."

He cranked his neck and pressed his nose against the windshield as I struggled with the chain on the old log gate. I finally got the link over the head of the nail and swung it inward. The wire hinge at the bottom was broken, and it was necessary to support the entire weight as it swung. I squeezed through the opening, set the cumbersome structure back on the piece of firewood it rested on, and left the chain dangling for my return.

"Hello, Honey."

Eleanor's dun quarter horse mare stood looking expectantly up into the lower branches of a wildly overgrown apple tree. I jumped up and grabbed two of the small apples that hung from an upper branch and held one out in the palm of my hand. The aging girl bit into it, covering my fingers with slobber and juice. Before I could give her the second one, her old mate O'Brian clumped his way over in hopes of a handout.

"So you think you need one, too, do you?"

I grabbed another apple from the tree and held it out for the antiquated bag of bones. He chomped down on the piece of fruit with incisor teeth that were almost parallel to one another, then lolled it around and around intending to crush it. Froth bubbled from the corners of his mouth as he sought the second half, eager to get it before Honey could steal it away. The tired old gelding was used to competing with the blonde mare for every blade of grass or mouthful of hay. They had been at it for more than twenty years now. According to Eleanor, O'Brian used to be the dominant one, but that was when his teeth were still growing—before he had to gum everything to death. If I remembered correctly, he'd be thirty-six or thirty-seven this year, an admirable age for a horse.

O'Brian's past was almost as colourful as his owner's. Eleanor loved to tell the tale of how he couldn't be ridden. He'd been a rodeo horse and she apparently acquired him after he killed a rider and was going to be put down. I had been sure he was a goner a few years ago in the dead of winter when he had a session of colic as a result of an impacted caecum and colon, but Eleanor had somehow willed him to carry on. I had spent a couple of days worrying, not only about the animal, but about the fact that Eleanor was making herself sick as she nursed her beloved horse through a snowstorm. Her health wasn't good at the best of times.

I looked at O'Brian's rough hair coat and protruding hips and shook my head. He'd make a fantastic specimen to teach veterinary students the anatomy of the skeletal structure. One could count every vertebra in his swayed old back and feel the protuberances of every bone. He wouldn't be of much value for studying muscle, though—he had little of that left on his frame.

I fed them each another apple, then carried on up the path to the house. It was a clapboard structure built back in the first decade of the twentieth century. Although it was probably state-of-the-art at the time it was erected, now the roof leaked and sagged in the middle as rafters rotted and the foundation timbers became one with the earth. An old wooden verandah with a few missing boards led up to the front door.

I could tell Eleanor wasn't in the house. There were no lights on and a piece of baler twine ran from a nail on the greying cedar-

panelled door to a nail on the jamb beside it. She had to have locked it from the outside.

"Eleanor! Eleanor…are you around?"

I continued past the house wondering if maybe her friend Chris Herchmer had picked her up for some shopping and kept her over for supper. It was getting dark and Eleanor rarely strayed far from the property at this time of day. Aside from Chris, she didn't have a lot of friends she chose to spend time with.

"Eleanor!"

I was ready to retrace my steps to the truck when I heard her.

"Over here!" Her silhouette appeared from behind a broken-down shed that listed dangerously toward the neighbour's property.

"Oh, Dave, thank god you're here…Could you take a quick look at Wee Jordie?" She was obviously perplexed. "He's hung up again."

I leaned on the top rail of the fence and stared at the shiny black stallion in the twenty-by-twenty enclosure.

Eleanor took a deep drag on her cigarette. It glowed cherry red against the darkening sky and accentuated the deep wrinkles around her eyes and lips. "I spent the afternoon brushing him hoping it would relax him." She sighed and ground the remains of her cigarette into the top of the cedar pole. "But you can see it didn't do a lot of good."

The horse stood bolt upright eating hay from the top of a wooden apple box that Eleanor had set in front of him.

"Do you think Morgans are prone to this problem?"

"I'm sure there are certain bloodlines that are," I replied, putting my foot on the bottom rail of the fence and starting to climb. "But we can see it in almost every breed."

"Watch out for that one." Eleanor pointed to the second rail from the top. "It came off earlier…I just finished pounding it back on."

I swung my leg over the top rail and dropped to the ground beside the little stallion. He moved his front feet to the side to avoid me, but his hind legs remained stationary in an absolutely upright position.

"I don't know how you're always able to get him to move," Eleanor said. "It's exactly like the last time. I massaged him and tried everything I could think of to get him unlocked and still can't get him to take a step."

"I've never seen a horse that locks up as bad as he does," I muttered. "Usually the groove only catches the edge of the patella to cause an intermittent lameness."

I grabbed a piece of twine from the top of the fence and looped it around Wee Jordie's neck. Pulling his head to the side, I attempted to make him take a step. He reluctantly sidled toward me using his front foot, but stayed frozen on the back. I stepped into his side and ran my hand up his leg. The patella was locked; the tendons on either side were so tight that they felt like part of the bone.

"It's happening more often lately," Eleanor lamented.

She flipped a package of Player's Light cigarettes from her pocket and plucked one out. Leaning under the corner of the building, she scrunched her head to her chest and struck a paper match. Her wrinkled face glowed brightly for a few seconds before she blew it out. She dragged on the smoke as if it were her first for the day.

"Well, he is getting older, and he doesn't have a lot of room in here to exercise. Why won't you consider castrating him so you can let him run with Honey and O'Brian?"

Eleanor looked startled. "You know that he's a pure-blood Morgan, don't you?"

"You mentioned that before…but this is happening as a result of a conformational problem, and I'd expect that at least a tendency toward the defect would be passed on to his offspring."

"I've always pictured him pulling my carriage in the Blossom Festival parade," Eleanor said dreamily. "He just has so much class."

I knew that my friend was a fixture in Creston's annual parade. Even with Honey's advanced years, they made an impressive pair when they were both duded up. I think Eleanor was the only person I had ever seen riding side-saddle.

"You could drive him as a gelding."

Eleanor inhaled more smoke and glared at me. I said nothing more. "I'm not sure what's going on when he stands there like that," she admitted reluctantly. "Isn't there something more we can do for him? I tried giving him some of that Butazone you left me for Honey, but it hasn't made any difference."

"That's not surprising. This is a mechanical problem. Horses have a much more complicated stifle than we do. Where we have one patellar tendon, they have three. I guess I'm not telling you anything you don't know, but when things are working properly, it allows them to lock their kneecap over a groove in the lower portion of the femur so they can rest and sleep standing up. That's all well and good when it works the way it's supposed to, but when a leg's as straight up and down as Jordie's, there's a tendency for the ligament to lock into place and impede his movement rather than strengthen it."

Eleanor wagged her head as she stared mournfully at her horse's motionless hind legs. "I was just going in to plug in the kettle and make him a hot bran mash when I heard you calling. I thought maybe it would help…" Her voice trailed off as if afraid I might ridicule her suggestion.

"I think that's a great idea," I said.

Eleanor brightened. "My dad was always big on hot bran mashes," she stated enthusiastically. "He was a real horseman."

As soon as Eleanor left the paddock for the house, I dragged the apple box from in front of Wee Jordie. Although the horse stretched his neck for a final bite of hay as the platform disappeared, he made no attempt to move his hind end so he could follow it. He chewed, swallowed, and looked with longing in the direction of the hay.

I carefully scaled the rickety rails again and broke off a switch from a clump of willows at the edge of the property line. Standing on the second rail behind Jordie, I brought it down with a sharp crack across his rump. The horse tensed and crow-hopped forward. He looked at me accusingly, then walked to his hay as though he had just decided he was hungry. I grabbed Eleanor's brush and zealously stroked the dusty imprint that showed evidence of the willow's contact with his rump.

It was well-documented in the veterinary literature that a quick fix for the locking up of the patellar ligaments was to startle the animal and get it to suddenly contract its quadriceps. Larry Kramer, our equine professor, had often related how a sharp crack with a stock whip when the owner wasn't around could be a temporary solution to a perplexing problem.

By the time Eleanor came back with the hot bran mash, Jordie was at the far end of the corral leisurely picking at his flake of hay. She looked up to where I perched smugly on the corral rail and raised her eyebrows. She shook her head, smiled, then bowed gracefully in my direction.

"Dr. Perrin, I don't how you do it. You've worked your magic once more."

I smiled in return, took the bran mash from her outstretched hands, and presented it to Jordie. We watched him consume the mash and return to his hay.

"It seems as though it's getting worse when it happens," Eleanor insisted. "It's hard to imagine that this is the same little foal I once had bucking and romping around my backyard. I wouldn't have believed that something like this could possibly befall him. He was my pride and joy."

"I still think that having him castrated and getting him out of this corral would make a big difference. Lack of exercise is probably a major factor, and he'd be so much happier if he could get out and graze with the others."

Eleanor ignored my suggestion. "Is there something that can

be done about it?" She was obviously unwilling to consider the fact that confining him to this small paddock could be part of the problem.

"The literature describes trotting affected animals up and down hills for half an hour three or four times a week as a form of physical therapy. There's a claim that it can help stretch out the ligaments. In severe cases like Jordie's, though, we might have to consider surgery."

"Surgery?" Eleanor's eyes lit up as if she had finally heard the right answer.

"Yes, it entails severing the medial patellar ligament—the one that catches on the head of the femur."

"Does that mean he wouldn't be able to sleep standing up anymore?"

I contemplated her question in silence. It made sense that he wouldn't be able to lock his joint, but I couldn't ever remember seeing a horse that had had the surgery done. "I don't know the answer to that one, Eleanor…It would make sense that he wouldn't."

She contemplated Wee Jordie for a moment longer. He was shifting his weight from side to side, eating as if nothing had ever been wrong. She shivered and pulled her buttonless jacket together across her breast. "I hate the thought that another winter's coming on."

"Not too fussy about this nice weather ending myself."

"Do you have time to come in and take the stitches out of Samantha? There's still enough hot water for a couple cups of tea, and it's getting chilly out here."

"Sure," I said. "I'll grab my suture scissors."

I went back to the truck and fished the scissors from the disinfectant tray. Lug stuck his nose against the driver's window hoping beyond hope that I'd let him out. I opened the door and gave him a pat.

"Sorry, old buddy…not yet."

I took a deep breath of the cool evening air and headed reluctantly toward Eleanor's house. As much as I enjoyed spending time with my friend, I could think of places I'd rather do it than in her house. I followed the ribbon of light that extended from her front window and stepped cautiously onto the verandah. It was almost totally dark now and I didn't want to take a tumble—several boards were either broken or missing.

I peered through the curtainless window. Eleanor was still scurrying around inside in pursuit of Samantha. She rushed past the window and began digging behind some boxes in the farthest corner. I pushed on the door, but when it wouldn't yield, stood waiting. It was several minutes before I heard the knife being pulled from the jamb. The door swung inward, scraping heavily along the floor as it opened.

"Get in quickly!" Eleanor gasped.

As I stepped inside, she quickly plunked her butt against the door. Still clutching a squirming bundle tight to her chest, she slid the butter knife under the jamb. She was bleeding from several parallel scratches running the full length of her forearm.

"She got you, eh?"

"She's never been a cuddly kitty."

I remembered how much trouble we had getting Samantha into a cat bag before doing surgery. That was ten days ago when she was toxemic from a pair of rotting kittens in her tummy. We had spayed her and removed several mammary tumours at the same time. I was thankful when I came in the next morning to see she had pulled all remnants of the intravenous off her foreleg. Neither Doris nor I had been looking forward to the task.

"What's the plan?" I asked. I was breathing very deliberately, trying to acclimate myself to the pungent odour in the room. I knew from experience that the first five minutes would be the worst—after that my olfactory senses and taste buds would simply give up and accept.

Eleanor shuffled to her kitchen table and plunked the swaddled burden next to a dirty plate. The cat was wrapped in her woollen jacket, and I quickly evaluated which end was which. I felt a prickly sensation on the back of my neck as a high-pitched scream emitted from beneath the cloth barrier. I firmly placed my hand on the cat's neck and pressed her to the table. I had clipped her nails after surgery to reduce the likelihood of injury to me and Doris, and to facilitate Eleanor's ability to administer antibiotics, but that hadn't prevented her from brutalizing Eleanor's arm. I felt vaguely reassured that I had scaled her teeth and extracted a rotten molar, but that didn't make a bite from her any more appealing.

"Keep your hand here, Eleanor."

She held Samantha's head to the table as I restrained her back legs and slowly worked my way into the jacket. The cat growled deeply and struggled when I folded back the flaps. I was cursing myself for not using subcuticular stitches—they didn't have to be removed—but at the time I felt it necessary to place drains to remove the inevitable seepage from the mammary tissues. I exposed her tummy and got Eleanor to take her hind legs. The wounds had healed nicely and only a bit of crusty material remained in the drain tubes. I rubbed her tummy with an alcohol swab, then started snipping stitches. The cat struggled briefly when I pulled the drain, then shot out a great stream of urine in protest. I continued to snip as the pee soaked into Eleanor's jacket.

"Okay, Eleanor."

The moment she let go of the cat, the creature tore off to the farthest corner of the room and disappeared under a cluster of cardboard boxes. There was a screech and a hiss and several other cats scurried to the centre of the room.

"You'd think we were killing her," Eleanor sighed. "I'd have thought after all these years of living here, she'd have settled down…Oh well, at least I won't have to worry about more kittens from her."

She wiped the urine from the table with her jacket and threw it into the corner. Plugging the kettle in, she pulled a cup from a cardboard box under the table and plunked it on the freshly washed surface. She retrieved her own cup from a shelf above her bed and set it next to mine. Pushing an old neutered tom from her only kitchen chair, she waved me to it.

"Have a seat."

She fumbled open a box of orange pekoe tea, put a fresh bag into her cup, and poured steaming water into both cups. Retreating to her bed, she pushed a pair of kittens far enough from the edge for her to sit down. She took a spoon from the table and began chasing the tea bag around her cup.

"I'm sure not looking forward to winter coming on," she repeated wistfully.

"Well, if it's any consolation, I'm hoping that this weather holds for a bit longer, too. We're putting the rafters up for my roof tomorrow."

"Oh, isn't that exciting!" Eleanor gushed. "You'll have to drive me over to see it when you get the roof on. I always liked that old house…It was so classy before they covered the logs up with those hideous asphalt shingles."

"Oh, you remember the old Ahlefeld house then?"

"Of course I do," she replied indignantly. "My memory may be selective, but it's pretty good. Sheila Ahlefeld was a Hood." Eleanor fished the tea bag from her cup, got up from the bed, and plunked it and the spoon into mine. "My dad knew the Hoods quite well…We were neighbours back in the old days."

"Neighbours?"

"Yes, we farmed on the reclamation flats for years. It was only after we were flooded out two years in a row that we built up here. Dad came with the first settlers to this property back in 1908."

"I never knew your father was actually a farmer…I gathered that he was sort of a dandy who got sent over here from Britain to get out of his older brother's hair. What did they call those guys?" I regretted the word "dandy" the moment I spit it out.

"My father was not a remittance man, and he certainly wasn't a dandy," Eleanor bristled. "He was one hell of a horseman. There are a lot of folks around here who think they know a thing or two about our four-legged friends, but Dad could have straightened them out in a hurry."

"Whereabouts in Britain did he originate?" I blurted, trying to deflect her wrath.

"He was a Scot," she said with less of an edge to her voice. "With a name like Campbell Blair, he couldn't have been anything else—born in Glasgow. He and his brother emigrated to South Dakota originally. They operated a farm and imported Clydesdales from the old country. Daddy went back to England when he was in his twenties and lived there until his mid-thirties—that's when he volunteered for service with the British Army in South Africa." Eleanor struck a match and lit another cigarette. Taking a drag, she tipped her head back and exhaled a jet of smoke toward the ceiling. "I envy Daddy, living when he did. The Victorian era would have been a great time to be alive...I'm sure I would have fit in a lot better then."

She sorted through a dilapidated cardboard box at the head of her bed and dragged out a tattered album. She rummaged through a stack of black and white pictures that fell onto her lap. Several empty stickers still remained on the black felt pages as evidence that they had once had moorings. She handed me a photo of a dozen people wearing English hunting garb. They were all mounted on horses and surrounded by hounds. She pointed to a distinguished-looking man in the centre of the picture.

"That's my father when he was riding with a royal hunt—just before he left for the Boer War. Here's one of Mom and Dad and I out here in Canyon."

I examined the photo of the people mounted on pinto horses. There were half a dozen other horses standing behind and the ground was covered with snow. I flipped the photo over. The notation on the back was "Canyon 1947."

"Here's one of Mom and Dad and I with Percy Watson and the rest of the crew threshing grain down on the flats. That would have been somewhere around 1927 or 1928."

"I had no idea your dad farmed there."

"My dad, hell—we all worked our butts off."

She passed me a photo of a young lady sitting on the back steps of an ivy-covered house. She was holding a kitten and three or four others were eating from the same bowl. "That's me in 1933 after I returned to Canyon from finishing school in Britain."

"So you were a star pupil at finishing school?" I joked.

"Certainly," she replied. "Can't you tell?"

She put her cigarette on the top of the cat food can she was using as an ashtray, flipped her head back, and elegantly patted her white hair. She grabbed a hardcover book from the box at the head of her bed. Standing straight as a pole, she placed the book on her head and walked about the room, balancing it perfectly.

"That's amazing, Eleanor…you're full of hidden talents."

"You have no idea," she said with a smile.

She set the book on the table—it was a tome of Milton's poetry—and sat down on her bed again. She sighed deeply, then picked up her cigarette and inhaled another big draught of smoke. She frowned.

"I wasn't much on the discipline. Adjusting to a proper British boarding school was quite a feat for a sixteen-year-old farm girl from the backwoods of British Columbia. Poor Father thought it would make a proper lady out of me. Up until I left, I had pretty much been allowed to run wild. Can you imagine going from running horses bareback across the flats to being prim and proper in a sidesaddle?" She stopped for a moment, picked up her copy of Milton, and flipped open the well-worn book. "I loved studying English literature, though," she went on. "Especially poetry."

"Funny how it goes…I hated having to learn poetry when I was in grade school, and now I spend hours trying to write it when I should be sleeping. It always seemed such an effort back then, when studying poetry meant regurgitating verses." I removed my tea bag and took a sip of the now lukewarm liquid. "You know, about the only line I can remember is, 'What is this life if, full of care...'"

Without missing a beat, Eleanor took over, "'We have no time to stand and stare.'" She recited the remaining verses without hesitation, her voice rising and falling dramatically. I listened with appreciation to this woman who never ceased to amaze me.

"The poem is *Leisure* by William Henry Davies," she said, "the poet of the tramps. He was a British lad who went to America and lived as a vagrant. He lost a leg while trying to jump on a moving train. He eventually went back to England and collected enough money begging on street corners to print a few copies of his first book of poetry. Once George Bernard Shaw got hold of one and showed interest in his work, everyone else jumped onto the bandwagon. He was all the rage when I was at school. He died in 1940."

I sat staring at Eleanor with my mouth hanging open. She smiled shyly and got up from her bed. Picking up a dinner plate from the centre of the floor, she scooped it full of dry cat food from a plastic garbage can. There were scurrying noises from every corner of the room as cats materialized and came meowing to her feet. She placed the dish down and picked up two more from the far corner.

"Good Lord, Eleanor, how many critters are you feeding?"

She looked at me with a mischievous glint in her eyes. "My dear doctor, there are some questions you just don't ask a lady."

By the time she finished doling out four heaping plates, a dozen cats at each location pushed one another in a desperate attempt to grab as many kernels as possible before the food was gone.

"So you came right back here after finishing school?"

"I went to college in Winnipeg for a year in hopes of getting my degree in literature, but there weren't many opportunities for women academics back then, and Dad always thought it wasn't a proper way for a lady to spend her time."

"What happened with your job at the newspaper? That should have been an ideal place for you to use your talents."

"Who told you about that?" she asked defensively.

"Chris Herchmer mentioned that you worked for the *Creston Review*."

"I did for a few months...till Herb Legg fired me."

"Oh, sorry to pry."

"It was kind of funny, actually." Eleanor lit a new cigarette from her dying butt. Holding it in her mouth with the smoke curling up around her face, she squinted and continued talking. "Herb and I got into a bit of a disagreement about an article I'd written. When he said he wouldn't print it, I punched him in the face. I argued with him and refused to leave, so he called the local constabulary. Of course, that was back in the days when the Royal Canadian Mounted Police still wore their parade uniforms for everyday work."

Eleanor flushed and her voice gained in intensity as she went on. "When the young pup of an officer came, he refused to listen to a word I had to say. He kept asking Herb questions and telling me to sit down and shut up. He finally made me sit on the floor in the corner of the office. He strolled back and forth in front of me with his spurs jingling, writing down everything that Herb said. I got sick of listening to that old bugger go on and on telling his side of the story, so I started chanting a little ditty that I made up. I'll never forget it: Twinkle, twinkle little spur / How I wonder what you're fer / Strapped about his boots so tight / And not a god-damned horse in sight...They kept trying to make me shut up, but I wouldn't. Finally, Herb told the officer he wouldn't press charges if he could just get the crazy woman out of his establishment. They ushered me out on the street and told me not to come back. I never spoke to Herb again, nor did I ever read another copy of the *Review*."

I shook my head and smiled. "You take the cake, my dear woman."

I chuckled when she tipped her head elegantly in my direction. We both sat quietly drinking our tea and watching the cats push and shove one another for the final morsels of Feline Feast. Eleanor got up and opened a door into a portion of the house that she no longer used. I guessed it had once been a bedroom.

When she disappeared from sight, I craned my neck to see what lay beyond the door—I was dying of curiosity. All I could see from where I was sitting were cardboard boxes heaped to the ceiling. When I asked Chris Herchmer why Eleanor only lived in one room of her house, she had told me that since her mother died in the late forties, the rooms had gradually been abandoned as they filled with trash. I often sat with my legs crossed while visiting, wondering where Eleanor went to the bathroom. There was definitely no longer a bathroom here as part of the house, and I had never seen an outdoor biffy. I presumed that was another of those questions you just didn't ask a lady.

"Damn it, anyway...I know it's here." There was a tremendous commotion as Eleanor rummaged. Several cats skittered out of the room. A box jammed full of empty cat food bags tumbled through the door.

"Do you need a hand, Eleanor?"

"No! No, I don't need any help..." There was a tone of desperation to her voice that kept me glued to my seat. "I know it's here somewhere."

Eleanor hissed and clapped her hands; six more cats hastily exited the room. A few moments later she came out clutching an object in the palm of her hand. She flipped a new cigarette from a pack on the table and struck a match to light it. With the cigarette drooping from her mouth, she scooped several cupfuls from the water bucket with her empty teacup and poured them into a washbasin. Squirting in some soap, she scrubbed enthusiastically at the object.

"I've been thinking of finding this for you since I brought Samantha home," she said, chastising herself. "I'm sure you know all about people and their good intentions...Darn cats, I don't know why they insist on pooping in all my boxes." Eleanor continued scrubbing at an encrusted mass on the front of the object. The cigarette still dangled from her lips, and she squinted as the smoke curled up into her eyes. "This was Daddy's flask. He carried it all the way through his stint in South Africa." She wiped it on the front of her shirt and handed it to me. "See," she said, pointing to an inscription still partially hidden under encrusted cat poop. "Campbell Blair."

I held the treasured possession reverently. "Are you sure you want me to have this?"

"I always pay my way," Eleanor said with pride. "And I'm sure that my father would approve."

I rotated the flask back and forth in the dim light of Eleanor's house. The first thing that caught my attention was the lion rampant in the centre above Campbell's name. I scraped at the lid and found another. This was a sterling silver riding flask. Who would have thought?

"What does that say at the bottom?" I asked, scraping at debris with my fingernail.

Eleanor rummaged through another ratty box and pulled out a pair of glasses with one of the earpieces broken off. She polished them on the front of her shirt, balanced them precariously on her nose, and reached for the flask. She clicked on a lamp at the head of her bed and sat down with her rag. After rubbing for a few minutes, she held it to the light. "Warwickshire Yeomanry...that must have been Daddy's unit." She took off her glasses and handed the flask back to me. "Daddy had such an adventurous life..." she said with a far-off, dreamy look.

"Did you have a good relationship with your parents?"

Eleanor suddenly became very serious. "What do you mean by that?"

"Well, I'm just getting to know my father by working with him now," I answered defensively. "When I was younger, I was always kind of scared of him—always afraid that I wasn't meeting his expectations."

Eleanor's face softened. "Sometimes, my good doctor, you think too much…My father gave me some very valuable advice before I left for finishing school. I was worried about going away—about how I would fit in. He said, 'You, my dear, are a race-horse and not a cow. Whenever you doubt yourself, remind yourself of that.'"

We sat quietly for several moments. I turned the flask over and over in my hand, thinking of the places it had been and the action that had gone on all around it. Eleanor sat watching me.

She broke the silence. "Some of us were not designed to follow the rules, Dave." She dragged on her cigarette, exhaled, and watched the plume of smoke dissipate on its way to the ceiling. She looked me square in the eyes. "You have to realize that there's a big difference between a racehorse and a cow…You, my fine friend, are a racehorse. Stop acting like a cow."

"Ice Cream Isn't Good for Dogs"

"Do you remember this big guy?"

I held the plastic carrying case steady as Betty Roper dragged her massive black cat out and deposited him on the table. The rotund critter made a desperate bid to claw his way back to his shelter, but when unable to get traction on the stainless steel table, he settled into a quivering mass.

"This is Sinbad."

"Hello, Sinbad." I patted my reluctant patient on the head and tried to settle him down. His intense yellow-green eyes darted back and forth searching for an avenue of escape. As I continued to stroke him, he became resigned to his fate and crouched reluctantly on the shiny metal surface.

Doris handed me the patient record. "Betty wants to bring him up to date on his vaccinations."

I began my examination while Betty and Doris chatted.

"The other day Ray and I were talking about the first time we met Dave," said Betty. "I don't think he'd been in the valley more than a week before we had to call him out for Sinbad. We thought his front leg might be broken. We live in a rough neighbourhood for cats—right next door to Eleanor Blair and her menagerie."

"I can just imagine how many invaders he'd have in his territory," said Doris.

Betty nodded. "It gets pretty hard on Sinbad some days. But you know what it's like with Eleanor feeding every stray that shows up—not many of them are neutered."

Sinbad sat quietly as I examined his ears and teeth.

"He's sure a lot better this time," Betty observed. She launched into the story of my first encounter with her pet. "You had to go back to your car for the straitjacket. You wouldn't have believed it, Doris. Poor Dave came in with this brand new cat bag—it was still in its plastic wrapper. He got Sin into the bag, shaved his leg, and started cleaning up the wounds. First, there was black hair everywhere. The next thing you know pus and blood were squirting all over the bag. Then Sinbad had a hissy fit and peed and pooped. To top it off, when Dave gave him his pill, he foamed at the mouth and got pink froth on everything..."

The two women doubled up with laughter.

"The poor guy left our house holding his brand-new cat bag out in front of him with two fingers. I don't think we've had Sinbad to a vet since, but living next to all those cats, we figured we better make sure he has protection."

I slipped the needle under the cat's skin to inject the first vaccine, then loaded the rabies vaccine into a syringe and administered it in the muscle of the hind leg.

"That's it."

"You mean you're finished already?"

I opened the carrier cage door and the cat disappeared inside. Betty almost seemed disappointed that Sinbad hadn't given us a repeat performance of our first meeting. As she settled her account, I moved to the waiting room and sat next to Fred Tady.

"Well," I asked optimistically, "is Rascal back to normal?"

The stocky gentleman shook his head dejectedly. "It's the same thing...he's constantly gagging."

Disappointed, I looked at the shaggy little mutt on his lap. Last week I had sent the terrier-cross home on my favourite concoction for gagging dogs, convinced it would resolve his problem. I had

169

found the remains of a burr in the long hair at the base of his tail and was sure he'd swallowed several of the stickers that made the seed pods so clingy. I couldn't count the times I'd seen the same symptoms in dogs that had tried to remove the pesky things themselves.

"Was he any better at all?"

"Maybe at first."

Fred self-consciously adjusted the black hairpiece that nestled in the grey hair at his temples. "He doesn't get to be around me as much these days...now that us newlyweds are running the restaurant and all."

"That must have been quite a change for you both."

"It sure has been, but it's a good change for me...I love being busy and around people again. Business has really picked up since we took over."

"That's good. You were swamped when I was in there last week. I guess it's like everything else...Give people good service and good food, and they'll keep coming."

Fred nodded, then looked sadly at his pet. "The only downside is not having much time for poor Rascal here."

The little guy licked his lips, swallowed, and peered up into his owner's eyes.

"Well, let's get him on the table."

Fred held his buddy to his chest as I reached for the thermometer. "Assume the position, old man...You know the routine by now."

The dog struggled further up his master's chest as I inserted the hated glass rod. Shivering as if thrown into a blizzard in mid-January, he clung to Fred's sweater with his claws.

"You'd think you were killin' him," Fred grumbled. "He's always such a baby."

I removed the thermometer and wiped it with a paper towel. "Just as I suspected—normal again."

I plucked Rascal from Fred's arms and cuddled him to me.

With the stethoscope to his chest, I strolled back and forth beside the table. By the second turnabout, he had settled enough that I could hear more than the rattling caused by his shivering. I listened intently to his heart sounds from first one side, then the other. The lub-dubs were crisp and clean—there was certainly no indication of a murmur. I moved the diaphragm higher and focused on the sounds of the air entering and leaving his lungs. There was no whistling, no bubbling, not the slightest indication of a problem.

Cases like Rascal's were so difficult to deal with. It was one thing to see something wrong and give an opinion on what to do about it. It was another when all you had to go on was an owner's interpretation of some nebulous problem one couldn't see.

"You say it's more of a gag than a cough?"

Fred scrunched his chin to his chest and extended it several times running. "He does this, two or three times in a row," he imitated, demonstrating the movements while holding his hand firmly on his hairpiece, "and then he goes aaaaaarrrrrrrgggggggu-uuuu." Rascal studied Fred intently while he vocalized and demonstrated the retching motions. "It's driving me nuts, I tell you…"

Fred shrugged his shoulders as I palpated the dog's throat in the hope it might activate a performance.

"I'd like to see him do it just once. I was sure when I found the burr on him last time he had an irritated throat from swallowing a couple of the barbs."

Fred shook his head in frustration. "I'd like him to do it for you, too. Look at him sitting there like Mr. Perfect—it's as if he's trying to make a liar out of me."

I rolled back Rascal's eyelids one at a time, then examined his gums. "He has a bit of tartar, but for a Yorkie-cross, it's not bad." I opened the dog's mouth and depressed his tongue with my finger. Both tonsils were red and yawning from their crypts. "His tonsils look inflamed."

171

"That's what you said last time. Wouldn't the antibiotics have taken care of that?"

"I hoped they would."

"Do you ever have to take the tonsils out of dogs?"

"The procedure is described, but I've never seen a case where it was necessary."

"Well, it might be necessary here...I'm not sure how much more of this nonsense I can handle."

"Tonsils are lymphoid tissue—they have a job to do. If they clear up with the antibiotics, then we should plan to put Rascal under anesthetic and clean his teeth to remove a possible source of infection."

"I listen to people talk about that with kids nowadays, too...they keep dragging 'em back and forth to the doctor every few months for more pills. They never used to do that. The first time I had a sore throat when I was a kid, the doctor sent me to the hospital. They slapped a piece of gauze over my mouth, put me to sleep, and I woke up without my tonsils. Never had any trouble since."

"There's no doubt they used to be quicker to remove them in humans than they are now."

"Have you still got yours?'

"No. I had a continuous battle with tonsillitis before they were finally removed."

"Well, there you go."

"Dogs certainly do seem to be different, though, Fred...Let's give him a try on a different antibiotic for a few weeks and see if that helps."

Fred looked worried as he plucked his pet from my arms. "This is really getting to me. It was after ten when we got in last night from the restaurant. I listened to him gag from the moment I got home until I finally put him in the spare room...How can you sleep when you have a dog gagging next to your ear? He usually sleeps right here." Fred patted his chest.

"I can imagine how distracting that would be."

Doris counted out Rascal's pills and saw my client on his way. The familiar woeful feeling of inadequacy settled on me as I moved to the waiting room.

"Hi, Audrey, Kev," I greeted my new clients. "Doris tells me you're having problems with Buttons."

The dark-haired woman adjusted her glasses and frowned. "There's definitely something not right with him. The last few days he's been lying under the coffee table doing nothing. Kevin tried to get him to play ball this morning and he wouldn't even get up."

"Has anything happened to him that you can think of, Kev?"

The eight-year-old regarded me thoughtfully and shook his head.

"He didn't run into anything when you were playing ball with him, or get bumped by a car?"

The boy looked directly at me with expressive brown eyes. "Nope, but he didn't want to play ball with me yesterday either."

"But he's worse today?"

He nodded seriously and stroked the yellow cocker that lay on the seat beside him. The dog was stretched out on his side with his head on Kevin's lap.

"Has he thrown up or had any signs of diarrhea?"

"He threw up a bit of yellow froth outside yesterday, and he wasn't very interested in his supper," Mrs. Vance offered. "But he'd been eating grass, and I thought that was why...Have you seen anything, Kevin?"

He glanced at me shyly, then whispered to his mother.

"Tell the doctor," she told him.

"Yesterday, his pee was really dark."

"Was it yellow dark or red dark?" I asked.

He shrugged.

I went to spray the exam table with disinfectant. Even though it was time to change gears and start dealing with a new case, my mind was still awhirl as to what to do with Rascal.

"Okay, Kev, bring him in."

The boy marched up to the table and deposited Buttons. The dog lay dejectedly with his head on his paws; this was not the spirited puppy I had vaccinated six months earlier. Then, he had been in danger of squirming out of his skin with exuberance, constantly jumping up as he tried to lick my face.

I knelt at the head of the table and rolled back his lip. The gums were pale with a yellow hue.

"Is there any possibility that he got into mouse poison?"

"Certainly not at our place," Audrey replied.

I held the dog's head in my hands and lifted his eyelid. His conjunctivae were pale—very definitely jaundiced. I inserted a thermometer, then grabbed my stethoscope. The cocker's heart was pounding like a trip-hammer, and I could hear blood squishing backward with each contraction.

I ran my hands over his body, searching for any swelling or bruising. Other than his hair coat looking a bit scruffy, nothing seemed abnormal. I removed the thermometer; his temperature was almost 40 Celsius.

"Problems?" Audrey could see I was concerned.

"Yes, I'm afraid so. Buttons is really anemic…and he's running a temperature."

"What would cause that?" she asked. "You remember my telling you about where this dog came from? I was so worried when I saw the place. It was dirty and there were dogs running all over. I kept telling Bob that we should just leave, but then Kevin saw this puppy and fell in love with him. Before we even told him he could have the dog, he had him named."

"We better get some blood and run some tests. There's no doubt something major is going on."

Kevin glanced toward his mother with a look of woe, took his hands off his puppy, and stepped back.

"I'm going to need your help, Doris. Get an IV set up."

I made a quick trip to the lab and returned with supplies for collection. By the time I got back, Doris had a bag of fluids hanging from the stand and a catheter on the table. The dog sat passively as I clipped the hair from his forearm and rubbed it down with alcohol.

"Hold off his vein for me," I whispered.

As Doris applied pressure at the level of the cocker's elbow, I pierced the cephalic vein and worked the catheter into place. I collected a sample as blood dripped from the end of the plastic cannula. Buttons held his head up for a few seconds watching the procedure, then settled his chin on Doris's hand. Too tired to complain, he closed his eyes.

Doris raised her eyebrows as I replaced the cork in the lavender tube and filled the two smaller capillary tubes. The sample was little more than pink water. I connected the intravenous and taped the apparatus to the cocker's foreleg. I left the capillary tube without anti-coagulant on the table to check clotting time, and quickly got the other one spinning in the centrifuge. As the machine built up to a high-pitched whine, I smeared a drop of blood on a slide. The sample was so dilute that it was hard to see much of a residue.

"Will you please stain this, Doris?"

She waved the slide in the air to help dry it and hastily made her way to the lab.

I turned to Audrey and Kevin. "His anemia is severe. That's why he's so tired—why he wouldn't play this morning. We'll have to find out what's up as quickly as possible."

"This sounds serious," said Audrey worriedly.

"Very serious, depending on what's causing it. We'll know more after Doris gets finished with that slide. The stain she's applying will let me evaluate his remaining cells and see if there are any abnormalities. Each different component of a cell attracts a specific stain, so they are coloured differently. We need to determine whether his red cells are in short supply because he's not making them, or because he's destroying them faster than they can be produced. A red cell would normally be in circulation for about four months. Anything that decreases that survival time can contribute to a condition like this. We can sometimes see a decrease in red cell numbers in an old dog with a failing liver or bad kidneys, but a healthy young dog like Buttons should have no problem cranking lots of them out."

I brought Kevin a chair and put it next to the table. "You just sit with Buttons for a bit, Kev, and I'll go and see what's going on with the samples."

I glanced at my watch. It was over four minutes since I had drawn the blood. I picked up the tiny glass capillary tube and broke it about a third of the way down. A fine strand of material spanned the broken pieces.

"His clotting time is pretty normal. That makes warfarin poisoning very unlikely."

I shut off the centrifuge and waited impatiently for it to quit spinning. Unscrewing the lid, I placed the capillary tube on the ruler for evaluation—it was as I suspected.

"It's under 10," I whispered to Doris. "How long before my slide is ready?"

She was wandering around the back room waving her arm in a wide arc to dry the glass strip. "It's just about ready but I'm wondering if I did something wrong when I stained it. There doesn't appear to be much on it."

"That's not surprising with the packed cell volume this low."

"I can't remember seeing a sample so watery," Doris whispered. She watched me intently as I slid the slide onto the microscope carriage and scanned it. "Well, what do you see?" she prompted.

"Give me a second while I increase the magnification."

I put a drop of oil on the slide, then switched to the emersion lens for higher magnification. The moment I focused on the sample, I was sure of the diagnosis.

"Very sad-looking red cells…Take a peek at this one." I leaned back from the microscope so Doris could squeeze in. "See the cell that's right above the pointer?"

"The big pink one?"

"Yup…that's a normal one, but right below it is one that's about half the size and much rounder."

"I see it," Doris said enthusiastically. "What's that?"

"That's a spherocyte."

"A what?"

"A spherocyte—a red blood cell that has had small bites chomped from it on the way through the spleen or the liver. When enough of the outer membrane has been removed, it loses the concavity that the cell above it has, and looks like a sphere—a little round ball."

I studied the slide a bit longer, moving from one group of cells to the other. "See that one." I set the pointer on a cell that had a pink perimeter with a large dark blue mass in the centre. "This one's a red cell, too—an immature one. There are so few normal ones left in circulation that the bone marrow's cranking them out long before they'd normally be released."

"So what does that mean?"

"It means that Buttons has a regenerative anemia—that's the

177

good news. The bad news is that for some reason, he's recognizing his own red cells as foreign and destroying them."

"Oh my, does that mean a trip to the Dairy Queen for Lug?"

"I'm afraid so. I better talk to Audrey and see what they want to do, but a packed cell volume of less than 10 on a dog is not compatible with long-term survival."

"I'll get a transfusion bag ready in case she wants to go ahead."

I smiled at Kevin, who sat stoically at the table with Buttons, and went to the waiting room to talk to his mother.

"We've got a very serious situation here, Audrey...I'm pretty sure Buttons has an autoimmune hemolytic anemia."

She gave me a blank look. "You better explain what you just said."

"When we're talking about an anemia, we're talking about a lower-than-normal red blood cell count. One of the most convenient ways to evaluate whether or not it's anemia is to spin a sample at a very high speed and determine what percentage is made up of red cells and what percent is serum. It's called a hematocrit. A normal count for a dog would be between the high 30s and the low 50s. For a healthy dog of Buttons' age, I'd expect it to be in the neighbourhood of 50. His packed cell volume is less than 10."

Audrey closed her eyes and shook her head.

"The yellow colour to his skin, eyes, and gums is caused from all the hemoglobin that's being released from the destruction of the red cells. The liver's doing its best to handle the breakdown products, and the kidneys are getting rid of as much as possible. That's why his urine is dark."

"What would cause things to go so wrong?"

"I guess the biggest miracle to me is that things don't go wrong more often. I'm afraid they still don't have all the answers with autoimmune diseases. What seems to happen is that the immune system recognizes a part of its own body as foreign and starts attacking it with antibodies. In the case of rheumatoid arthritis, it's a protein in the joints. In this case, it's the red blood cells."

"Do you think it has something to do with where this dog came from? I heard someone talking about puppy mills on the radio. I'm sure the place we got Buttons was one of them. I don't think the woman even knew which dog was his father."

"Well, that's certainly a possibility. There's lots of talk in the literature about inbreeding as a predisposing factor. Have you given him any medicine lately? Dewormed him? Given him an Aspirin or any other anti-inflammatory?"

She shook her head to each of my questions.

"The theory is that something—a drug, a toxin, or a parasite—binds to the outside of the red cell. At first, the immune system tries to get the foreign agent, but then it gets confused and keeps destroying the membranes of the red cells themselves…Is there any possibility of his swallowing a penny?"

Audrey sighed in frustration. "Puppies are always chewing or swallowing something. I have no idea about that."

"Well, regardless of the cause, we have to make some major decisions right now. We'll start him on steroids to suppress his immune system so it'll stop destroying those red cells…but the effect of the steroids can take as long as a week to completely kick in, so we'd really be gambling to go with that option alone. I think he needs a transfusion. His blood is so dilute that his heart isn't pumping efficiently. He has an anemic murmur from blood squishing back through the valves each time the heart contracts."

"I've never seen Kevin so attached to a pet before," said Audrey. "We've had other dogs and cats, but from the moment he laid eyes on that pup, we couldn't pry him away. He's our third child, so up until now, he's been used to dealing with hand-me-downs. This is the first time he's ever had a pet of his own."

I nodded in sympathy. I knew what it was like to be third in line, and I could still remember the thrill of getting my own puppy. My Cindy was a cocker, too, except she was black. I knew how Kevin felt; there had been something so special about knowing that Cindy was really mine and not just a family pet.

Audrey shrugged her shoulders. "I guess you better do what you can to save him...Kevin would be devastated if he lost the dog now."

Although Lug came thundering down the stairs when I called him, he immediately picked up that something was not quite right.

"Come on, Lug...Come here, old buddy."

With his ears flat and his tail down, he plodded to the surgery and looked to Doris for rescue.

"How does he always seem to know?" she asked.

"I don't know, but his body language says it all."

Lug began shivering when I picked him up and plunked him on the surgery table.

"You get to go for an ice cream!" Doris told him exuberantly.

I applied a tourniquet to his elbow, doused his foreleg with alcohol, and readied the collection apparatus. As Doris held his leg in extension, I felt for his vein. Lug looked away as I drove the huge needle through the skin.

"There's a good boy," Doris chimed as a steady flow of blood ran to the collection bag on the floor.

I held the needle in place and massaged the bag with my foot as the blood slowly started mixing with the anticoagulant. I massaged Lug's foot and intermittently flexed his carpus to keep the flow going.

Over the next twenty minutes, he stared out the surgery window, refusing to make eye contact with me. I always felt so mean using my own pet, but it beat scouring the neighbourhood for someone who had a dog big enough to part with a bag of blood. There were eleven different blood groups in dogs, and although it was not as critical to crossmatch dogs as it was for cats, it always made me feel safer knowing that Lug was type A negative and supposedly a universal donor.

As the bag got closer and closer to bulging fullness, it got harder for me to persist with tormenting him. "I think we'll call this quits, Doris." I pulled the needle from his leg and quickly applied pressure. "There's a boy! You survived another one."

Lug's tail wagged furiously as I taped a strip of gauze to his leg and lowered him to the ground. He whined and jumped up on me with his front feet, licking at my hands as if I had just done him a great favour.

"He's telling you it's Dairy Queen time."

I had no doubt Doris was right—he'd been through this procedure often enough to know the routine well. I grabbed the bag and headed for the exam room. Tying off the collection tube, I plugged in an administration set and readied the line for the transfusion to Buttons.

Kevin's eyes widened as he watched Lug's healthy red blood slowly work its way down the plastic tube and begin dripping onto the table. I connected the line to the catheter.

"This'll get Buttons feeling better."

The boy nodded passively and watched the blood drip through the filter into the chamber.

"Help's on the way, Buttons."

The Vances left shortly after the transfusion started. By the time it had run its course and we had finished the other appointments for the day, our patient was looking much brighter. Before leaving the office, I repeated his hematocrit. I was delighted to see that the packed cell volume was in the low 30s. The main thing now was to hope that the prednisone would do its magic and suppress Buttons' overactive immune system. All we could do was wait.

It was after six when I called upstairs for Lug. "Okay, old man, it's Dairy Queen time!"

He thundered down the stairs and ran past me for the front door. When I caught up to him, he twirled round and round, yipping excitedly. As soon as I opened the door, he tore around the corner and was gone. When I caught up to him he was sitting at the driver's door of the truck, staring up expectantly.

"You'd almost think you were in a hurry to go somewhere."

He wagged and waited impatiently for me to let him in the truck. As I pulled onto Canyon Street and headed east, Lug peered intently out the window. The moment I clicked on my signal to pull into the Dairy Queen, he started making noise.

"You can't be hungry…"

I parked in the lot and headed into the popular hangout. As I opened the glass door I glanced back at the truck. Lug's nose was pressed against the driver's side window; he was watching every move I made.

"A double-patty burger with no veggies. Hold the mustard and the pickles—just mayo. And two small soft ice creams."

Lug's head was bobbing up and down as I approached the truck with the goodies, and although I couldn't hear him, I knew he was whining. His tail thrashed wildly back and forth as I opened the door and handed him the burger.

"Hey, slow down enough to taste it."

Within seconds the patties were gone, and he was working on the half of the bun that had somehow gotten lost in the shuffle. I savoured my ice cream as Lug licked the remainder of the mayonnaise off the seat. I pretended to ignore him when he looked to me for more.

"Ice cream isn't good for dogs, you know." He nudged my arm with his nose. "Okay…but be civilized." I held out his cone and he licked at it voraciously. "You'll be upset when you finish yours and I won't give you any of mine," I warned.

My reasoning did nothing to slow the rate at which his ice cream disappeared. When he had it worried down to the top of the cone, I passed it to him. He devoured the remainder as I turned the truck around and headed toward the farm.

I decided to stop at Jack and Sandy's on the way. It seemed strange to have them living next door now. Their deal with Verna had gone through and they had taken possession of the farm a couple of weeks ago. I enjoyed having them as neighbours, and it gave Father somewhere to go for a coffee and warm up when he got tired.

I was thankful that we'd made good progress with the roof during October while the final aspects of the deal were being pounded out, because since he'd become a farmer, Jack had no time to spare for activities away from the homestead. Fortunately, Sam Hoodikoff, a carpenter from Erickson, had finished work on the Veitches' house and was able to take over the final framing.

I pulled into Jack's and stopped at the house. When there was no answer to my knock, I headed for the barn. I was almost to the milk house when I heard a scream. I rushed into the barn, expecting the worst. Sandy was standing next to a farrowing crate with a shovel in her hand. She was dressed in a sloppy denim shirt and a pair of Jack's old jeans cinched up with a piece of baler twine. Her brand new gumboots were plastered with pig manure.

"She killed him, Dave!" she shrieked. "The poor little guy went up to the front and this horrible creature just bit into him and kept chewing...Look! Look, there's still half of him left."

"When did she farrow?"

"Earlier this afternoon."

Sandra still held the shovel as if expecting to give the sow another rap.

"Pigs are sometimes like that," I half-heartedly explained. "Some mothers are really protective of their offspring; others would kill the whole litter. Have the babies all sucked?"

She nodded. "Jack fooled with them all morning to make sure. He was so happy to get eleven live ones—he was already counting them as part of our December cheque."

"That was probably a bit premature..."

I kicked the back half of the dead piglet from in front of the sow, picked it up, and threw it on the manure pile. "I don't think we better be counting that one," I said grimly. "Let's confine the rest of the babies under the heat lamp."

Sandra and I chased the remaining piglets to the back of the crate and slipped a piece of plywood between them and the sow to keep them from wandering.

"You'll have to supervise their feeding for a couple of days...Hopefully, she'll settle down." I smiled at Sandy. "How's it been going otherwise?"

"Hairdressing sounds pretty good right at the moment," she said meekly.

"I can well imagine...I better go see how Father's making out."

"He was over for coffee a half-hour ago. He sounded pretty happy about things over there."

"Where's Jack?"

"He's out back moving a couple of sows to the boar."

I found him behind the barn leaning over a fence constructed of upright mill slabs. His right foot rested on an empty five-gallon bucket.

"Well, farmer, how's it going?"

"Look at that, Dave," he said gleefully. "Money in the making."

An immense brown boar was mounted on a sow in the middle of the pen. Neither of them moved as they stood joined in porcine bliss.

"I swear he has a smile on his face," Jack mused.

I chuckled. He was right.

"I tell you, David, if things got any better, I'm not sure I could handle it."

"So you made out all right on your trip to Pincher Creek?"

Jack smiled broadly. "It was a real treat sitting through that auction."

"You did pretty well, then?"

"Can you multiply forty times seventy-five?"

"You got seventy-five apiece for them?" I asked excitedly. "The bank has to like that."

"We both do...You know, I can't remember being so tired at the end of the day, but I sleep like a baby and I love every minute of it."

184

"I sure hope the prices stay where they are."

"So do I. A good year with prices like this under my belt, and I'll be able to set up my own finishing operation. I'm sure I can streamline things around here and free up a lot of time for building."

Father was on the roof when I got to the house. He had accomplished quite of bit of sheeting, and Sam had made considerable progress on the bridging between the two roofs. As Lug took off to explore the surrounding bush, I started throwing boards to the second floor through the holes Jack had framed for the windows.

"As soon as we get this roof closed in, we'll get Sam to work on those stairs."

Father leaned back onto a rafter. "It'll go a lot quicker when we use up the rest of this old lumber...a few sheets of plywood covers a lot more ground."

I nodded and examined the pile of boards in the yard. I hoped they lasted a little longer. Marg Rogers had taken me aside for a talk this morning, informing me that I was stretching her abilities. She wondered if I'd won a lottery she hadn't heard about. Apparently, creative financing was not the total answer to my fiscal problems.

I tapped gently on a nail to start it, then drove it in. It was amazing how hard it was to get a nail through these hundred-year-old larch boards. Jack kept telling me I should save them and peddle them in the city where people were willing to pay big premiums for old barn boards. Although that may have pleased my bookkeeper, it wasn't about to happen. I needed a roof up before all the plywood on my floors was ruined. We had already had several autumn downpours after getting the rafters up, and it was painful to watch water drip relentlessly from one floor to the next until it collected in puddles in the basement.

I placed another board and pounded in more nails. I was excited with how each little job brought me one step closer to completion. I focused on the bathroom dormer in the new addition and tried to imagine how the whole roof would look when it was all covered with the same golden-brown shakes. Father and I had made several trips into the bush with his old truck and returned with heaping loads of cedar blocks for shake material. I had split enough to cover the dormers, but it was proving to be a time-consuming venture. The way the seasons were advancing, I had decided to cover the rest with rolled roofing and leave shake splitting for a winter project.

I leaned back against a rafter and scanned the rugged face of Thompson Mountain. There were a lot of similarities between building this house and building my practice. Although I was always impatient with how slowly things progressed, somehow, I had a deep-down certainty that if I kept driving in one nail after the other, I'd create something special in the long run. Maybe someday both this house and my practice would be finished to the point I'd be satisfied with them. I smiled ruefully as I grabbed another board and began pounding. No matter how good things eventually got, there was bound to be the odd day when the cat bag got shitty.

Kinky Cases

Jean Partington wasn't one of my more patient clients.

"Have you heard anything from Pullman yet?" she asked, her intense brown eyes burning into me.

"Dr. Sande was supposed to be back today, but it was too early to call before I left the office."

"John thinks we should just put Saiawna down and be done with it," she said in a melancholic tone.

I took a deep breath and moved the cherry pit from under my tongue. This time the cherry pit was for real. I hadn't been looking forward to this ongoing discussion about Jean's old mare. The Partingtons were great clients and I didn't want to say something I'd later regret.

"I know how you feel about Saiawna, Jean, and believe me, I wish I knew what was wrong with her." I deposited the pit under my tongue again and tried to focus on the job at hand. We had a dozen cows to check yet. I grabbed Mabel's tail. Jean continued to glower at me as I evacuated the cow's rectum. "What's the story on this one?"

"She was bred thirty-eight days ago," she responded tersely. "It's the second breeding…She calved a hundred and ten days ago."

I could understand Jean's frustration with me, but it wasn't helping me get closer to finding out what was plaguing her horse.

187

I had done everything that seemed logical to investigate the animal's lameness and was still trying to come up with a diagnosis. Half a dozen times during the last year I had examined Saiawna, and each time I left her paddock feeling bewildered.

I returned to the moment. Whenever I started browbeating myself about my inadequacies, it invariably detracted from the immediate task. I flipped over Mabel's uterus and searched for a bulge in the horn. I gently ran the organ between my thumb and my forefinger. There it was—the familiar slip of the membranes.

"She's pregnant."

I made my way to the next cow and opened the parlour gate behind her. Shifting her back end over a few feet, I began the usual procedure.

"Dodie calved forty-six days ago," Jean informed me. There were a few moments of silence as she focused on making notations and I palpated. "Do you think they might want Saiawna at Pullman if I were to donate her as a teaching case?"

"I'm not sure," I replied hesitantly, "but I can ask."

"At least if they had her there, someone might be able to figure out what's wrong with her."

I felt the familiar burning sensation at the back of my neck. I knew my ears would be a fiery red. I shifted the cherry pit, bit on it a few times, then returned it to its original place. She was right, and I wanted to know as badly as she did what was going on with that horse.

"This cow's in good shape. Her uterus has contracted down nicely…her right ovary is three and a half centimetres with a corpus luteum…her left is three with a developing follicle." I moved to the next cow.

"Trixie has been calved a hundred and eight days and we haven't seen signs of a heat." Some of the tension had left Jean's voice.

I thought back to the first time I had examined Saiawna for this problem. Back then, her lameness was barely perceptible and she was still usable as a mount. Jean had ridden back and forth in front of me on the field.

"See…she just did it!" Jean had leaned back in the saddle and hollered over her shoulder. "It's a clicking sensation!"

I was unable to come to any conclusion then, or for that matter, during the next two or three inspections. My inability to come up with a diagnosis only fuelled Jean's determination that there was something wrong with her old mare, and I wasn't sharp enough to pick it up.

Then, six months ago, I finally came to a spark of understanding as to the mechanism of Saiawna's lameness. Jean had ridden the horse down a trail she frequented that ran from their farm to the Goat River bottom. She insisted the horse was doing fine until she started descending a steep embankment toward the river; then Saiawna seemed to lose control and stumble her way to the bottom. Although Jean stayed on board, she'd been badly shaken by the incident. She had dismounted and walked the horse home.

She called me as soon as she got back to the farm. After ten minutes of her parading the horse back and forth in front of me, I was totally disconcerted. Just watching Saiawna move, I was unable to detect anything abnormal. It wasn't until I suggested taking her on a downhill slope that I finally picked up on what was going on. Every once in a while, when the animal placed weight on her foot going down a steep hill, her pastern joint—the first one above the hoof—gave way and knuckled over with an audible clunk. I was almost certain that the horse flinched with the pain of the event.

"Hear that now?" Jean had questioned. "That's what I was feeling on her back."

I repeated the maneuver on the sidehill several times, walking in a stoop position beside the horse with my hand resting on her fetlock. There was a palpable click on both sides with almost every step. On the last trip down the hill, the joint folded forward, causing the fetlock joint to collapse as well. Saiawna threw her head in reaction to the pain and stumbled out of control the rest of the way down the slope.

"See!" Jean shouted, almost gleeful that I had finally seen what she'd been trying to explain to me. "That's what she did when we were going down the riverbank."

I had never seen anything like it before, and I couldn't remember hearing it addressed in any of my lameness classes at veterinary college. I called the equine specialists at the colleges in both Saskatoon, Saskatchewan, and Pullman, Washington, hoping that they'd instantly recognize the symptoms. After a long session in which I talked and they listened, I wondered if they were questioning my sanity. Neither of them offered me the slightest insight.

Saiawna's condition had gotten progressively worse until now, even when she was walking on flat ground, I could hear a decided click. Last week, I had taken X-rays of both limbs in the hope that hard images would shed some light on the situation. Arthritic spurs proliferated between the second and third phalanx of both feet, the exact area where we were seeing the strange knuckling movement.

"What would you do if she were your horse, Dave?" Jean sounded tired and discouraged as we finished palpating the last cow. "She's been such a good horse—always did whatever I asked of her. Now look at the mess she's in. If I thought she was suffering I'd agree with John...Do you think she is?"

"I don't know, Jean. It's certainly not looking good at the moment. I guess if I were a horse that was used to running freely, and ended up like that, I wouldn't be very happy about it. I'm as frustrated as you are. I keep talking to other practitioners about her hoping that someone will recognize the symptoms, but when I tell them about her, all I get is silence. I sometimes wonder if we aren't living on a different planet...Surely, something like this has happened to other horses."

Jean shrugged and sighed deeply. "John wants you to have a look at a cow out in the free stalls. She freshened four days ago and seemed to be doing fine. We just let her out of the calving pen yesterday, and this morning she was down in her stall with milk fever. John treated her and she's looking brighter, but we can't get her up."

We went through the milk house and out into the free-stall area where seventy cows milled about. Most were congregated around the feed bunk, eating; a few were lying down; some were standing idly in the alleyways. John was on the tractor at the far side of the building scraping manure from the concrete and dragging it to the manure pit. When he saw us, he jumped off his machine and met us at the end of the first row of stalls.

"This is one of our best cows," Jean lamented. "We've had a lull in our calving schedule…been struggling to make quota. Wouldn't you know that we'd have trouble with her."

I entered the stall adjacent to the big black cow. She was lying down but was bright and alert; both hind legs were positioned comfortably beneath her. As I approached, she looked at me and made a half-hearted effort to stand.

"She's been trying," John noted glumly, "but that's about all she can do."

The cow stuck out her tongue and stretched her neck forward as I felt her ears.

"They're warm." I plucked the thermometer from my coveralls and stuck it in her rectum. "She's got herself worked right up to the front of the stall," I observed. "That doesn't give her much of a chance to get a run at it." I pulled the thermometer out and read it. "It's normal."

I palpated the cow's udder. All the quarters felt soft and pliable. I squirted a jet of milk from each teat onto the toe of my boot. The milk looked perfectly clear.

"How much calcium did you give her?" I asked John.

"I gave her one in the vein at five and one under the skin…just finished giving her another one in the vein when you got here."

"Let's give a good try to lift her."

I jammed myself between the big cow and the two-by-sixes

that separated her from the next stall. I quickly depressed my knees, jabbing them into the cow's rib cage, and strained on the tail as she struggled to get to her feet.

"That's the best she's done," John noted as the cow made it about halfway up, then flopped back into her recumbent state.

"Well, we best get her out of here."

John shot me a disgruntled look. "I was afraid you'd say that."

He brought me a crescent wrench, and as I removed the bolts from the partition, he positioned the tractor and the plywood stoneboat in the alley beside us. I jammed myself between the cow and the wall. With my feet planted against the concrete and my back against the cow's chest, I heaved. After fifteen minutes of grunting, pushing, and pulling on the cow's tail and ears, we had her laid out on her side on the plywood. I lay on top of her and pulled her head up as John maneuvered the tractor down the alley. The cow lay still as the plywood slid easily over the thin layer of manure on the concrete floor. Once we left the holding area and proceeded over the bumpy gravel roadway, she began to struggle.

"Hold on a minute, girl...save your energy." Her eyes widened and she proceeded to blow snot down the front of my coveralls.

I strained to hold her down as she struggled to straighten her neck. John finally brought the tractor to a stop in the middle of a hay shed that was only half full of hay. This time when the cow attempted to stand, he pulled the plywood away and I grabbed her tail and lifted. She got up, her hind legs unsteady and her whole body trembling.

"Oh no...she's got kinked feet," Jean moaned.

"Kinked feet" was not a diagnostic term one would have found in *Blood, Henderson and Radostits*, the bible of large-animal veterinary medicine, but it was certainly a term I had come to recognize here in the Creston Valley.

"Not another one of these," John groaned.

I gradually relinquished my hold on the tail as the cow showed signs of being able to hold herself up. John glared at her hind legs.

Both were bent in the shape of a lazy S, with the pastern joints knuckling forward. The cow trembled and lifted one hind foot after the other as if they were numb or causing her pain.

"Well, it looks like we better get some more blood."

I had been struggling to comprehend this condition since I'd started practising in the valley. It almost always occurred secondary to a mineral imbalance and resembled peroneal nerve paralysis. So far, most cows like this one had tested low in both phosphorus and selenium. Deficiencies of selenium and copper seemed consistent over the entire valley, but here in Lister where the Partingtons farmed, calcium to phosphorus ratios in legume forages were often as high as twenty to one when they should have been somewhere around two to one. That inequity necessitated the addition of high levels of phosphorus to rations for both dry and lactating cows. Without it, many more cows developed milk fever and went through long periods without showing heats. The district agriculturist and I had developed a mineral supplement that we were hoping would improve the situation.

On my way back to the office I began thinking of the similarity between Saiawna and the cow we had just treated. Could it be that there was some sort of predisposing factor in both cases? There was obviously a big difference in the timing and the circumstances leading up to the presentation. I was sure that many veterinarians would argue that the cow's symptoms were the result of damage to her peroneal nerve while she was in her hypocalcemic stupor. Yet, I was certain I had gotten a response to dispensing both phosphorous and selenium to similar cows in the past, and would have felt negligent leaving the farm without administering both.

What if the cause of Saiawna's condition had a similar origin? After all, it was the same joint on both animals, and it seemed to involve the same nerve. Why shouldn't I consider supplementing the horse? From what Jean said, they were on the verge of putting her down anyway.

"You look like you're a hundred miles away."

Shirley, my usual waitress at the Depot Restaurant, was trying to get my attention. I was sitting alone at the corner table. I smiled vacantly as she slipped the clubhouse sandwich in front of me. She was right—I had been a long way off.

"Your coffee's getting cold. You haven't even touched it." I took a sip to please her. "Looks like you've had a hard morning."

I wanted to match Shirley's cheerfulness with a pleasant remark, but she was off to the next table. She refilled the cups of an elderly couple who sat across from one another, each engrossed in copies of the *Vancouver Sun*.

I took a bite of my sandwich and returned to my conjecture. What was the difference in mechanism between Saiawna's knuckling over at the pastern and the Partington cow's hind-leg problem? I sighed and chewed thoughtfully. I was still not convinced kinked feet in dairy cattle was selenium-related—all I knew was that when I treated them with selenium and phosphorous injections, they usually returned to normal.

I finished my sandwich and paid my bill. By the time I got out on the sidewalk, I had made up my mind. I'd give Ron Sande a call as soon as I got back to the office. If he couldn't come up with something I'd missed on those radiographs, I was going to start Saiawna on our mineral mix to see if it would make a difference. I felt like a quack for inventing a new syndrome, but I couldn't sit back and do nothing. I felt strangely lighter as I tripped across to the office. I may not have come up with a diagnosis, but I'd made a decision. Right now that seemed like a victory.

Ron had spoken to us several times at our Kootenay veterinary meetings, and I felt comfortable dealing with him. Whenever I referred films, I always requested that he be the one to view them. It was more like sending them to a friend than a specialist. When we were at the barbecues, swapping stories and tipping back beer, he was one of the boys, but when he stepped in front of an X-ray view box and started interpreting films, he was not mortal. The

man could wring more information from a radiograph than anyone I knew.

I crashed through the door on the way to the phone and
almost tripped over a leash. It appeared I had a few immediate
things on my plate—the office was full.

"Thank goodness you're on time," Doris said, chasing me to the
back room. "We have a full afternoon. Buttons Vance is here for
his recheck and Fred Tady hopes we can fit him in…Poor man, he
sounds like he's at his wit's end with Rascal."

"Who's first?"

"The Vances have the one o'clock appointment…I told Fred
we'd fit him in as soon as we could."

I slipped into my smock and tied it up on the run. "Okay,
Buttons, let's have a look at you!"

The little cocker bounded into the examination room, tugging
at his leash. Kevin was all smiles as he followed him in. His father,
Bob, brought up the rear.

"So how are things going at home?"

"He seems to be doing all right," Bob answered. "But he's eating everything in sight and wants to go outside for a pee every five
minutes."

"That's the side effect of the prednisone, I'm afraid. You'll have
to put up with it until we can get his dose tapered a bit more."

Kevin lifted Buttons onto the table and stood seriously at his
side.

"So, has he been playing ball with you, Kev?"

The boy nodded and burst into a big smile. "He sure has…and
he's nice and pink, too. I've been checking him a couple of times
a day, just like you showed me."

I took the cocker's head in my hands and rumpled his ears. The
moment I bent down for a look at his gums, he jumped up and his
tongue lashed at my face.

"Well, you sure look like you're back to normal."

The boy moved closer and held his pet still as I examined his mucous membranes. Kevin was right—they were nice and pink. I pressed firmly on the gum above his canine tooth, then quickly removed my finger. The colour came back immediately.

"Isn't that a pretty sight...It's all that good German shepherd blood," I joked.

Kevin wrinkled his brow. "Do you think that most of the blood is still Lug's?"

I smiled reassuringly. "I'd bet that almost every drop of this is cocker blood now."

The boy beamed from ear to ear and his big brown eyes lit up.

"So when can we get the dog off this medication?" his father asked.

"That's going to depend on the response we get when we start to decrease it...Some dogs can eventually be taken off everything, but some may have to be on low doses for the rest of their lives."

The look on Bob's face left little doubt that long-term therapy was not an option he relished. "The dog isn't even a year old. It doesn't seem fair for him to be having pills crammed down his throat for the rest of his life."

"I know, but we don't have much choice. We'll draw a blood sample today and have a quick look at his packed cell volume...If it's as good as I think it is, we'll cut his dose of prednisone by half and see how he manages."

"That stuff can't be good for him," Bob mused. "It's turned him into a bloody beggar—if he isn't after food, it's water. If we forget to fill his water dish, the next thing we know the toilet bowl is empty."

I nodded sympathetically. "I know it's a real nuisance when they're on high doses of prednisone. Their increase in thirst and appetite can really get to you."

Bob looked at me skeptically. "What else is it likely to do to him?"

"Well, I'm hoping we'll be able to taper him to a low dose soon—maybe get to the point we only use it on alternate days. If we can manage that, then you may not see anything else."

"And if we can't?"

I felt uncomfortable as Bob and Kevin continued their scrutiny. "If we have to keep up high doses for the long term, you can bet he'll have considerable weight gain. You may also see muscle weakness and an increase in susceptibility to infections because of the immune system suppression."

Kevin was stone-faced. He stroked his pet and stared at the tabletop.

"Long-term usage at higher doses can sometimes also affect liver function."

Bob ran his hand through his hair. His frustration was palpable. Kevin gave his father a sad look and pulled Buttons toward him.

"Well, we'll see what you find."

Kevin watched intently as Doris and I drew a sample. I revelled at the difference a few weeks could make as the rich red blood filled the tube. While Doris held a gauze on the puncture wound, I grabbed my stethoscope and had a listen to the dog's heart. The sounds of regurgitating blood were gone, replaced by a reassuring lub-dub, lub-dub, lub-dub. I filled a capillary tube and started the centrifuge.

"We're going to give you a new prescription of the same drug, only smaller pills. As soon as I've had a look at the sample, I'll give you a call and we can decide on the dosage."

Bob nodded in resignation. I could appreciate his conundrum. Although everyone with a pet realizes they've taken on a long-term commitment, who would welcome news that their puppy might need to be medicated daily for the rest of its life?

I prepared my slides and had a quick look at the hematocrit while Doris welcomed Rascal and checked his temperature.

"I tell you, Doris, this dog is going to drive me nuts," Fred started.

"So, he's no better?"

"If anything he's worse."

I closed my eyes and tried to shut out their conversation as I dipped Buttons' slide into stain, then rinsed it under the tap. I measured the hematocrit—his packed cell volume was up to forty-eight. I placed the slide on a paper towel to dry and took a deep breath. What was I going to do with Rascal? I moved to the doorway and stood listening to their conversation. Fred nodded at me and continued with his story.

"We got home about ten-thirty last night after we closed the restaurant…We had the biggest day since our grand opening, and we were so happy with the way things are panning out." He looked from Doris to me. "You know how it feels—we were dead tired from running all day, but everything had gone so good that it all felt worthwhile."

Doris smiled her encouragement.

"We were going to have a little nightcap and relax for a few minutes before hitting the sack." Fred paused, sighed loudly, and gave his pet a look of disgust. "The moment we stepped in the door, this little bugger came over and started his routine. He jumped up on my legs yipping away, so happy to see me…the next thing you know he started gagging, then puked on my foot."

I stared down at the scruffy little mutt. What in the world could be causing him to gag like that? "Has he been eating well?"

"Yeah, he seems to be—especially when we bring him something special from the restaurant."

"And he never vomits right after he's eaten?"

Fred thought about it, then shook his head. "He sometimes does it right after he eats, but even then he just brings up this white frothy stuff. He's only thrown up his whole supper a couple of times."

Doris read the thermometer. "It's 38.5."

"Well, I've been here often enough to know that's normal," Fred noted with a hint of discouragement.

I picked up my shaggy patient and gazed into his eyes.

"What's gotten into you, Rascal?"

"It's those tonsils," Fred insisted. "He's just like a kid…bugger around with 'em and bugger around with 'em, and then finally take 'em out."

I listened to Rascal's chest, trying to focus on the sounds of his heart and lungs as Fred went on about all the problems they had had with his nephew's tonsils—how they finally took them out like they should have to start with. I removed the earpieces and set down my stethoscope with a sigh. Sometimes normal sounds were so disgusting.

"He's been pooping and peeing normally?"

Fred nodded. "Never been the slightest problem there."

"Does he gag when you have him outside?"

"No, he doesn't," Fred mused. "After I got home last night, I took him for a walk and he was his old self, wandering around lifting his leg on everything and sniffing for god knows what."

Rascal shivered as I pried open his mouth and looked down his throat. His tonsils were still distended from their sheath—no different from the last time he'd been in.

"Do they look better?"

"No."

"I knew it…I want to leave him with you 'til you take 'em out."

"Are you sure you don't want to take him home and bring him back another day? We won't be able to do anything today if he's had something to eat and drink."

Fred shook his head adamantly. "I've had it with 'em. I want 'em out."

"Okay," I agreed grudgingly.

Fred gave his little buddy a pat. "I'll call you tomorrow and see how you made out."

I picked Rascal up off the table and cuddled him. He shivered and stared longingly after his master as he retreated out the door. I looked to Doris for sympathy. "I sometimes wonder if it's like this for other vets."

"What do you mean?"

"I listen to other vets talk about running their practices. This one seems to run me."

"Oh pooh," she said.

It was after three when I finally got a chance to call Pullman about Jean's horse. By that time, red blood cells and bulging tonsils were as much on my mind as collapsing pasterns.

"It is an unusual presentation, Dave," said Dr. Sande. "As you've noted, there's extensive arthritic changes involving the margins of P2 and P3. I can't say I've ever seen anything quite like it before. It's not surprising that she's showing signs of lameness."

"I guess that's my problem," I interjected. "What came first? I wasn't the least bit surprised to see those changes—not after walking beside her with my hand on her foot. The way that joint is abused with the constant collapsing, it would be a miracle not to see arthritic changes...And it doesn't seem logical to me that arthritis could cause her to collapse the way she does. You have to see it to understand what I'm talking about—she actually tosses her head in pain when it happens."

"I had a talk with John in the clinic. He vaguely remembered your call, but without looking at her he doesn't have anything to suggest."

"Do you think there'd be any advantage to hauling her there to the college as a teaching case? She's a twenty-year-old mare and the owner would consider donating her."

"I can check with the powers that be," Ron answered. "It sounds like she might be an interesting case, but we're pretty plugged up down here at the moment."

"Have you ever heard of this sort of thing being a result of a mineral deficiency?"

"Nooo...can't say I have."

"I'm feeling like a bit of a quack even talking about it. I remember when I was still a student and going out to visit with older practitioners...it always seemed each one of them had some special cure for a pet peeve in his own area. I guess I didn't think I'd get into it."

"There's been a lot of progress made in vet medicine by guys who listen to their instincts." Ron chuckled. "But, I have to say that the first bunny to poke his head out of his hole is the most likely to get it blown off."

"Yeah…"

Doris signalled me with a hand across her throat and held up a patient record to indicate that someone was waiting. I hung up the phone determined that it was time to experiment.

"Jennie Ibbitson is waiting…Her dog is having eye problems."

I tried to take the card from her. She held on to it and gave me a stern look. Peering through her horn-rimmed glasses, she raised her eyebrows. "She's been taking the dog to see Cory." I flushed. "Please don't make a big issue of it," Doris went on. "Mrs. Ibbitson is really uncomfortable about the situation."

I took the card from her and retired to the lab. I studied the six-by-four page as if it were suddenly going to enlighten me. I could see by the notations that I had given the dog her first vaccinations as a puppy. I stared at the record, not thinking about her case but about what I might have done to upset the Ibbitsons. There must have been something, or why had they taken the dog to Cory?

I took a deep breath and read on. In Doris's hand, with today's date, was written: *Ovariohysterectomy at another clinic. Has eye infection that is not improving with the treatment they prescribed— Pentamycetin ophthalmic.*

I sat on the counter, closed my eyes, and took another deep breath. My heart was pounding. This was ridiculous. I had to accept the fact that Marcie and Cory were here to stay, and people were going to go where they were going to go. I couldn't take it personally. Doris brought my next patient into the exam room. By that time my heart rate had almost returned to normal.

"We're ready for you, Dave," she said quietly.

I opened my eyes, inhaled deeply, and took the plunge. "Hi, Jennie."

"Hello."

"What's up with Mandy?" The springer spaniel's tail wiggled at top speed as I patted her.

"It's her eyes," the lithe blonde reported. "I noticed they were red when I took her in to get her stitches out."

Mandy's eyes were definitely pink and her third eyelids were prominent. The dog peered at me with a strange expression as I examined her more closely.

"He gave me some stuff to put in," Jennie went on, "but it hasn't made any difference. I took her in right after lunch today and told him she wasn't getting better, but he said to just keep putting the drops in. He said that I was too impatient."

She hesitated, then continued. "He looked kind of worried, so I started wondering if she caught something when she was there to be fixed."

I stared at my patient with her distinctive red and white markings, trying to quantify what was bothering me about her. There was something about her expression that wasn't right. Her eyes were peculiar with the whites ever so prominent, and her ears were strange, too—as if they were laid back farther on her head than they should be. It was as though a bizarre force were pulling her face back on her body.

"Did she have a discharge before you started putting in the medication?"

"A discharge?"

"Did her eyes water, or did pus come out or accumulate in the corners of her eyes?"

"No," Jennie said thoughtfully. "She was like this—just not quite as bad."

I rolled back the dog's eyelids and examined the conjunctivae looking for some indication of matter or inflammation.

"What are you giving her?"

She handed me a tube of chloramphenicol ointment. "Do you think it's the wrong stuff?"

I stared at Mandy for almost a minute without responding. "Do you notice something strange about her?"

"What do you mean, strange?"

"Well...is she carrying herself the way she usually does?"

"She's been kinda stiff when she walks, but I thought it was because of the surgery."

"What about her face?"

"Well, that's different, too, now that you mention it. She looks a bit oriental—her eyes are usually more rounded."

I clapped my hands together suddenly in front of the dog's face. Jennie jumped back, startled by my sudden movement.

"Did you see that?" I asked.

"What?"

"Look at her third eyelids."

"What's a third eyelid?" asked Jennie.

"Most animals other than primates have a protective flap called the nictitating membrane. It comes out from the corner of the eye to prevent damage to the cornea."

Doris and Jennie leaned in to look at the pink structures that had emerged suddenly from the corners of the dog's eyes—they covered almost a third of her corneas. As we watched, they continued to spasm as if they had a will of their own.

"That's gross," Jennie lamented.

"Why's she doing that?" Doris asked.

"If she were a horse or a cow, I'd say it was because she had tetanus...We were told in college that we'd never see it in a dog, but—"

"How would she get tetanus?" Jennie interrupted.

I avoided her question and began palpating Mandy's shaved tummy for some indication of an infection. The surgical wound from her ovariohysterectomy had healed beautifully. I found it hard to imagine its being the source of problems. I palpated deeper in the abdomen, convinced there must be a problem with either the uterine stump or the ovarian ligaments. The dog seemed relaxed; I couldn't detect any indication of discomfort. I ran my hands over her body looking for any signs of abnormalities or evidence of an old wound.

"Has she had any cuts or injuries that you're aware of?"

Jennie shook her head.

"Let's put her down for a second, Doris. I want to see how she's walking."

Doris lowered the dog to the floor and stepped back. Mandy stood stock-still, shifting her eyes to focus on her owner.

"Maybe head out to the waiting room, Jennie."

The dog stood there for several seconds after her mistress's departure as if wondering what to think of the situation.

"Here, Mandy…Come on, girl."

She stood like a statue shifting only her eyeballs, then with a concerted effort, trotted toward Jennie.

"She's sure not running around like she usually does," she noted. "If anything, she's been a more hyper dog than we expected. That's one of the reasons we were anxious to get her fixed…Don and I were hoping it'd settle her down a bit. What's going to happen with her? Do you think it'll get worse?"

"I hate to tell you this, but I don't have a clue…I've had mixed results with treating tetanus in horses and cattle. Dogs and cats are supposedly resistant to the organism, and it may not get any worse than it is right now. Usually, with large animals it depends on how many bacteria are growing at the site of infection."

"Infection?"

"Yes. Tetanus is caused by a bacterium that loves to grow in an oxygen-deprived environment. That usually means it's somewhere in a deep wound."

"So you think she got infected when she was fixed?"

I flushed. I had been avoiding that question. The two women watched me expectantly.

"It's not impossible that she stepped on a thorn or a nail and the wound has healed."

"How long after she was injured would she start showing symptoms?"

"I know in the horse and cow it's usually between three and ten days, but they claim it can be three weeks or longer. I assume it would be similar in other species."

"Do you think she could have gotten dirt in the wound when she was lying out in the backyard? Don did tie her out there for the first few days after her surgery."

I shrugged. "It's certainly possible."

After Jennie left, I gave Mandy a massive injection of penicillin, retired to the back room, and began plowing through my small-animal textbooks looking for advice on treatment. When I found nothing, I went back to the notes from my medicine classes. I searched until I found the section on clostridial diseases. Under the heading of tetanus, I found only one line: "Dogs and cats are extremely resistant to this condition—will not see it in practice."

In desperation, I dug out my trusty copy of *Blood, Henderson and Radostits* and skipped through the portions of text I had underlined in red pen when studying for my exams. The section on tetanus started with: "Tetanus is a highly fatal infectious disease of all species of domestic animals caused by the toxin of *Clostridium tetani.*" Although it wasn't a surprising statement, it wasn't overly encouraging either. I read on wondering why, if large-animal clinicians knew it involved all species, they hadn't informed the small-animal pundits of the fact.

The further I read the more discouraging it got. They quoted the mortality rate in farm animals as eighty percent—higher in horses, sheep, and swine, lower in cattle. My eyes skipped from one underlined passage to the next until I reached the section on treatment. "The main principles in the treatment of tetanus are to eliminate the causative bacteria, neutralize the residual toxin, relax the muscle tetany to avoid asphyxia, and maintain the relaxation until the toxin is eliminated or destroyed."

I pondered Mandy's situation. Removing the source of toxin made sense in the affected animals I had seen to date. I could remember three cases since I had arrived in the valley. Two had been horses with deep puncture wounds—they had died within days of diagnosis. Only one, a two-hundred-pound calf, had survived. He had started showing symptoms after his owner had performed a crude castration. I had aggressively removed all remnants of the infected cords and injected massive levels of penicillin. We kept him sedated for over a week before we could get him to stand again. By the end of a month I couldn't distinguish him from the other calves.

Did that mean I should go into Mandy's abdomen to remove the stump of her uterus and the remains of the ovarian ligaments? It wasn't as if we'd be dealing with an overwhelming infection. Maybe she wasn't going to get any worse, and antibiotics and anti-toxin would be all that were required.

According to the text, anti-toxin was considered of little value once clinical symptoms were seen. Somehow, it made sense to me that if there was still toxin circulating in the bloodstream, it would be best not to let it attach to yet more neurons. Frustrated that I couldn't find any literature about treatment in the dog, I decided to call Pullman one more time.

I dialled the small-animal clinic and asked for the internist in charge. I was informed he was away until next week, but I could speak with a resident. As I waited, music I recognized as a Mozart sonata played over the phone. I continued to read. The authors talked about optimal results for horses when 300,000 units were given every twelve hours for three injections. I wondered how that dose would translate for a thirty-five-pound dog.

There was a click on the line and the music stopped in the middle of a crescendo. "Dr. Wiley speaking." His voice was high-pitched and squeaky, and the picture of a wet-behind-the-ears chap who had still not framed his diploma popped into my mind. "How can I help you?"

"Yes…this is Dr. Perrin from the Creston Veterinary Clinic. I'm hoping you can offer some suggestions on how to handle a case of tetanus in the dog." After an uncomfortable silence, I went on. "I'm having difficulty finding references on case management. Have you any idea as to the dose of anti-toxin that I would use?"

Dr. Wiley cleared a frog from his throat and I imagined the young buck rolling his eyes, thinking that he had a real loonie on the line.

"Dogs and cats are resistant to tetanus," he stated confidently. After a brief pause he went on in a tone that told me he knew he was dealing with a crackpot. "What made you suspect your patient has tetanus?"

"I just don't see what else it could be," I began hesitantly. "It's a ten-month-old springer spaniel that was spayed ten days ago. She's stiff…her ears are erect at the base…her facial muscles are drawn up in a forced smile…her eyes are slanted, and she's pro-lapsing the third eyelid."

Silence prevailed for a full half minute. "Has she had seizures?"

"Not yet. She was presented because her owner was worried about her eyes."

After several more minutes of interrogation, the resident took leave promising to get into the literature, discuss the case, and get back to me. After he hung up, I made the call I was dreading.

The phone rang twice before the familiar voice answered, "Veterinary clinic."

"Cory…it's Dave calling."

Another uncomfortable silence.

"I'm calling to tell you that the Ibbitsons brought Mandy into the office this afternoon…I think she has tetanus."

"Dogs don't get tetanus!" he blurted.

"That's what everyone keeps telling me…I just wish someone had told Mandy that."

Never Say Die

I was tired. I flicked on the light and glared with bleary eyes at the alarm clock as it emitted its dying rattle. I had intentionally put it out of reach on my dresser so I wouldn't inadvertently shut it off and go back to sleep. I gave Lug a pat on the head, pushed him unceremoniously off the bed, and swung my feet to the floor. I didn't trust myself to lie there for even a second longer or I'd be drifting off. This was the second time I had been up to medicate Mandy since I had fallen into bed at nine o'clock. My sleep had been fitful at best, and it seemed as if I had just drifted off from my last session.

This was the tenth day since Jennie had brought Mandy in with her eye problem, and unless she was constantly sedated, every muscle in the dog's body went into rigid contraction. The previous night I had slept through this three o'clock alarm and not checked her until six. I had woken with a start a few minutes before six and rushed into the spare room of my apartment where we now kept her. My heart was pounding. She was motionless and my initial impression was that she was dead. When she finally drew a breath, I sighed with relief and hurriedly grabbed for a syringe and a glass vial of Valium.

The first few days I was sure she would continue to give me her sardonic smile and be able to deal with a bit of stiffness, but

209

by the third day, there was no doubt she would have to endure the full range of tetanus symptoms. Initially, her behaviour had been almost humorous to watch. Then, she had only shown signs of increased muscle tone and had been in no real danger. We had kept her in the surgery kennel with a blanket over the doors to cut down the light and reduce the amount of stimulation she received from our movement.

We were still able to take her outside for a walk, and we allowed her the run of the clinic. By the third day, however, she could no longer get up on her own, and when assisted, could only stand in a stiff-legged, sawhorse stance. When she was ready to lie down, she'd lift her feet from the floor as if they were suspended on wooden stilts and rotate her body until she could see us. She'd give a tiny wiggle to a tail that stood almost upright, and beg to be lowered onto her bed.

If we didn't reach her on time, she simply toppled from her full height to land flat on her side. When she was standing, she was able to open her mouth and slurp at water we held for her. She could still lick her nose and was eager to swallow big bites of canned dog food.

By the end of the fourth day, she could no longer stand but lay prone, with her head fully stretched out, her ears erect, and both front and hind legs extended. She could open her mouth enough to eat and had a good appetite for delectable treats. After she became totally recumbent, we were able to feed her with a syringe and get her to swallow a slurry of canned dog food and warm water. Although she had to concentrate to swallow during these feedings, she did her best, and actually gave me the impression she was hungry.

On the sixth day, I came to appreciate the layman's term for her condition—lockjaw. I had just given her another injection of tranquillizer and was trying to feed her with the syringe I had modified by drilling out the tip so it would allow blended dog food to pass through more easily. I found that when I got the device well

211

back in her mouth, she could still manipulate her tongue enough to swallow. I had already emptied the fourth syringe and had developed a bit of a routine for positioning it. Although it took quite an effort to get her jaw pried open enough, once the syringe was there I could push it further back in her mouth, even though she clamped down on it with considerable force.

Perhaps it was the repetitive nature of the job that got me into trouble, or maybe it was plain carelessness. Somehow, when I pulled the syringe out, my index finger got trapped between the dog's incisor teeth. I quickly evaluated my situation. With one hand incapacitated, I was unable to pry her jaw open again. My finger hurt like heck, but it was obvious that if I yanked on it, I'd peel the skin off the entire tip. I could tell by Mandy's expression she knew I was in a bad way, but at that point she was unable to help me out by slacking off the tension of her jaw.

That's when I hollered for Doris. I must say I didn't appreciate the twinkle in her eye as she manipulated the gauze over Mandy's canines and pried open the vice that held me captive. She vehemently swore that the expression on her face was not amusement, but she sure could have fooled me. Although the skin wasn't broken and the finger regained feeling fairly quickly, there were indentations in it for hours after to remind me of my carelessness. The next day I installed a tube that entered Mandy's mouth through the back of her cheek to facilitate feeding her.

As she got progressively worse and the scope of her treatment settled on me, I spoke with the Ibbitsons about taking her to the veterinary teaching hospital at Washington State University where she could have round-the-clock surveillance by students. I feared that if her condition worsened, she would develop a respiratory paralysis from an inability to relax the muscles of her thorax and abdomen enough to fill her lungs with air. In that case, she would probably need to be on a respirator for a few days.

Both Don and Jennie worked full time, so transporting her to Pullman presented a problem. When we discussed how much it was likely to cost, they made up their minds. If things worsened, they'd have Mandy put to sleep.

They had been upstairs to visit her yesterday, and I didn't like the look on their faces when they left. It was tough for them to view their pet, the perpetual-motion machine, as she was now—stretched out on her side with a pharyngostomy tube poking from the back of her cheek and an intravenous dripping into her leg. Although I couldn't say she had worsened over the last few days, there was absolutely no improvement either.

I felt like a fool when they questioned me about her likely outcome. I still hadn't found anyone who had treated a case of tetanus in a dog; all I could do was assume that the course of her disease would be similar to what it would be in other species. Every time they asked me if I thought she'd get better, I'd shrug and meekly tell them I hoped so.

I traipsed through the living room in my undershorts with the same trepidation I had on each visit to Mandy. She was still alive, stretched out, with every muscle taut and quivering. She wasn't as rigid as she'd been last night after I slept through her treatment, but I was sure the Atravet and Valium combination was not as effective as it had been initially. Although I'd been uncertain about administering Valium on top of the phenothiazine tranquillizer, the pharmacologist from WSU had given his blessing.

Mandy looked up at me with pleading brown eyes as I gave the first injection into the port of her intravenous line.

"You poor thing…I wish I could magically end your torment."

Her tail wiggled ever so slightly as the medication took effect. The light in her eyes faded and some of the tension left her body. I manipulated her front leg back and forth. I knew she wasn't relaxing the way she had in the beginning, and I dreaded that I might have to start using barbiturates. It wasn't so much a terrible alternative, but it was an admission that things were getting worse rather than better.

I stumbled to the kitchen. Still in a fog, I turned on the hot water tap and stuck my finger into the flow. Once it turned hot, I poured several cups into the blender, spooned in canned dog food, and flicked the switch. I closed my eyes as the machine whined away. I wanted to sleep and sleep and sleep with no interruptions.

I returned to the spare room and knelt beside my patient. Even though she didn't react to my presence, she still looked uncomfortably rigid. I lifted under her chest. Her eyes immediately popped open, her neck arched like a bow, and her legs extended stiffly.

"You poor baby…your muscles must be so sore."

Mandy's outstretched body was unyielding as I held her to my chest and removed the soiled blanket she'd been lying on. Lifting the plastic sheet, I fluffed her feather pillows and repositioned them on the thick layer of foam rubber. We had kept our patient on a soft bed to try and avoid problems with pressure sores. So far, at least that plan seemed to be working. I replaced the plastic, put down a new blanket, and positioned her at the join of the two pillows.

During the time it took me to flush the slurry down her feeding tube, she remained rigid with her head cranked back and her legs extended.

"Oh Mandy, we can't leave you like this."

I made up my mind. Without dressing, I tiptoed downstairs to the drug cabinet. Leaving the lights out so as not to be an exhibition for strangers on the street, I unlocked the door and withdrew a bottle of phenobarb. Was I just wasting my time? Was there still reason to hope that Mandy would turn some magical corner?

"You look terrible, Dave." Doris's eyes brimmed with concern.

"I feel worse than I look."

"Is she any better today?"

"I had to start her on phenobarb last night…It seemed as if the acepromazine and Valium weren't quite enough."

"Did the Ibbitsons talk to you yesterday about putting her to sleep?"

"I managed to steer them away from the topic."

"How much longer can you keep this up?"

I shook my head dejectedly.

"They know you've tried hard, Dave. They just don't want to see her suffer any more."

"I know, but where there's breath there's life. I've read about putting human cases on respirators for long periods of time before they rallied. At least Mandy's still breathing on her own."

Doris sighed and pointed to a notation she had made on the edge of the day page. "We had the morning booked for surgeries, but Phil McGraw called about a horse. He says he's breathing hard and coughing. He apparently wasn't looking good last night, and he treated him with penicillin. He says, if anything, he's worse this morning...he mentioned something about his skin crackling."

"Crackling? What do you mean by crackling?"

"I'm not sure. I thought maybe you'd know."

"Let's pre-med the first spay and I'll get out there."

After injecting an eight-month-old poodle with tranquillizer and atropine, Lug and I headed to the truck. It had snowed during the night, but the way the rain was coming down now, there would soon be little evidence of the white stuff. I drove leisurely toward Lister. Slush sprayed in a rooster-tail to the side of me as I passed the golf course in the direction of the mountains. I had started signalling for the turn onto Sinclair Road to get to McGraws when I changed my mind and headed up the hill toward my place. For several days now I had been ignoring the house and just feeding the cows. Last night I had stumbled around in the dark with a flashlight.

I drove slowly past the house as if I were sightseeing. The log structure looked so peaceful and serene back there in the trees. Lug whined and twirled on the seat in anticipation of stopping. I braked the truck and squinted, trying to picture the house with the stone portion finished and shakes on the roof. When would I ever get the chance to split the rest of those shakes?

"Not now, boy."

I hit the accelerator and headed south on Canyon-Lister Road. There was work to do and this little junket was not helping me get it done. Lug stared at me in obvious disappointment. I turned down 12th Street and continued on Sinclair until I reached a stone monument that was built in tribute to the Huscrofts, the area's founding family. Halfway down the hill, I pulled up outside a barbed wire fence and parked. I stuffed a thermometer and my stethoscope into my coveralls and got out.

"You stay," I warned Lug as he tried to push his way out the door.

I hesitated at the gate and grabbed a soggy piece of grass to test the wires. I had learned from experience that all was not as it appeared on the McGraw farm. The last time I entered unawares, the jolt from the fence knocked me flat. When I was satisfied that it wasn't electrified, I cautiously lifted the wire from the post and stepped through. I hadn't taken more than six steps when I was greeted by a cacophony of barking from the house across the draw. I took a deep breath as the pack of dogs descended upon me. The words of Phil's neighbour flashed through my mind. Early in the spring when I was there for a calving, he had told me: "Living next door to Phil, I never know from one day to the next whether I'm going to be shot, run over by a herd of horses, gored by a wild boar, or eaten by a pack of dogs."

I held my breath and marched on as yipping spaniels, growling Dobermans, and an assortment of Airedales and Irish setters charged toward me.

"Enough!" A booming voice sounded from the corrals ahead. "Don't worry about them, they're a bunch of pussycats."

"Do you think you have enough of them?"

"They're cheaper by the dozen," came the jovial response.

"You must buy your dog food from a different place than me."

I counted as the dogs milled around me, sniffing my pant legs and sticking their muzzles into my hand for attention. Phil wasn't exaggerating—including the five cockers and a matted poodle, there was an even dozen.

"He's in the back corral," he noted as I approached the barns. "It's the damnedest thing I've ever seen. Poor Gray's coughing, wheezing, and carrying on like you wouldn't believe. I was going to give him another shot of penicillin this morning, but when I went out there, his skin felt funny—all crackly and puffy."

"Crackly?"

"Yeah, just wait and see."

I swung my leg over the rail fence and was halfway to Phil when I halted in my tracks. A humongous boar that had to weigh five or six hundred pounds sauntered out from the barn.

"Don't worry about him," Phil laughed. "Beep's a real pet." The animal sidled up and my client rubbed his back. The massive pig arched his broad back and emitted a high-pitched bleeping sound. "Hear that," Phil went on. "That's where he got his name…He beeps whenever you scratch him."

"I'm not sure I'd want to hang around to find out what noise he made if I didn't know he was friendly."

"That's what my neighbour's wife thought, too. Old Beep has a thing for bicycles. He got out a couple of weeks ago and went for a walk over to their place. Poor woman must have thought she was done for. She was out on her bike and Beep took after her. You'd have thought the devil himself was chasing her the way she was screaming and carrying on. I about died laughing." Phil chuckled as if he were viewing the scene all over again. "I don't think even she knew she could pedal so fast."

I skirted Beep and headed in the direction of the horse.

"Be sure and keep an eye on old Bummer," Phil warned.

"Bummer?"

"Yeah, he's our mascot."

He pointed to a goat with an impressive set of horns that stood just inside the barn door. The animal raised and lowered his head as if trying to get me in better focus.

"A couple years ago we found a fawn on the side of the road and brought it home. I got Bummer to keep her company...bought him from a woman out in Arrow Creek who said he was de-scented. The deer's long gone, but Bummer's still here." Phil grabbed a shovel and watched over his shoulder as we headed to the corral. "That's how he got his name."

"What do you mean?"

"Well, life's a real bummer when you smell like he does. Not sure what he'd have smelled like if he hadn't been de-scented, but he smells pretty rank right now."

As we approached the back paddock and my patient came into view, I lost interest in the goat and focused on the gelding. I couldn't take my eyes off him as I climbed to the top rail of the next fence. I paused there to watch him. The horse was standing with his neck extended and his head so low that his chin rested on the ground. His sides pumped frantically as he worked to move air.

"How long has he been like this?" I asked in disbelief.

"He wasn't this bad last night. When I gave him the shot at about seven, he was just breathing a bit faster than normal and coughing now and again. He had a bit of snot in his nose, so I thought he might have picked up a bug." Phil climbed the fence and sat on the top rail next to me. "I called your office as soon as I saw him this morning."

I dropped to the ground and slowly circled the horse. The hair coat around his neck and withers was wet and slicked flat to the skin. Phil was right—the horse looked puffy. I slipped a thermometer into his rectum and ran my hand along his back to his withers. The gelding's skin crackled under my fingertips.

"What's causing that?" Phil asked. "Been around horses all my life and never felt anything like it before."

"It's air," I answered vacantly. "He's got air between the muscles and his skin."

218

"How could air get in there?"

I didn't answer him, but leaned back against the fence to watch the animal breathe.

"What are you doing?" Phil asked impatiently.

"Watching. See how he's breathing?"

"Yeah, he's puffing a lot."

"His breathing's a bit faster than normal, but not much. Look closer at how he's breathing—he takes a quick puff in, then works hard to push it out."

I watched several more breaths; each was a struggle with a quick inspiration and a prolonged expiration when every muscle in the horse's abdomen tensed in an effort to force air out of his lungs.

I removed the thermometer. Gray's temperature was only slightly elevated at 38.4. With my stethoscope I listened to lung sounds that were surprisingly distant on the left side, while loud squeaks and whistles were present on the right. The heart was muffled but its rate was almost twice normal.

I thought back to pathology lab and the lungs of a horse that had died from acute emphysema. They had been blown up like a balloon that would not collapse. I was ready to bet that Gray's lungs were in a similar condition.

I removed the stethoscope and lifted the horse's head. He appeared reluctant to hold it up on his own, and I wondered how it could be more comfortable for him to breathe with his jaw literally resting on the ground. The mucous membranes of his mouth and eyes were a dirty grey. I pushed on the gums and couldn't see a return of colour. The gelding shook his head free of my grasp, extended his neck, and gave a low, protective cough.

"He's in rough shape, Phil."

"I can see that…What can we do about it?"

"You've heard of people with emphysema?"

"Yeah…you think that's what he's got? How's that different from heaves?"

"We accept that they're the same thing in the horse."

"Why would he suddenly get heaved? He's never showed signs of it before."

"It's pretty well accepted that emphysema results from an allergic response of some type...What sort of hay have you been feeding him?"

"It's a mix of grass and alfalfa—some I put up myself."

"Is it dusty or mouldy?"

Phil's eyes averted mine. He looked at his feet and scuffed at the dirt. "Well, some of the bales were a bit dusty...mostly the bales from the draws that got put up a bit tough."

"Well, from now on, Gray gets nothing but your best hay. I want you to wet it down before you give it to him, and feed him in an open area—somewhere up off the ground. And for the next few days, you may be best to try feeding him cubes."

Phil was glum. "I still don't understand why he's breathing like he is."

"The theory is that an allergen causes the smooth muscles around the airways to constrict. Just watch what you do when you take a breath; all the effort is when you suck air in. Breathing out is usually no work at all—the rib cage collapses automatically when you relax."

Phil took a deep breath and nodded his understanding.

"When the tubes the air flows through get smaller, it's more difficult for the horse to force air out of his lungs. That's why you see him pushing with his tummy muscles."

Phil rested his hand on the tense muscles of Gray's abdomen as he strained to push the air out.

"The smaller the passages get, the harder he has to push to empty his lungs, and the more likely it is that air will break out of the normal channels. Once it does, it dissects through the interstitial tissues and forms pockets. He's probably got a big bolus of air on the left side where I can't hear much."

"How's it getting out under the skin?"

"Probably through the lymphatic system. I've seen it once or twice before with cows, but this is the first time I've ever seen it in a horse."

Phil looked longingly at his gelding. "What are we going to do? He's a hell of a fine animal—the best mountain horse I've ever had. I don't want to lose him."

"We'll get him on atropine, antihistamines, and steroids to try and relieve the spasm of the smooth muscles that are causing the bronchial constriction…and you can continue the antibiotics you started yesterday."

"Okay."

"Do you have a cutting torch?"

He gave me a questioning glance and shook his head. "A cutting torch? What do you need to cut?"

"Nothing…I was hoping you might have some oxygen here. Gray could use it right now."

Phil nodded as I scaled the fence to return to my truck. Scurrying over ahead of me, he grabbed his shovel and chased Bummer into the barn. I loped toward the far fence as Beep followed behind me like a puppy dog. There was something about his size that commanded my respect and lent a spring to my step. I was met by the pack of dogs as soon as my feet were on the ground outside the corral. They followed me to the truck and milled around as I gathered the medications I'd require to treat Gray. Lug got up on the seat, growling menacingly; soon there was a bedlam of barking with each creature making a determined bid to defend its territory.

"Enough!" I bellowed as two dozen front feet scratched at the paint on my truck. "Lie down, Lug! And shut up!"

My faithful buddy slunk to the floor in total dejection as I circled the vehicle and pushed the dogs down one after the other. Phil was waiting at the fence with a broad smile when I returned with the medications. I passed him a bottle of antihistamine.

"I want you to give him a shot of this every twelve hours and

one of dexamethasone every four hours until we see improvement."

"I work up on the summit tonight so I won't be here in four
hours…I've got a job with highways now."

"Well, I'll come back and check him as soon as I get done at
the office. The shape he's in, we have to make sure he's treated
properly."

The morning and lunch hour passed in a whirl as Doris and I
caught up with the surgeries. By the time our last appointment left
shortly after four, I was exhausted. It seemed as if the entire afternoon had been spent in catch-up. The busier it got, the more I
thought about how I'd like to go hide out in my basement at the
farm and split shakes. There was something therapeutic about
making the thick wooden shingles. Maybe it was watching the
steel blade disappear into a block of cedar, or maybe it was swinging the heavy homemade birch mallet. Whatever it was, I was
craving the opportunity to get back at it.

"You've got some calls to make," Doris informed me. "I warned
them you'd be tied up 'til late afternoon. Jean Partington wants to
talk to you about her horse, and Jennie Ibbitson is waiting for an
update on Mandy."

I glared at Doris, as if she were in some way complicit in select-
ing my phone calls.

"What are you going to do with Mandy?" she asked.

"What do you mean?"

"When I was up there checking her this morning, I left feeling
so hopeless…and Jennie Ibbitson sounded really down today. She
told me they'd talked things over at home and they're ready to let
her go." I continued to glare at her. She gazed at me with tears
pooling. "Is it because of Cory that you won't give up?"

I looked away from her. "I won't say that his involvement has
no bearing on this, but I want more than anything for that dog to
walk out of here under her own steam. There's something that tells

me she's not ready to be stuffed in a black bag yet…Even when she was as stiff as a rock, there were moments when she looked at me with that light in her eyes. She doesn't have a clue what's happening to her, but I'm convinced she's not ready to give up."

"Well, you better be prepared to convince the Ibbitsons of that…You might be a never-say-die kind of guy, but they're rapidly losing faith."

I took a deep breath and decided to phone Jean Partington first. I dialled the number that I knew off by heart and waited as it rang. I wasn't looking forward to this call.

"Hello." It was Jean who answered.

"Hi, Jean…it's Dave."

"Dave, you wouldn't believe what happened today!" Her voice was brimming with excitement. "I've been feeding Saiawna the mineral mix like you suggested. I never had much hope it would make a difference, and haven't paid very close attention over the last couple of weeks. When I put her feed out tonight, she came galloping over like there was nothing wrong with her. She bucked and chased around with the other horse just like she used to."

A shiver ran up my spine and tears came to my eyes. "Are you serious?"

"I am…I couldn't believe it myself and ran into the house to call you. When Doris said you were out, I went back and ran her around on a lunge line. I even took her out on the hill where she kept collapsing, and she charged up and down like it was no big deal."

"Oh man, Jean, did I need this news."

"I thought you'd be happy…I couldn't wait to tell you."

I hung up the phone with a smile on my face, closed my eyes, and inhaled as much air as I could. "Thank you, Lord…you always drop a pearl before me when things are looking black."

I picked up the phone again and began dialling, but halfway through the process I hung up and wearily trudged up the stairs. Lug met me with his tail wagging.

"What would I do without you?" I asked, stooping to give him a big hug. He licked my face, then rested his head in my arms. Lug was the one being who never judged me or blamed me when things didn't go to his liking. I needed to learn from him. I made my way to the living room and slumped into the recliner. I tipped it back and closed my eyes. Lug stuck his cold nose on my hand and I rumpled his ears without stirring.

What in the world was I going to do with Mandy? Doris's challenge about Cory kept bugging me. Was I stubbornly hanging on to prove something to him and the rest of the world? Was I still trying to convince myself that I could do something he couldn't?

I focused on my breathing, driving all thoughts from my mind. Within a few moments, I felt the familiar numbing at the bridge of my nose that announced I had reached my desired state of relaxation. I lay there for ten minutes—not asleep, but not fully awake. When I stirred, I knew for certain I had to persist with Mandy. No matter what happened, she deserved the chance to prove she could make it. Humans had survived this horrible disease after weeks on a respirator. She could do it, too.

Reluctantly, I roused myself and went to the spare room. Mandy was stretched on her side in a barbiturate-induced coma. I placed my stethoscope on her chest and listened intently. Her heart rate was normal; there was no indication of abnormal lung sounds. Doris had changed the intravenous bag while I was tending to my last appointment; it dripped away as regular as clockwork. I slipped a thermometer into the little dog and rolled her onto her other side. She stiffened briefly and her neck arched for almost a minute before she returned to a relaxed state. I sat for a while with her head in my hands, then checked the thermometer—still normal.

I finally went downstairs and called Jennie. I could tell by the tone of her voice that her mind was made up.

"It looks so hopeless, Dave. Each time I see her, I leave asking myself why I didn't tell you to end it. Don and I have talked it over, and we think it's time. Even if she survives all this, how will we know she'd be normal?"

"I wish I had the answer to that, Jennie. I keep going over things wondering if I could have done something different. Maybe if I'd removed the stump of the uterus and cut back the ovarian ligaments, she would have absorbed less toxin. According to the literature, once the nerves are affected, you have to wait for them to regrow...that takes time. I'd hate to give up on her now." She didn't respond so I stumbled on. "I've got her totally out of it with barbiturates now, and she's not aware of anything around her. Give me two or three more days to see if there's a change."

"I don't know," she replied uncertainly. "We had our minds made up. I cringe to think what this has already cost us."

"If the truth be known, Jennie, I couldn't possibly charge for all the time I've spent on her." My voice took on a pleading tone. "I'll continue on at my own expense...Just give me two or three more days."

"Two days," she answered resolutely, "and if she shows no improvement, we'll put her down."

"Okay," I mumbled.

I hung up the phone before she could change her mind. I could take this for two more days, and with a bit of help from the ultimate power, so could Mandy.

"It's all up to you, Lord," I muttered. "Drop me one more pearl."

I drew up the dexamethasone for the McGraw gelding and headed for the door.

"I'm off, Doris!"

"Did you make your phone calls?" she queried with suspicion.

"I did."

I opened the door. Lug rushed to follow me, but I stopped him. "Not this time, big guy...I've had enough scratches on that poor truck for one day."

I drove to the McGraw place in a daze. I couldn't remember a time even during calving season when I'd been so tired. My eyes burned and constantly wanted to close as I made my way through Lister. It was snowing again and the flitting of the wiper blades across the windshield kept me in a hypnotic state. I was to the stone monument before I realized it, and came to a complete stop to ask myself what I was doing there. I so needed a good night's sleep; every bone in my body ached for it.

I drove on, pulled over by Phil's fence, and sat in the truck for five minutes with my head in my hands. It never failed that all the physically draining cases happened at the same time. I popped the syringe of steroids into my pocket and opened the door. It was time to find out if Gray was still with us. It wouldn't surprise me in the least to get there and find him lying in a heap.

I got out of the truck and tipped my head up to the darkening sky. Snowflakes settled gently on my face. With a sudden resolve, I climbed the fence and jumped down onto the wet pasture grass. I had taken at least a dozen paces onto the property before the dogs clued in to my arrival. Trying to ignore them, I continued walking as they barrelled across the pasture and surrounded me with a barking fury.

"Enough!"

The cockers pulled back at my rebuke, and the Airedales and Irish setters widened their circle, but the three Dobermans maintained an aggressive stance and continued on a collision course straight for me. I trekked toward them as if I were walking on my own turf and not theirs. It was when the burly black and tan Dobie crammed his nose into my crotch that I came to a screeching halt. He withdrew a few inches and barked with sufficient authority that the vibrations were detected by very sensitive parts of my anatomy.

"Enough now! Get to the house!"

The Dobies retreated a step and parted, so I continued straight on to the corral fence. I breathed a sigh of relief the moment my foot hit the bottom rail. I sat on the snow-covered ridge with my eyes closed. Why did everything have to be so difficult? When I opened my eyes the dogs had dispersed. I dropped to the muddy ground of the corral and was halfway across when Beep sauntered from the barn. I stopped as the massive creature ambled toward me, grunting softly as he came.

"My god," I mumbled, "what a menagerie."

My heart pounded and my pace slowed as Beep continued on a steadfast course. I looked longingly at the far fence, then again at Beep. There was no way I could make my destination if the boar had any ill intent. As he walked toward me, all I could focus on were the tusks that curled from his lower jaw and protruded beneath his lips on either side of his snout.

"Hey there, Beep," I blurted nervously. "How you making out this afternoon?"

When I came to a stop, the boar maneuvered his long body alongside me like a yacht gliding up to a dock. I hesitantly reached out to scratch his side.

"Beep, beep beep," he squeaked in the high-pitched tone that was so foreign to a huge beast like him. As my fingernails scraped over his rough, thick hide, he leaned into me, raising and lowering his hind end. "Beep, beep, beep." He continued communicating his approval as the flat of my hand rubbed over the prickly hairs that covered his side.

Sudden movement at the barn door distracted my attention and brought Beep's massage to a halt. Bummer took two strides beyond the confines of the building, then raised and lowered his head. His beady eyes squinted at me between his massive curling horns.

I had never been much of a track star, but thank God I started sprinting across the muddy corral a few seconds before Bummer did. I reached the fence in full stride with one long leg stretching toward the second rail. I grabbed the top plank, pulled up with all my might, and flipped up my legs. I was fully extended on top of the uppermost rail when Bummer's head hit the fence. My belly screamed in protest as the entire structure vibrated from the concussion of his contact, and I toppled into the mud on the other side.

"You stinky son of a bitch," I growled.

The buck raised and lowered his head and peered through the rails at me. Strangely enough, the expression on his face had changed. The malice that had been so evident before his charge became an almost gleeful sparkle. He curled his upper lip and gave a playful little blat. If I didn't know better, I'd swear that goat was laughing at me. I lay there in the mud trying to convince myself that nothing more important than my pride had been injured. My right butt cheek ached from my contact with the ground; my belly burned from where it had scraped across the top rail.

I propped myself up on my elbows and looked over my shoulder. Gray stood next to the fence a few yards from where I had landed. His sides still billowed, but his head was up. I glared at Bummer. The buck defiantly peered through the rails. He gave several intimidating blats as if daring me to return.

"Laugh, you bugger...I'll get even with you one way or another."

I hauled myself erect. My coveralls and jacket were soaked and plastered with mud. Trying my best to ignore the obnoxious creature on the other side of the fence, I attended to Gray. The horse was gaunt and looking weary, but the urgency that was present earlier in the day had eased. I ran my hand under his blanket over his neck and back. The skin crackled as bubbles of air were displaced, but it appeared that the size of the air pockets had diminished.

I plucked my stethoscope from my pocket and stared at it with disgust. Both earpieces were packed with mud. Screwing the tips off, I blew through them to dislodge the muck and polished them on the inside of my jacket. Bummer continued to taunt by snorting through his nose and rolling up his lip as I worked on the instrument. I made a conscious effort to ignore the beast.

By the look of the flake of hay in front of Gray, he had actually eaten something. His breathing wasn't as laboured as it had been earlier, but I was disappointed to detect little change in the sounds emanating from his lungs—they were still wracked with a chorus of whistles and crackles.

He stood rock-still as I gave his injections. I surveyed the route I had come and decided I'd walk through the pasture and take the long way around to the truck.

I plodded up the stairs and fumbled through the pocket of my muddy jacket for the keys to unlock the door. I had come up the back stairs so as not to leave a trail of mud behind me on the office carpet. Lug yipped happily as I stood on the landing peeling off my boots, jacket, and coveralls. He jumped up on me with his tail wagging when I entered the kitchen. Poor dog, he was missing his long runs at the farm.

I stroked his head and talked to him for a few minutes before I went for a peek at Mandy. She was sleeping peacefully, oblivious to the world. Her face was the only betrayal of restfulness. With ears still perched at an abnormal angle and her eyes mere slits, it appeared as if an invisible hand were pulling everything backward.

"How're you doing, girl?"

I slipped my hands under her and lifted her. Her muscles tightened momentarily, but after I changed her blanket and rotated her to her opposite side, she lay still. Was she really beginning to improve, or was it the barbiturate concentration accumulating?

"Please, Lord…just one more pearl."

Too Ornery to Die

"Isn't there something else we can do, Dave?"

Phil stared intently at me as I removed the stethoscope tips from my ears. "Gray's too good a horse to just stand around in a pen wheezing like a winded old man. I've never had a better horse than him in the mountains...Me and my buddy went hunting in Elk Valley last month, and you wouldn't believe the places he took me."

"We've done everything that we can do conventionally," I responded defensively.

"The crackling might be gone from under his skin, but you know yourself he wouldn't be good for much more than a walk around the block the way he is."

Phil was right. I watched as Gray exhaled jets of steam from flared nostrils. Even standing at rest it was hard work for him to breathe. He'd be in no shape to handle a trek on rocky uphill terrain.

"There's only one thing we haven't tried."

"Why's that? What're you waiting for?"

"Well...it's not exactly a treatment that's been written up in the textbooks."

"I should give a damn about textbooks! All I care about is having a horse I can use again."

"I've had good luck with it on several horses," I said hesitantly, "but it hasn't worked on them all."

"What is it?" Phil asked impatiently. "Do you have some with you?" I nodded. He eyed me with suspicion. "Why are you being so secretive about it?"

"Because it's an off-label use of a drug."

"Off-label? Does that mean illegal?"

"No, not exactly. It means that the product has a label claiming it's used for something else. This one actually has a claim as a dewormer in cattle."

Phil was skeptical. "So, you're suggesting Gray has worms that are affecting his lungs? If that's what you're thinking, it couldn't be. I dewormed him at the beginning of September with stuff I bought from your clinic."

"I doubt it has anything to do with worms. A couple years ago, a veterinarian working in a federal slaughter plant somewhere in Quebec wrote a letter to the editor of the *Canadian Veterinary Journal* claiming that the drug was a cure for heaves. He apparently rescued a number of horses that were afflicted badly enough for people to sell them for meat. He suggested in the letter that heaves might have something to do with a lungworm infestation. The poor guy was bombarded with ridicule from other veterinarians. Most people who read the letter laughed his suggestion off as a dumb idea…I decided to try it on a few non-responsive cases. I was really impressed with the results. Some of the horses I tried it on had lung sounds just like Gray has now, and they seem to have returned to full function."

"So if it isn't killing worms, what's it doing?"

I could see by the look on Phil's face that he was miles ahead of me; his mind was already made up about trying the treatment.

"I suspect it has something to do with immune modulation. The drug is doing something to dampen histamine release or in some other way diminish the animal's response to an allergen."

"Can you give it to him today?"

"Only if you're going to be around to watch him for the next while. For some reason, treated animals have more trouble breathing for the first few days after giving the drug. They bear watching. Besides, you need to be around to rub the injection site every couple of hours. I've never known the stuff to cause a reaction in cattle, but it sure does in horses. I've seen welts the size of my fist when they weren't tended to."

Phil nodded assertively. "I'm just starting four days off, so it's perfect timing."

"Well, we'll give it a try then."

I pulled on my gloves, grabbed the metal bar from my calving jack, and climbed the fence Gray was tied to.

Phil grinned broadly. "Bummer's got you a bit nervous, has he?"

"You could say that."

I picked my way across the crusty, frozen corral, daring the caprine demon to challenge me. Beep was curled up sleeping in a corner inside the barn, but Bummer had me on the radar screen from the moment my foot touched the ground on his side of the fence.

"Well, what're you waiting for?"

The obnoxious buck took a step in my direction and continued to watch me. His demeanour was disconcerting to say the least. He flared his nostrils, lowered his head, and ejected several jets of steam. I stopped and waved the metal bar in his direction.

"Come on, you SOB...I'm ready for you this time."

Phil laughed. "He's too smart for that. Just put it down and see if those long legs of yours can get you across fast enough."

I turned my back on Bummer and was soon climbing the fence on the opposite side. The dogs had seen so much of me in the last week that only a few of them barked, and none of them bothered crossing the draw.

I pulled off my gloves and sorted through my medications. I stared in amazement at the frozen bottles of penicillin, calcium, and dextrose. The sudden drop in temperature had caught me totally off guard. I'd have to sort through things and winterize my kit later this evening. I found the levamisol, filled two syringes with the sluggish material, and stuffed them in my inside shirt pocket to warm them. Grabbing a squirt bottle of alcohol and my trusty bar, I headed back across the field.

Bummer viewed my passing from his vantage point at the doorway to the barn. Peering at me with great interest, he raised and lowered his head, then took an ominous step forward. I shifted the bar from hand to hand in anticipation of a fight.

Phil stood on the second rail of the fence watching my progress. "Come on, Dave, be a sport...That bar gives you unfair advantage!"

Ignoring his taunts, I was soon over the fence tending to my patient. I soaked a spot on Gray's belly several times with alcohol, then waited for a minute to pop a needle under the skin.

"Why're you giving it there?" Phil asked.

"This injection sometimes causes quite a reaction and if there's a problem with an abscess, best that it be somewhere it can drain well and not leave a disfigurement."

Phil watched intently as I injected the material under the skin. As soon as I removed the needle, I began massaging.

"See where this is? The other one will be a hand's breadth away."

"How often do I rub them?"

"Every chance you get—best if you do it every couple of hours until we see how he's going to react. If he gets really swollen, then come in for an anti-inflammatory to rub on it. If he's going to have problems, you'll know by tomorrow."

I drove leisurely to the farm. It was great not to feel that I was rushing to meet a deadline, or keeping someone waiting—this was Saturday and Phil's was the last call booked. I turned onto 12th Street and Lug started his whining and twirling.

"It's been a while since we spent any amount of time here, hasn't it, fella?"

Over the last couple of weeks, going to the farm had become just one more chore that had to be done before I could crawl into bed and pull the covers over my head. The cows would be surprised to see me in the daylight hours. Most nights I had driven to the hay shed and left Lug in the truck to keep him from getting muddy. I stumbled around in the dark yanking on bale strings with one hand and shining the flashlight with the other.

Lug howled excitedly and scrambled over me when the door swung open. I stretched my legs to the ground and snugged up my jacket. It felt good to have my feet planted firmly on the ground I loved. It felt even better to know that there was nothing to rush off to—the rest of the day was mine. This peaceful afternoon had been a long time coming. My friends at the ashram would be quick to point out that every day would be peaceful if I were at rest with myself and my intentions.

That had been the problem. So many times in the past month, I had been riddled with doubt and troubled by my motivation. Most of my conflicts originated with Mandy. I came to wonder if she had been sent just to test my resolve. Not only was her case the most difficult and troubling I had ever handled, but it brought me face to face with all the negative attributes I learned to recognize while at the ashram. Pride, self-doubt, self-pity—all dominated my daily thoughts.

Never had I been so confused about whether or not to give up a battle. It was gut-wrenching to watch poor Mandy's ordeal day after day. Was her struggle all for naught? Several evenings I picked up the phone determined to tell the Ibbitsons that the time had come. On each occasion, I hung up, deciding to see what the morning would bring.

The fact that Mandy did walk out of the clinic on her own steam mitigated some of the self-criticism. Dealing with her illness was a bit like trying to navigate an oil tanker on the Kootenay

River. I kept hoping I would wake up one morning and find her standing at the bedroom door wagging her tail. But that wasn't to be. Her recovery was agonizingly slow.

The day after my consultation with Jennie, I was able to discontinue the phenobarbital. Two days later I cut out the Atravet and removed her pharyngostomy feeding tube. I took her off the Valium two days before she went home. That morning she stood upright, her legs stiff as posts, and took a few hesitant steps. She was rail-thin. Her facial expression was still grossly distorted. Although she had great difficulty opening her jaw, she was ravenous and forced down a whole can of dog food.

It was strange watching her leave—sort of anticlimactic. Why wasn't there a band playing or a politician pinning a medal on my chest for valour beyond the call of duty? At the very least, there should have been a reporter there taking pictures of the dog who had been to hell and back and simply wouldn't say die.

I cinched up the top button on my coat, filled my lungs with cold mountain air, and slowly rotated to take in a panoramic view of my surroundings. The sky was an azure blue, without a cloud in sight. The hay fields to the south bumped into the tree-covered hills along the Idaho border. The mountain at my back formed a mosaic—the white of snow outlining its peak and streaking its ridges. Its face was the grey of granite with blotches of blue and green where trees clung to the rocky cliffs.

I turned to face my yard. The area under the trees was covered with a crust of snow, but the rest was bare dirt where the cows had cropped off what little grass there was. From here, the fir and larch trees almost hid the house. I focused on the log structure. I loved its profile against the forest, but the darkness inside and the lack of windows left it feeling lonely and neglected—an empty shell waiting to be filled. I had to get back to work on the place. It was time for it to become a home—my home.

I grabbed the caveman's club I had fashioned from a piece of birch wood and the shake knife that Bill Irvine had made for me from a car spring in his machine shop. Keeping the sun at my back, I perched on a block of wood in front of a stack of cedar blocks. I placed the blade on top of a three-foot bolt and pounded until it was buried full length. Pulling toward me on the handle, I popped off an even slice of cedar that tapered from an inch at the top end to half that at the butt. I picked up the block, flipped it, and repeated the process.

I worked for several hours, splitting and flipping until a block was whittled to a thin wedge, then choosing another block and starting all over again. When my feet got numb from the cold, I stomped them on the frozen ground until I could feel them again.

It was getting dark when I decided I'd had enough. I trimmed the edges of my last batch of shakes with a hatchet and carried them to the pile that I made against the logs on the south side of the house. My shoulder and back were tired from swinging the birch club, and my forearm had pulled enough shakes for the day. Lug lifted his head as I headed to the truck. He had scouted around the property for most of the afternoon and had been content to lie on the ground and snooze while I worked.

"Let's hit the road."

He beat me to the car and twirled in a slow dance until I opened the door.

After the weeks of sleep deprivation and an afternoon of physical exertion, I was happy to hit the bed early. My butt cheeks were pink when I finally hauled myself from the tub—I'd been soaking for more than half an hour. The hot water was a good antidote for the cold that had crept into my bones.

I set the alarm for seven-thirty and hopped into bed. I had been sleeping so deeply that it almost worried me. This morning, I had still been sound asleep when my first appointment arrived at nine. Poor Doris pounded on my apartment door for several minutes without waking me. It was her hollering in my kitchen, "Dave! Dave, are you here?" that finally got through to me.

I didn't remember drifting off to sleep tonight either—only that I had a dream about the persistent ringing of a telephone. I lay there for a long while after my eyes opened, willing the annoying noise to stop. Finally, I jolted awake and pushed Lug to the floor.

"Hello," I croaked.

"Is this Dr. Perrin?"

"Yes."

"I'm sorry to call at this time of night. This is Ron Draper. You don't know me, but you've been to my dad's place a few times...Lyle Draper."

"Yes, right."

"Dad's away for a few days and I'm looking after his cattle."

"Okay."

"He's had me watching a couple old cows he bought from a sale in Pincher Creek. I went down to check them when we got home from the bar. One of 'em—an old Simmental-cross—already calved out, but it looks like she pushed all her guts out behind the calf."

"Is she still down?"

"No...she got up and put the run on me for being too close to her calf."

"You sure it's not just the afterbirth hanging down?"

"It's not like any afterbirth I've ever seen. It's all red and knobby-looking...real bloody."

"It sounds like she's prolapsed her uterus." I looked at my watch—it was a few minutes after one. "Where have you got her?"

"She's in the big corral across the road from Dad's place."

"Did you get a rope on her?"

"No. As soon as I saw her, I ran in and called you."

"Well, you better get right back out there and get a halter on her. It's really important to keep her confined. If she starts walking around with the weight of her womb dangling, she may rupture one of the big arteries that supplies the uterus. If that happens, she'll be dead in minutes."

"Okay, I'll do that."

"It's not comfortable for a cow to stand with that whole mess hanging out, so she'll probably be lying down when you get there. Take a piece of plywood or cardboard to put underneath the uterus to keep it clean...And take down a couple five-gallon buckets of hot water and some old blankets or towels. Soak them down and keep applying them to the womb so it stays as moist and warm as possible."

"All right."

I was still in a daze as I hung up. It was only November—calving season seemed to be starting earlier every year. Lug watched expectantly as I dragged on my long johns.

"Are you sure you want to come with me? You'll just have to sit in the truck and steam up the windows."

He wagged his tail yes as I finished dressing and collected my thoughts. I filled a five-gallon bucket with hot water and carefully sealed the lid—it seemed there could never be enough water to clean up after messing with a prolapse. Most veterinarians wore a rubber suit to keep from getting soaked with the blood that inevitably leaks from the surface of the cotyledons. I had never been able to find one to fit my long frame, so just accepted the fact that when I treated a prolapse, I'd get bloody.

A shiver ran up my spine as I stepped out the door. This was January weather. In the Creston Valley it was unusual for November to start in such a harsh manner.

I checked through the truck to make sure I had everything I'd need for the procedure. Lyle lived just this side of Yahk on Highway 3, so it was a long way back if I happened to forget something. He had moved to the area over a year ago and had slowly been building up a herd by buying cows a few at a time in Alberta.

I chastised myself as I glanced at my watch. It was 1:20. A prolapsed uterus was right at the top of a large-animal veterinarian's list for immediate treatment. Although there were exceptions, the condition usually couldn't be corrected fast enough. The organ was extremely vascular, with huge arteries pumping vast amounts of blood through it. In cold weather like this the organ acted like a radiator, dispensing an animal's body heat to the surrounding environment.

On the way out to Lyle's, I thought back to a prolapse I had treated late in the spring. It had been a black Angus heifer that had pushed out her calf bed shortly after delivery. The farmer had seen it happen and called me right away. As it turned out, I was at a herd health appointment on a nearby farm and arrived within twenty minutes.

I thought it would be a simple fix. The animal was standing, and the farmer had her tied to the corral with a halter. I gave her an epidural injection, cleaned her up, and manipulated the organ back into her body. The moment I unfolded it, the animal shivered violently, gave a bellow, and collapsed in a heap. She gasped a few times as we struggled to untie the rope from the corral post. Before I could worry more about treatment, her eyes rolled back in her head, she gave a few kicks, and lay still. I stood speechless as the farmer looked at me in horror. I was sure that the middle uterine artery must have ruptured and she bled out internally, but a post-mortem proved that was not the case. All I could think of was that the sudden rush of cold blood trapped in the dangling uterus had put her into shock or caused a heart attack. I did not want a repeat of that disaster. I stepped on the gas.

When I got to Lyle's corral, I couldn't see anyone around and wondered if they had gone back to the house to warm up. I filled a syringe with lidocaine and threw a couple of extra needles in my pocket.

"You stay here," I told Lug as he tried to follow me out the door. He was obviously forgetting our agreement.

There was no moon, but the sky was clear and the stars were brilliant. I clicked on the flashlight. My boots crunched on a few inches of crisp snow as I retreated to my canopy. I slipped a half-litre bottle of soap into my pocket, grabbed a spool of umbilical tape, then filled my stainless steel bucket with water from the five-gallon pail. I left it and my instrument tray on the tailgate.

As I made my way to the corral, I began wondering if I had misunderstood Ron's directions. I scaled the fence and wandered among the twenty-some cows sleeping there. Nothing looked awry with any of them. At the far end I came across the calf. Only his head poked out from underneath a grey woollen blanket. I lifted it to find a healthy shivering bull bedded on a layer of straw. I shone the flashlight toward the far gate—there was the afterbirth. The cow must have calved right here. I checked the fetal membranes. They were cold but still not frozen.

"There she goes!" cried a voice way off in the distance.

"Oh no," I groaned.

I left the corral following a well-trodden trail that parallelled the highway. I shone the light to first one side of the path, then the other. Specks of blood dotted the snow in an irregular fashion. I could just picture the cow running down the path, her uterus swaying back and forth like a gigantic garbage bag filled with blood.

"Right there!" came a distant voice.

Then another: "Rotten bitch…I almost had her!"

I was a hundred yards down the path when I saw a flash of light to my left.

"There."

"Yeah, I see her."

"Can you get the rope on her?"

"Not in all that brush, I can't!"

I veered off the trail in the direction of the voices and was picking my way through a clump of willows when I found a red blob several inches in diameter in the Y of a branch. I shone the flashlight on it; it was one of the cotyledons from the cow's uterus. Another big splotch of blood in the snow showed in the beam of light.

"Hello!" I bellowed.

"Over here," came the reply.

"I'm the vet!"

"Thank God you're here...Have you got a tranquillizer gun?"

"No."

"Damn! We still haven't caught her!"

"So I gathered!"

"We sort of have her cornered in this brush but can't get a rope on her. We've been back and forth to the corrals a dozen times, but we can never catch her."

"Well, see if you can keep her standing quietly until I can get there."

"Stay to the left...You'll avoid the swamp."

"Okay."

I pushed my way through the underbrush trying to forget that a cow with her uterus hanging out had just done the same thing. Within a few minutes I could see the light from the men's flashlights reflecting through the trees and hear the pair talking about their strategy. I was almost there.

"She's on the move again! Make some noise, she's coming right for you!"

A huge red and white cow with horns curling down over her face came crashing through the brush. Her nostrils were flared, her eyes fixed straight ahead. Seeing me, she veered to her right and charged past. The last thing I saw was a massive pink sac flopping from side to side as she disappeared. There was no doubt as to the diagnosis.

"She's heading for her calf!" yelled one of the men.

"Get ready with your rope!" yelled the other. "She'll come back toward us when she can't cross the creek."

I came face to face with one of the errant cowboys. "I'm Ron," he said, pulling off his mitt and extending his hand.

"Dave." I shook his hand.

He was over six feet tall, solidly built, and probably ten years my junior. His face was flushed and covered with scratches from his enthusiastic chase. Running his fingers through shoulder-length red hair, he shook his head in frustration.

"Sorry we don't have her all tied up and waiting for you. I should have shut the corral gate before I tried to get her. She was just layin' there when we came back, and I thought it'd be no big deal to get the rope on her. I sort of had it half on but didn't get by those darned horns. She got up, almost bowled us over, and ran off with her guts floppin'. We've been chasin' after her ever since."

"Maybe we should work her back to the corral where we can corner her," I suggested.

"We were thinking that, too, but she's a foxy old thing and always seems to be one step ahead of us."

"Let's try to slow things down a bit. That uterus wasn't designed to be hanging out a cow's back end like that."

"Maybe you should tell her that...It sure hasn't slowed her down much."

We skirted a clump of willows and moved off in the direction the cow had disappeared.

"She's over here!"

"Keep her going toward the corrals, Frank!"

"She's headed for the creek!"

I followed Ron back to the trail. We were retracing our steps to the corral when we heard brush crashing ahead of us.

"She got by me, Ron! She's heading straight for you guys."

Ron and I separated and stood either side of the trail waving our arms as the cow plowed resignedly through a clump of willows toward us.

She veered to the right and took off across a patch of ice on the edge of the creek. Her feet went out from under her, and she flopped in a heap. The ice gave way and there she lay.

"Damn," Ron grumbled. "What now?"

"Get the rope on her."

While he affixed the lariat to a now subdued cow, I made my way out to examine the uterus, which was resting on a thin ledge of ice in several inches of water. It was surrounded by a pink halo of blood.

"Do you think she can get up?" asked a short dark fellow I assumed to be Frank.

"I'm not sure she's got enough left. Could you run back and get the stuff on the tailgate of my truck? There's a stainless steel tray and a bucket of water that I hope is still warm."

The cow lay in a passive heap as I rotated the uterus to determine the extent of the damage. There were several tears to the lining, but none of them was full-depth. Most of the blood loss was coming from the pedicles of cotyledons that were no longer there.

By the time Frank came huffing back down the trail, I had scrubbed up the womb and given the cow an epidural to deaden the feeling to her back end. My hands were already numb from working in the frigid water, and I plunged them into the bucket to regain some feeling.

I threaded a needle with catgut and began suturing immediately. Although the current blood loss from the wounds wasn't great, I had no idea how much that would change if the cow survived the shock of my replacing this massive mound of flesh. The stricture on the vessels with the uterus hanging inside out acted like a massive tourniquet. Warm the organ up again and remove the impingement to flow, and blood could start pouring out. A quick ligature around the base of the pedicles was enough to stem most of the bleeding. Standing in mud and water halfway to the top of my boots, I sutured until all of the rents were repaired. My hands were freezing, my feet were cold, and I could only imagine the rate at which this cow was losing her own body heat.

I hung my coat on a snag beside the creek and asked Ron to wade out with me and hold the tail. I began positioning the uterus for replacement, then lay on my side on top of the ice. My coveralls quickly soaked through; my body screamed in protest. I focused on the cold flesh of the uterus, manipulating it with both hands until it started to disappear into the cow's vagina. I placed my fist at the furthest tip of the organ and maintained a constant pressure. The moment this portion began to invert, the part I had already replaced started creeping out.

"Push over there, Ron."

I indicated the pink balloon of tissue that was slowly enlarging. He lay next to me on the ice, spread his fingers, and began pushing. I withdrew my arm and pressed with both hands on the double fold of uterus until it gave way and followed what had gone before.

I looked at Ron who was now as bloody and wet as I was. "Can you believe they call veterinary medicine a white-collar job?"

I knelt behind the cow and gasped as icy water invaded my boots. I pressed both hands and my body against the remaining bulge until it gave way and disappeared within the cow.

"Thank God," groaned Ron.

Dousing my arm with surgical soap, I unfolded the uterus inside the cow as best I could. My hands were aching and my fingers were moving in slow motion.

"Can you give me the instrument tray?"

By the time I was finished with the foot-long needle and umbilical tape, a suture of 3/8-inch cotton looped the vagina. I tightened it and tied it off. Hopefully, it would prevent the old crock from pushing the mass out again.

I sloshed my way to my coat with my teeth chattering. "We better get her out of there quick—that water's cold."

"Let me get my rope on, too," suggested Frank. "Maybe we can pull her out."

He threw his rope for the cow's head, but it merely batted her in the face and fell ineffectually onto the ice. He hauled in his lariat for a second throw, but before he could recoil it, the cow struggled to her feet.

"Let her have her head," I suggested as Ron tried to pull her to shore.

"Maybe we should just get out of her way," he said.

The cow stood shivering as we gave her space. With a concerted effort, she turned and stumbled onto shore, dragging the rope behind her.

"It's amazing she's still alive," I muttered.

"She's too bloody ornery to die," said Frank.

Ron shook his head in bewilderment. "The thing that puzzles me most is what Dad loves about having cattle. When we sold the farm out in Saskatchewan and bought here, all he could talk about was how much he missed having cows around."

I shivered my way back to the truck wondering what gave some animals such a strong will to live while others seemed to give up so easily. Whatever the mystical quality was, when the good Lord was doling it out, he certainly gave Mandy and this old cow more than their share.

Coming to Terms

"It's Fred Tady again."

Doris held the phone out to me at arm's length.

"Not now, Doris."

Doris covered the mouthpiece with her hand. "Dave, this is the third time he's called this morning."

"But I don't have anything new to tell him."

"Well, tell him that." Doris continued to point the phone in my direction.

"Tell him I've gone for an early lunch," I whispered.

Doris stood unwaveringly with her arm extended. Giving her the evil eye, I slunk toward her and took the receiver.

"Hello, Fred," I said as nonchalantly as I could manage.

Doris rolled her eyes at me and returned to the surgery where she resumed folding the never-ending pile of laundered surgical drapes.

"So...what do you think?"

I paused, not knowing what to tell my client. "I can't find a thing wrong with him."

There was an uncomfortable silence, and I could picture Fred turning a multitude of different shades of red.

"You've had him there six days now," he finally said tersely.

I sighed. It was just over a month ago that I had been railroaded

into performing the tonsillectomy. I shouldn't have gone against my better judgement.

"I know, and he's been eating well and hasn't thrown up once."

"I can't believe that," he said defiantly.

"It's true, Fred. Nobody here has seen him gag. The kennel boy had him out for a long walk this morning; I fed him and walked way down to the school and back. I haven't seen anything that would resemble a gag—not even when he was pulling on the leash." I paused. When my client said nothing, I went on. "I don't know what else to tell you."

"Are you sure you didn't leave part of his tonsils in?"

"I'm sure, Fred...and I've just about worn his throat out looking down there. I can guarantee you there isn't the slightest remnant of a tonsil left."

"What are you going to do with him then?"

"I'm at my wit's end, Fred. I can't see any reason for us to keep him longer. Why don't you come take him home?"

"He's not leaving until you find out what's wrong with him." Fred's voice had the same edge to it every time we talked. "I can't put up with this anymore. I've had him in to you a dozen times in the last six months and he's no better than he was at the start."

I took a deep breath, tensed my jaw, and held the imaginary cherry pit firmly against the side of my mouth. This was not the moment for an inappropriate response.

"Do you have someone you could leave him with?"

"What do you mean, leave him with?" Fred's voice was gruff.

"What would you think if he spent some time at a friend's place and didn't gag?"

Fred was silent again and I wondered if he was thinking about my question or just too angry to reply.

"Are you suggesting this is my fault?"

"I can't find anything physically wrong with him, and I'm really beginning to wonder if this isn't some sort of behavioural problem."

"To get attention, you mean?"

"Yes…to get your attention."

"I don't know—"

"Fred, look at it as if Rascal were your son, and up 'til seven months ago you spent every waking moment with him. How do you think he'd feel if you got married and brought a new woman into his life, then took on a job that kept you away from six in the morning until ten at night."

Fred was silent.

"How many hours do you spend at the restaurant now?"

"Not that long," he replied defensively.

"I was in there for breakfast last week at seven-thirty and you were there. Who closes up?"

"I do."

"And where is Rascal all that time?"

"At home," Fred grudgingly admitted.

"Would you consider giving it a try?"

"I'll call up Glenda Davis and see if she'll stop in there to visit him."

"Do you think the Davises would take him home for a bit?" I liked that idea—Glenda and Murray Davis were no-nonsense farmers who lived on a farm out on the Creston flats. They were good with animals but wouldn't be likely to coddle Rascal the way Fred did.

Fred skirted my question. "I'll call Glenda."

When I got back from lunch, Glenda and her eleven-year-old daughter were sitting in the waiting room. Rascal was on the bench soaking up their attention.

"What do you want Rochelle and I to do with him?" Glenda asked.

"I was sort of hoping you'd take him home with you and see how he behaved there."

"Oh, I don't think Fred would like that…He just asked us to

come in for a visit. Rascal's like his little baby, you know. I think you hurt his feelings when you suggested that the dog live with someone else. He was terribly upset when he called this morning."

"I can understand that, but I think Rascal's attachment to Fred is part of the problem. Let me find a lead and you can take him for a walk. Pay attention to what you're doing if he starts one of his gagging sessions. Fred keeps talking about how much he does it, but I've never seen it myself."

"He did it one night when I was there, Mommy," Rochelle volunteered.

"I don't doubt that he does something…You take him out and see what happens."

The trio returned a half-hour later. Rascal's tongue was hanging but his tail was wagging furiously.

"Well, how did you make out?"

"He was as good as gold," Glenda replied, "even when he was tugging on the leash."

Thank you, Lord, I thought in relief. It would have been just my luck that he had one of his spells as soon as my back was turned.

"Can I see if I can get him to play like he used to, Mom?"

Glenda looked at me and I nodded my assent.

"Have you got an old towel?" she asked.

After I produced one from the kennel room, she gave it to her daughter. "Be careful not to get carried away, Rochelle. You know Rascal's been sick."

Rochelle took off across the clinic dragging the towel in her wake. Rascal was a bit slow to catch on, but after the second lap from the waiting room to the surgery, he grabbed hold and was literally being towed along on the carpet. After a few minutes of this raucous play, I called the restaurant and asked Fred if he was free to come to the office for a bit.

I put on my jacket and waited outside until his car pulled up beside the clinic. I led him to the window. "Just watch for a few minutes."

Rochelle stumbled across the surgery floor pulling her enthusiastic little buddy behind her. Rascal was shaking his head and even through the window we could hear him growling with sheer pleasure. Fred stood there slowly shaking his head. I knew he was baffled, but he also looked hurt.

"Let's go in," I suggested.

We waited until the two were out of sight, then entered the waiting room and sat next to Glenda. We watched as the dog and his eager friend tore back and forth. Rochelle was obviously tiring. Dragging Rascal over with the towel, she plunked down beside her mother. The mutt continued to jerk away on the towel, totally unaware that his owner was present.

"Hi there, Rascal," Fred offered tenuously.

The dog quit tugging and squealed with delight. Running to his master, he jumped up and down at his legs. Before Fred could stoop to pick up his pet, Rascal stopped, put his head down, and began to retch. Emitting a tormented gurgling sound, he deposited a great gob of mucus on the toe of Fred's shoe. All eyes were on Fred as he scooped up his errant baby and cuddled him.

"I really don't understand, Dave," he protested after Rascal had finally cuddled up on his lap. "Why does he puke every time he sees me?"

"Because whenever he pukes, you give him what he wants. Just look at what happened. He retched and you picked him up and cuddled him—more positive reinforcement. Remember the first time you brought him in to me in the summer—when he was gagging and I found that burr in his tail."

Fred nodded and continued stroking his dog.

"Well, I think that's when all this started a vicious cycle. You lavished him with attention because he was gagging. Rascal got the message that all he had to do to get Dad to pay attention to him was start retching."

Fred groaned. "What do I do now?"

"It makes sense to me that you try and reverse the strategy. How about putting him in a room all by himself as soon as he starts gagging?"

"You mean, walk away and leave him?"

"That's what I'd do...and try to pay him more attention when he's just being Rascal."

I brought the birch club down on the knife, pulled toward me with the handle, and split off one last shake. I threw the remaining triangular scrap of cedar into the waste pile and leaned back against the wall. Trimmed shakes were stacked to the level of the floor joists. A huge pile of rubble from trim and waste material occupied the centre of the basement. I'd have enough kindling to last me for years once I moved out here.

I glanced enviously at Lug who was stretched out on the floor sleeping. I tilted my watch toward the trouble light dangling from a nail on an overhead floor joist—quarter to eight. I could work for at least two more hours. I wearily grabbed a new shake bolt from a stack against the wall and began pounding. Five whacks and the blade still hadn't gone halfway in—another knot. I pulled ineffectually on the handle, hit the knife a couple more times, then stopped in defeat. My arm was sore. The continual pounding with my caveman club and the repetitive motion of pulling on the handle to flip off the shake was taking its toll.

"Come on, mutt...I've had enough."

Lug scrambled to his feet, ready for anything. I grabbed my flashlight, clicked off the overhead light, crossed the mucky surface of the courtyard, and carefully picked my way up the slippery clay bank.

It was unseasonably warm for this time of the year. All of November and early December had been colder than normal, and farmers had been predicting damage to alfalfa stands and next year's fruit crops. The third week in December it had warmed up,

253

and for days the weather was more like late October. Christmas Eve had been sunny and so warm that I spent the entire day nailing on shakes. After a few minutes on the roof, I had stripped off my jacket and worked comfortably in a long-sleeved shirt.

As I drove past my neighbour's place, I could see long rectangles of light streaming from the side windows of the squat farmhouse. I turned down the long tree-lined lane. I left a disappointed Lug in the truck and knocked at the back door.

"Come on in!" Jack hollered.

I pulled off my boots, kicked them in with a collection of others in the stairwell, and stepped into the kitchen. Neither Jack nor Sandy moved from their chairs at the table. They were seated across from one another, both looking exhausted.

"Pour yourself a coffee, Dave." Sandra took a drag on her cigarette and motioned to the cupboard. "You know where the cups are." I poured myself a cup then made a round to refill theirs. "Thanks, Dave, I'm too tired to move...Jack had me holding the baby pigs up by the hind legs while he did the castrating. My arms are so tired I can hardly lift my cup."

"Were you working over at the house today?" Jack asked.

"I put in a couple hours splitting shakes, but my wrist is getting sore from all the pounding."

"Haven't seen much of your dad lately...How's he been?"

"Doing great. Hibernating for the winter at Riondel—curling up a storm. I saw them at Christmas dinner. They're both just fine."

Jack added sugar to his coffee and stared morosely at his spoon as it swirled round and round in his cup.

"Why so glum today? You both look like you lost your best friend." He passed me an opened envelope. "Oh, you got the cheque for your last shipment?"

"Yeah," he said flatly.

I took the cheque out of the envelope. "Three hundred and two dollars? How many did you send?"

"Fifty-six."

"Fifty-six?"

Jack nodded.

"That can't be!"

"Nine bucks apiece minus the commissions and trucking."

"That's ridiculous. The price of fat hogs hasn't come down that much…What did you get last time?"

"They averaged thirty-five."

I sipped my coffee and continued to stare at the auction's breakdown of the deductions, not wanting to look at either Jack or Sandra. After all, I had encouraged them to take the leap and buy Verna's farm.

"What are you going to do?"

Jack shrugged. "We're selling a few off the farm here for forty or fifty dollars, but that doesn't begin to keep up with what we're producing."

"We sell enough milk from the two cows to keep us in cigarettes and buy a few groceries," Sandra added brightly.

"Gary has the right idea," Jack went on. "He feeds them all the way up to slaughter and doesn't have to worry about a bit of a fluctuation in the number of weaner pigs that are available. Fat prices are pretty good." He shoved a copy of the *Western Producer* at me and pointed to the prices listed for finished hogs. "There's got to be a good buck in there for finishing them…The price of barley hasn't changed."

"What are you going to do?"

"I'll drop in to the banker tomorrow and see if he'll spring for enough feed for me to start finishing some."

"Where'll you feed them?"

"I guess I'll stick them wherever I can find room. I can drag the baler and stuff outside and put a few in the machine shop. The hay shed's half empty and I can run a hose up there for water."

"Can you think of anyone else you could get to feed a few pigs?"

"Blackmores bought a few from me the other day…Maybe I can make them a deal."

"There's got to be a way."

"Your hay shed's half empty," Jack noted dryly. I didn't respond—just stared across the table at him. "You have to come out here every day to feed the cows anyway."

"I can hardly keep up with what I've got to do now!"

"What does it take to run the hose to fill a trough a couple of times a day? You're doing it for your cows already…I could help you out if you get too busy."

"Oh man, Jack, how would I get time to build pens and feeders?"

Jack was getting excited that I would even consider his proposal.

"I'm making some feed bins up for myself, so it'd be no hassle at all to build a few extra."

"What about watering troughs?"

"No big deal. I'll burn a few more water tanks in half."

"I don't know, Jack…We've got a lot of winter left yet, and I'm just coming into my busy season—pretty soon I'll be up all night doing calvings."

Jack was looking right through me with stars in his eyes. "I'm going out to Powell's mill in the morning for a load of slabs—a couple days with a chainsaw and hammer and you'll be in business. Can I borrow your post-pounder?"

Heifers from Hell

"This is the last thing you needed, Dave."

"I know."

"Then why are you doing it?"

I grabbed another slab from the pile, lined it up parallel to the last one, and began nailing it on to the cross-member of the new pig run.

"I've been asking myself that since I made the deal with Jack."

Father stared at me intently. "Where do you get this from?"

I stopped hammering. "Get what from?"

"This notion that you have to take on enough jobs for a dozen men…as soon as you get something half done and get a moment's peace, you're looking for more."

"This is different. I sort of encouraged Jack and Sandra to take the plunge and buy that place…I sure don't want to see them sink."

"I can understand that, but you can only do so much. There are twenty-four hours in a day, and you have to sleep some of them. Besides, the few pigs you're buying from Jack will be a drop in the bucket for them."

"I guess it's just that I have to try something."

We each went back to work pounding on boards and didn't speak again until the pile was depleted.

"Looks like a couple more loads should finish this run."

Father nodded and we headed for his old green Ford pickup. We had pulled down the fence that Verna had constructed between our two farms, so now we could exit through Jack's driveway rather than go the entire length of the property at the back.

I pulled off my soggy leather gloves and rubbed my hands together over the heater vent. The moment Father had arrived last night, we attached the post-pounder to the tractor and started driving posts into the ground. First thing this morning we brought a load of scrap two-by-fours from the building site for cross-ties and began work on the first run.

"Have you given up the notion of doing your own hay this year?" Father asked as he pulled onto the main road.

"I think we can still manage it. We have the tractor and it shouldn't be too difficult to pick up an old swather and baler. How much trouble can it be to put up sixty acres?"

Father said no more until we rounded the bend at the bottom of the Canyon hill and drove across the bridge. I peered over the metal railing at the swirling waters of the Goat River.

"You know, Dave, you scare me half to death...the way you jump into things with both feet. All my life I've had to scratch for every nickel I got, and each time I was sure I was getting ahead, there was always someone or something to knock me back. Even after I started working for Cominco, lots of opportunities came along. Some of them I've kicked myself for passing up. Instead, I hung around there for thirty years waiting for a pension. I guess it got to the point I was afraid to try something new. When you started out to become a vet, I didn't want to discourage you, but I really had a hard time convincing myself you'd actually make it."

His voice trailed off as if he'd just spit out something he didn't mean to say. He turned right onto the highway and headed east. I watched him intently as he shifted gears and got up to speed, expecting him to say more. I was disappointed; he never looked at me again until he pulled up next to the slab pile at Jim Powell's

259

Arrow Creek mill. Then he simply pulled on his gloves and began pitching suitable boards into the pickup box.

We were both exhausted when we got home to my apartment. Father cooked supper while I had a bath. After we'd eaten, he collapsed in the reclining chair in front of the television. By the time I finished the dishes, the sound of his snoring was drowning out the voice of the announcer on the six o'clock news.

After Father went to bed, I settled into the chair to watch an episode of *Beachcombers*. Just as Nick was getting into a rant about Relic's stealing one of his logs, the telephone rang.

"Hello."

"Bob Rogers here, Dave."

"Hi, Bob, what you got going?"

"I've got a critter here that looks like trouble. She's one of those bred heifers I bought from Ben Ahlefeld—this one's a Limousin-cross. She broke her water a couple, three hours ago, and there's still nothing showing but front feet."

"Has she been pushing hard?"

"She doesn't seem to want to settle in. She's been up and down ever since the water broke."

"How is she for size?"

"You know, it's strange…she was the same as the rest when I bought 'em, but she just didn't grow like the others. She's definitely the smallest of the works."

"Have you run her into the chute to check her yet?"

"I thought about it, but I don't like the look of her. I think you should come out if you can."

"Okay, I'll get my long johns on in case it turns into a Caesarian."

"Good idea."

I wearily hung up the phone and began digging through my drawers for a clean pair of long underwear. I glared grudgingly at Lug where he had curled up on the foot of the bed. He jumped to the floor, ready for action. "Not tonight, old boy. You stay home with Grandpa."

I shivered when I stepped outside; it was a drizzly night in February and a thick mist hung in the air. I unlocked the canopy door of the truck, checked through the surgery box, and threw in the new bottle of lidocaine I had brought out from the surgery.

The streetlights shimmered eerily through the fog as I drove through town. Visibility improved when I headed down the hill toward the John Deere dealership, and I picked up my speed across the flats. I made good time until I approached the bridge over Kootenay River. There, the fog was thick, and I had to slow to a crawl. I watched carefully for the lights of the gas station as I passed under the last metal arch of the bridge. When I turned left off the highway, I leaned forward to peer into the thick cloud that hung in beside the river. I poked along at thirty miles an hour, staring into the white void trying to recognize a few landmarks.

I was relieved when I finally spotted the floodlights of my bookkeeper's family feedlot and turned a hard right down their drive. I could see Bob coming out of his mother's house as I made my way to the long hay shed that parallelled the feedlot. He calved all his cattle here at the old homestead and consumed buckets of Marg's coffee.

"Boy, she's thick tonight," I said.

"Sure is," Bob agreed, setting down the old galvanized bucket he produced on every trip I made to his corral.

"This critter's pretty flighty," he reported as I scaled the rail fence and perched to watch the heifer on the other side.

She stood with her ears forward and her eyes riveted on me. I hopped down and edged along the enclosure to get a better view of her hind end and gauge the progress she was making. Every time I took a step, she turned to face me. When I climbed the rails, she flipped her head at me and snorted.

"I think she likes you," Bob joked. He walked to the far end of the holding pen and opened the gate at the head of the chute. The creature held her head high and shifted her focus back and forth between us. "I changed the gates around here last week, so we'll see if they work any better. There always seemed to be a bottle-neck there at the head of the chute."

He moved along the thirty-foot runway pulling out two-by-fours and metal bars and leaving them at the ready. He lifted the sliding gate at the end of the catch pen, opened the self-closing head gate, and made his way back to me still carrying the last tim-ber he had removed. "I'm ready when you are."

I climbed the corral railing and dropped to the ground inside. My patient lifted her head, snorted, and pawed at the straw with her foot. I hesitantly took a step toward her and waved my arms.

"Yah! Get up there!"

"Watch yourself with her," Bob said, following me with his two-by-four. "I don't like the look of her."

At that moment, the heifer turned and disappeared down the runway. When I reached the entrance to the alleyway, there was a rattling as the end gate crashed down behind her, then a tremen-dous clattering as she struggled to get free.

"Her head's loose!" Bob hollered, running around the outside of the corral in an attempt to catch her.

The heifer suddenly dropped to the ground, then thrashed to her feet beneath the end gate. The metal barrier lifted with her and slid ineffectually along her spine. The moment she realized she was free, she backed up as fast as her legs would carry her.

"Look out!" Bob shouted.

I made a mad grab for the timber that sat at the ready at the end of the alley. I got it in place seconds before she made contact with it. She hit it with such force that it gave way with a sickening crunch. I grasped the top rail and hefted myself up just before the enraged animal made contact with me. The force of her blow lifted my legs off the ground, and I held on tenaciously as she skidded beneath me. I flopped to the ground after she rolled past, strug-gling to regain my balance.

"Get out of there!" Bob yelled.

Before I could get turned around, the heifer butted me with her head, lifted my feet from the ground, and shoved me against the boards. I felt a terrible burning and grinding sensation over my rib cage as she pushed me again and again into the plank wall. I turned my head to meet eyes that were filled with fury. Her attack continued as she pummelled my back and side. With each blow she dealt, I became acutely aware of the pain in my side that inten- sified each time she backed away.

"Get out of there!" Bob yelled again. "She's going to kill you."

I struggled to turn and beat her off with my fists. "I can't...I'm stuck!"

Hollering and swinging his plank, Bob came to my rescue. As the heifer continued her assault, I clawed desperately at the cracks between the boards, trying to lift my weight off the metal hinge that had hooked under my ribs. When a solid whack between the eyes with Bob's two-by-four convinced the crazed animal to retreat, I was left dangling and struggling for breath with my feet six inches from the ground.

"God, man...are you all right?" Bob asked, trying to evaluate the situation.

"No, help me get off this damn hook," I gasped.

While he lifted my legs, I pried my ribs free and pushed away from the wall. Bob stumbled backward, my coveralls gave way with the sound of tearing cloth, and I flopped like a sack of barley to the ground.

"Oh man, Dave, I'm sorry...When that other hinge broke off, I just left this one, thinking I could always replace the bottom one and move it back." I lay there struggling for breath, trying to convince myself that nothing major was damaged.

"Are you all right? Maybe I better run you into the hospital," Bob went on in a worried tone.

"I'm not sure—but keep that crazy critter away from me."

I worked myself into a sitting position and gently probed my ribs. My breaths were coming easier. I unzipped my tattered coveralls and lifted my shirt. There was an angry-looking black hole where the skin had been crushed, but it didn't seem like something that could be sutured.

After five minutes of sitting with my head in my hands, I picked myself up and hobbled to the corral fence. I struggled to the top rail and glared at the heifer.

"Let's get a look at that miserable witch."

"Are you sure you're up to it, Dave?"

I watched her as she continued to toss her head and pace back and forth at the farthest reach of the enclosure.

"We can't just leave her like this."

"You're the doctor."

Bob made his way around the perimeter of the corral and began banging his two-by-four on the rails. The heifer ran past me at a dead run, huffing and snorting her way down the alleyway. Bob jogged around the outside and jammed a metal pipe behind her before she could back up again. When he lifted the end gate, she charged forward and the head gate slammed shut. She was caught. I gingerly followed her path and stood behind the metal barrier waiting for Bob to bring the water. This part of his setup was not under cover, and a fine drizzle settled over everything. I shivered uncontrollably and clutched my hands to my side as a girdle.

"Please, God," I muttered under my breath, "let this be one we can pull."

Bob lifted the bucket over the rails of the chute and lowered it toward me. I held my breath, grabbed it with both hands, and set it on the ground. My entire body screamed with pain, and I stood there for several minutes without moving.

"You're not looking too hot," Bob noted dryly. "Are you sure you can handle this? Maybe I should call Cory."

I shook my head and began scrubbing the heifer's rear end. The calf's front feet were just visible; there was no evidence of the head. I squirted soap over my arm and slid my hand in on top of the feet; even that simple movement sent pain shooting through me. The moment I examined her, I knew we were in trouble. A bony ridge jutted into the birth canal, forcing the feet upward toward the base of her tail. There wasn't enough room to get my hand in. The calf would have to come out the side.

"It's hopeless, Bob. It feels like her pelvis was broken somewhere along the line and it never healed properly."

"How could that happen?"

"Hard to say, but maybe she ended up getting hip-locked at birth. You know what it's like when a calf gets stuck—you keep applying pressure until something finally gives. In this case, maybe it was her pelvis."

"Are you in any shape to be doing a Caesarian?"

I took a deep slow breath. "I think I'll be all right as long as I don't have to do anything quickly. I hurt all over, but every time I move, it feels like someone's twisting a knife."

"Where'll we do it?" Bob asked.

"If she were half sane, I'd suggest we slap a halter on her and take her back to the pen where there's shelter. I've never been fond of working in a chute in case they fight and go down…but with her, we have no choice. We'll do her here."

"I'll get you some power for your clippers," Bob said, heading off for the house.

I made my way back to the corral, laboriously climbed the slippery rails, and lowered my feet to the ground. I was now acutely conscious of how many different muscles were involved with every little move I made. I gingerly reached in, grabbed my surgery box, and dragged it to the end of the tailgate. I stood staring at it, trying to summon the courage to lift it.

"Let me take that, Dave."

Bob looped an extension cord over his shoulder, scooped up the box, and headed for the corral. By the time I was back, he had the clippers plugged in ready for me to use.

The ancient chute clattered and banged as the heifer protested my shaving her. Every time the clipper touched her, she struggled to pull her head free or tried to kick me in defiance. Twice when her hind foot went over the side panel, Bob grabbed a steel pipe and pried it back inside.

"Do you think maybe you should give her a tranquillizer to settle her down?" Bob puffed after an extended battle with a thrashing leg. "She's about got me played out. I've never seen a critter so intent on doing you damage."

"Don't think it hasn't crossed my mind. We either do her here or take her back to the pen and knock her flat with Rompun. If we gave her Rompun here and she collapsed in the chute when her abdomen was open, we'd have a heck of a mess."

Focusing on every minute movement, I persistently clipped away until my patient's left side and tail head were shaved to my satisfaction. Washing her was almost as bad as shaving her. Each handful of water, each daub of soap solicited a reaction.

We closed all the bars in the side panels and squeezed them in tightly to restrict her movement while I injected the local anesthetic for the nerve block. With the rattling and banging and bellowing that went on with each prick of her skin, anyone within a two-mile radius must have wondered what the Rogers were up to. By the time she was frozen to my satisfaction, all three of us were ready to call it a day.

I couldn't believe the pain that even lifting my arm could create. Slowly and methodically, I worked toward one elusive goal—putting an end to this procedure and stretching my long frame out in bed. I kept thinking that the pain would surely lessen if I could get off my feet and stop moving.

Bob watched with bated breath as I picked up the scalpel and made my incision. Surprisingly, the beast stood without a single protest until I cut through the last layer of muscle, and air rushed into her abdomen. After a few moments of thrashing, she settled down and I severed the remaining muscles. I had located the baby's hind feet and was steeling myself for the pain of lifting the calf to the incision when we heard Marg's voice.

"How's it going?" she asked.

"Not too good," Bob said quietly. "This heifer's taken a decided dislike to Dave."

"Do you want me to put the coffee on?" My bookkeeper stood stoically as my ornery patient clattered away at the chute and I battled to bring the hind feet to the incision site.

"I think Dave's going to need something stronger than coffee."

I was reaching for my scalpel to incise the uterus when she spoke again. "The answering service called a few minutes ago. Cliff Schofer needs help with a calving...He's afraid it might be a Caesarian."

I dropped the scalpel back onto the instrument tray. Bob regarded his mother grimly and shook his head.

"Did I say something wrong?" Marg asked.

Bob looked away as tears trickled down my face. "I've got the chains ready, Dave," he said calmly.

I nodded and picked up the scalpel.

I was in agony by the time I got to Schofers. Every muscle in my body was competing for its fair share of attention. I sat like a zombie in the truck, surveying the landscape in search of my clients. I was beginning to wish I had taken Marg's offer of a good stiff drink. I knew from experience just how therapeutic my bookkeeper's refreshments could be.

I pried myself from the vehicle and rummaged through the back for another pair of coveralls. Hunching my shoulders, I struggled to get the wet ones off. By the time I had them stripped to my waist my eyes were smarting, and I stood like a little kid with his soggy snowsuit hanging at half-mast. Finally, I pulled off my boots and stepped alternately on the ends of my pant legs so they fell around my feet.

By the time I had on clean coveralls there was still no sign of

Cliff, so I decided to announce my arrival at the house. I had convinced myself to take a step in that direction when I saw a flashlight bobbing along through the fog in the field west of the feedlot. I thought it strange, because the beacon was well beyond the fenced area where the Schofers normally kept their cattle. I held my rib cage with one hand while I leaned on the truck door to watch the light. I could finally make out a shadowy figure—it was Cliff.

He looked about as good as I felt. His tattered canvas coat was soiled, his jeans covered with mud. He climbed the rail fence in front of me, clicked off his flashlight, and sat there a few seconds to catch his breath.

"Hello, Dr. Perrin. Sorry I'm not all set up for you, but this heifer is something else. When we saw she was having trouble, we tried to bring her in from the field where we're calving them. She took off like a deer and broke through two sections of fence."

I avoided Cliff's gaze, not wanting him to see the disappointment his words brought.

"We finally got her cornered down in an old hay shed at the far end of the property." He paused and glanced at his feet. "It's not an ideal situation. There's no power, and it's too muddy to get there with a vehicle…we'll have to walk."

I closed my eyes, determined to focus my thoughts. This was not the time to surrender to negativity. "How far is it?" I asked glumly.

"About a quarter of a mile."

"Do you think we'll be able to calve her out?"

"I doubt it—she's not very big. She got bred out on pasture when she was still sucking her mother. The only thing that really grew well on her was her horns."

"Horns?"

"Yeah, she's one of the ones we didn't get around to doing when she was a calf."

"I have to warn you, Cliff, I'm not in very good shape tonight…I got worked over pretty good by a heifer at Bob's and it's all I can do to keep breathing."

Cliff raised his eyebrows and frowned. "What do you suggest?" he asked soberly.

"I guess we'll check her and see what we can see."

"We've already carried water out. Janet's on her way there with another bucket now."

I sighed and tensed as the pain from my chest intensified.

"I'll carry your surgery box," Cliff offered. I grabbed my calving jack, slung it over my shoulder, and took a hesitant step in his direction. "Can you bring your lariat, too?"

"My lariat?"

"Yeah, we still need to catch the darned thing, and as you know, I'm not the world's best roper."

"I thought you said you'd already caught her."

"No…I said we had her cornered. She was dumb enough to run into the old shed, and we dragged the gate closed. She's loose inside."

I slogged unhappily into the mist behind Cliff. The ground was mucky; each time I picked up my foot, a big clod of gumbo dragged along with it. Several times Cliff stopped and waited for me to catch up. When we reached our destination, I was questioning if I'd ever be able to make it back to the truck.

"Hello, Dr. Perrin." Janet's voice floated in the darkness. "Welcome to the rodeo." She clicked on her flashlight and shone it on my patient. "I shut the light out, hoping she'd settle down a bit."

We all recoiled as a tiny heifer with long curling horns charged the fence and stopped a few feet short of us. She tossed her head and snorted aggressively.

"As you can see, it hasn't made a lot of difference," Janet added.

"How are we going to catch her?"

"We were hoping you'd have a suggestion," she said quietly. "You're pretty good with a lariat, aren't you?"

I groaned and shone my flashlight around the interior of the enclosure. The far end of the shed was piled to the ceiling with bales. Stacks of hay still remained on both sides. The centre area where the heifer stood was open and covered with a layer of loose hay. I headed for the far edge of the structure. I was calculating my chances of making it to the hay bales when she charged again.

"I wouldn't count too much on this gate," Cliff said nervously. "It was built to keep cattle out of the hay when we pasture this area, not keep a critter like her in."

I silently prayed: Please, God, make her charge right through this gate. If she got away now, surely they wouldn't expect me to run through the dark searching for her. All I felt capable of was limping my way home and crawling into bed. With a bit of luck, the crazy yearling would jump into the Kootenay River and drown herself.

I made my way along the side of the building. A couple of hours ago, I could easily have scaled the fence and hopped over onto the stack of bales where the animal couldn't get to me. Just the thought of doing it now had me quaking.

"What do you think?" Cliff asked.

"I think her twin sister is at Bob Roger's place."

"He has one as bad as this?"

I clutched at my ribs. "If you only knew." I leaned my calving jack against the fence and started scaling the wall. "Maybe if you get on the bales on the other side and I get on this side, one of us will be lucky enough to land a rope on her."

Cliff nodded. "Maybe you better stand here and guard the gate, Janet."

Cliff was in position long before I was.

"You missed her by a mile!" Janet hollered as her husband failed his first attempt.

"It's not easy throwing from up here," Cliff answered in his defence.

I shone my flashlight into the gap between me and the stack of bales and balanced precariously on top of the fence. I knew I could easily make it, but the dread of the pain that would inevitably come with the landing kept me frozen in place. It took several minutes to summon the courage to jump. I landed on my hands and knees, lowered my head to the bale in front of me as pain wracked my body, and clicked off my light. I could do this.

For the next thirty minutes, Cliff and I took turns flinging our ropes into the darkness while the heifer performed in the arena beneath us. Beams of light streaked from three sides as we each tried to keep tabs on her movement. A lucky fling from my haystack finally settled around the horns.

"You caught her!" Janet exclaimed.

Caught her, indeed. The moment the rope made contact, she bellowed and charged toward the far end of the shed. The rope burned through my hands as I made a half-hearted attempt to stem her retreat, then disappeared into the darkness.

"What now?" I asked.

"Can we get the end of the rope wrapped around a post?" Cliff suggested.

"Good luck." I stared into no-man's land.

"We could always wait until she goes to sleep," Janet chimed sarcastically.

We got down from our perches and studied our adversary. She faced us, her rear end backed against the stack. The rope lay on the ground between us.

"I think I can get in there and tie my lariat onto the end of yours," said Cliff. "Then we can pull her all the way over to that pole."

With his flashlight, he indicated an upright that was exposed near the corner of the shed. We dragged the gate open just far enough for Cliff to slide through, then shone our lights into the heifer's eyes. She tossed her head in a threatening fashion as Cliff quickly knotted the two ropes together. He wrapped the tether around the upright and handed the end to Janet.

"Get her to come after you so we can take up the slack," Janet suggested.

"Yeah, right," Cliff grumbled.

"We'll pull in the rope as she comes," Janet assured him. "She won't be able to reach you."

Sure enough, the moment Cliff passed the halfway mark in the barn, the feisty little beast took up his challenge and charged toward him. By the time he squeezed out the gate, Janet and I had pulled her to within ten feet of the pole.

"We're stuck at the knot!" Janet yelled in frustration.

The heifer bellowed as if her throat had been slit and bucked from side to side in an effort to pull free. Finally, she planted her feet like a mule and refused to move. I walked in behind her and tried to push her forward, but she continued to resist.

"If she's going to stand there like that, I'll take advantage of it."

I shaved over her tail with a razor blade and scrubbed her up while she lay back against her anchor. Even when I popped a needle between the vertebrae of her tail and injected a whopping dose of lidocaine, she didn't move.

"This'll slow you down, my dear."

Most times I only used enough anesthetic to numb a calving animal's back end to keep her from straining; this dose would temporarily paralyze her whole back end. Within a few minutes, my patient was swaying back and forth on her hind legs. Her ankles buckled, and still leaning against the rope, she toppled over. I hobbled up to the post and worked the knot until it was free.

I had just accomplished my task when Janet screeched, "Watch out, she's coming after you!"

The heifer pursued me, determinedly dragging herself with her front legs. I ducked behind the post as she flipped her head in a desperate attempt to skewer me with her horns. Janet kept tugging on the rope as the animal trundled toward me. By the time I got out of her way, she was snubbed tight to the post.

The remainder of the procedure was drudgery and persistence.

I shaved the heifer's side bare with nothing but a razor blade and performed the surgery by flashlight. As beams began to fade, we resorted to shining only one light at a time to make sure that at least one of them lasted. Fortunately, the calf was tiny and I was able to manage the birth with a minimum of discomfort.

I woke up the following morning with most of my clothes still on, so sore that scratching my nose was a major undertaking. Both the Schofers and Bob Rogers remember their respective animals as the wildest critters they had ever dealt with. I remember them as the heifers from hell.

A Nasty Drunk from Alaska

"Not you again, you ornery bugger!"

I chased the fat little pig around the corner of the run into an alcove in the hay. He stood motionless, his beady eyes focused on me, as I crept closer and closer. I pulled off my gloves and made a dive for a hind leg. My fingers closed around his hoof a second before he yanked free and took off like a sprinter charging from the starting block. I was left sprawled full length on the hay-shed floor.

"Damn."

I lay flat on the ground for several minutes. My ribs still throbbed from the encounter with the heifer at the Rogers farm, but most of the other aches and pains were now history. I had cancelled all my herd health appointments for the week following the incident, trying to avoid getting physical with big animals. Although I was sure ribs had been broken, I never bothered getting them X-rayed. What could have been done about them, anyway?

I picked myself up and brushed some of the hay off my coveralls. I had just finished pregnancy testing a group of heifers at the Weins' farm and was already splattered with manure. I snuck around the corner in search of my errant piglet, knowing full well there'd be no hope of catching him in the open. I crept past the shack where I stored all my feed, certain I'd find him there. I was disappointed.

"He's over here, Dave!" Jack stood smiling outside his milk house. He hollered and waved his arms; a few seconds later the fat fugitive came streaking around the corner. He whipped past me and scooted along the slab fence. About halfway along, he pushed on a board he obviously remembered. It flopped inward to allow him entry, and he disappeared.

"That was easy!" Jack hollered.

"Yeah, this time it was…but this little rat has been out every other day for weeks. If he comes over to your place again, catch him and keep him. I've run out of patience."

I went to the shack, grabbed my hammer and a can of nails, and pounded the board back on.

"Do you want to come in for coffee?"

"I better not…I'm supposed to be at the office in a few minutes. I was in the neighbourhood, so I thought I'd check on 'em and fill up their water troughs."

Jack nodded, grabbed his pitchfork, and returned to the barn.

"Where have you been?" Doris asked in an agitated tone. "Mr. Vance has been sitting here waiting for you."

"I stopped at the farm to check up on things."

"That's what I thought…Bob was about ready to leave."

I pulled off my boots, my heavy woollen socks, my vest, and my dirty coveralls. I grabbed a smock from the drier and was about to throw it on when Doris grabbed my sleeve.

"No, you don't. You've got muck on your neck and a high-water mark on your arm. Go wash up."

I scrubbed in front of the mirror in the lab until I had removed all visible evidence of my previous engagement. By the time I was cleaned up with my smock on, Doris had Buttons on the table.

"Like I said, Doris, he looks all right to me, but Kevin insists he's just not right," said Bob.

"Well, best to be on the safe side," Doris reassured him.

"I guess," he replied sullenly.

I leaned against the wall while Doris finished getting Buttons' temperature. "Hello, Bob...Sorry to keep you waiting."

He tipped his head at me, then watched Doris with interest as she removed the thermometer. She raised her eyebrows when she read it. "It's 39.8..."

"Is that up?" Bob asked.

I nodded and knelt beside the table for a closer look at my patient. "What made Kevin think something was wrong with him?"

"He played out really quickly when he was throwing the ball for him yesterday, and he left some of his dog food this morning."

The dog sat in a docile fashion while I rolled up his eyelid and pressed on his gums. "He's pale again."

"Do you think it's coming back?"

"I sure hope not...but maybe I should have kept him on a higher dose of prednisone for longer."

Bob glanced at the floor. "We ran out of pills five or six days ago."

"Oh..."

There was an uncomfortable silence as I examined the dog. When I removed the stethoscope from my ears, Bob continued, "There's been a lot of upheaval in our family lately. Audrey and I have separated and a lot of things have gone by the boards...Buttons was looking so good that I didn't think he really needed those pills anymore." He directed his gaze to the floor again. "There's not a lot of spare money kicking around these days."

"I can understand that, but prednisone is one of those drugs that you don't just quit cold turkey. That might be part of the reason he's feeling so punk. If we were going to discontinue it, we'd have tapered the dose for weeks and gone on alternate-day therapy first. Giving high levels over a long period of time makes him

dependent on the drug. It takes a while for him to be able to produce his own cortisol again."

"Are you sure it's the same thing? Could his temperature be up
because of an infection? You mentioned that the drug weakened
the immune system."

"No, I can't be sure without doing blood work…and I'd like to
get a urine sample, too."

Bob sighed and looked morosely at Buttons. "I guess you better do what you can to find out what's going on…Kevin's got
enough on his plate without having his dog sick, too."

Bob retired to the waiting room while we collected blood.
Doris took our patient to the back alley to get a urine sample and
I did my workup. I filled the tiny glass capillary tubes and popped
them into the centrifuge. While the machine was whining away, I
smeared out a slide and dipped it in stain.

Bob lifted his head from his hands when I approached him.
"What did you find?"

"It certainly seems like the same thing again, but hopefully we
can manage without a transfusion. His packed cell volume is still
around 30. We'll keep him here for a bit until I can finish my
workup."

He frowned as I opened Buttons' mouth and popped a large
tablet of prednisone down his throat. The dog had a sad look of
resignation—and so did Bob.

"Dave, there's a fellow on the line who's concerned his dog might
have gotten into antifreeze."

I had finished vaccinating a kitten and hurriedly signed the
certificate that Doris thrust in front of me.

"Hello."

"Yes, Dave…Jack Schwartz here…I've got a few questions for
you about antifreeze. You'll probably think they're stupid, but
Lynn insisted I call and ask anyway."

"Not a problem. Shoot."

"What happens to a dog if he swallows some?"

"It damages the kidneys."

"I should see something by now if he got into it around noon, though, shouldn't I? He's happy enough, and his nose is still wet."

"No."

"No?" he asked with concern. "Why not?"

"Because initially they look and feel fine. It won't be until the ethylene glycol starts being metabolized in the body that he'll start showing symptoms."

"Oh...maybe I better bring Shiloh up to see you then."

"What makes you think he got into it?"

"I finished my shift at the bar and came home to find the garden shed open. The kid that we hired to shovel the walks must have left it ajar."

"Did you leave some out in a bucket or something?"

"No, it was in its original container. I don't have a clue how much was in the jug to start with, but I found it all chewed up and empty, lying in the backyard."

"I think you better bring him in, Jack."

I made a quick trip upstairs to unearth my small-animal medicine notes. I was aware of most of the concepts of treatment but wanted to refresh the details in my mind. I had just pushed the binder aside when my client arrived.

Jack Schwartz was the owner of the Kokanee Inn, a landmark pub a block below the tracks in Creston. He was a jovial fellow in his mid-forties with curly black hair and dark horn-rimmed glasses.

"Well, here he is," he said, extending his arm to a handsome Alaskan malamute. "You remember Shiloh. My wife, Lynn, brought him in for his vaccinations last month."

"Yes, I do remember Shiloh." I paused and had a quick look at the record Doris handed me. "What's the longest it could be since he got into the antifreeze?"

"I'd guess about two hours, but it could be three or four." Jack nervously pushed up his glasses and forced his dog's butt to the sitting position.

"Have you noticed anything unusual about him up to now?"

"I hadn't when I called you, but on the way to the car, he walked like he'd had a few drinks. In my line of work, I get to see a lot of people in that state."

"I imagine you do. They talk about animals acting a bit drunk in the early stages after getting into antifreeze—it apparently affects the brain in a manner similar to ethanol."

"Could he die from this?"

"I hope not, but it'd sure be possible if he's not treated. My medicine notes suggest that between fifteen and fifty thousand dogs die every year in North America from accidental exposure to antifreeze."

Beads of sweat formed on Jack's forehead and he gave Shiloh a concerned look. "It's in every car and truck in the country...Why in the world would they use something so poisonous?"

"That's a good question. Veterinary associations around the world have been lobbying industry and government for years to make a change. There are less toxic products available—like propylene glycol—but they're more expensive and most people don't want to put out the extra money. The biggest trouble with ethylene glycol is it's sweet. Dogs and cats really like it. You'd think they could put something in it that would at least make it taste terrible."

"So what's the plan for Shiloh?"

"Let's get him on the table and check him over. We'll get some blood and urine. There's a new test I brought in a few months ago that'll tell us if he's absorbed any."

Jack rolled his eyes. "I'm not looking forward to this...Shiloh's a handful at the best of times."

I followed the pair to the exam room and helped Jack lift the dog onto the table.

As soon as his feet touched the surface, Shiloh struggled to jump overboard. Doris and I came to Jack's aid, and our combined efforts kept the malamute from bailing out. Between his attempts to escape, I was able to give him a cursory examination. His heart rate and lung sounds were normal. I agreed with Jack—Shiloh appeared the picture of health.

After several minutes of struggle, we were finally able to subdue him enough to collect a blood sample. He grumbled deep in his throat when I rolled back the lower lid of his eye and slipped in a little grey pill.

"What's that?" Jack asked worriedly.

"Apomorphine."

"Why'd you put it in his eye?"

"Because there's lots of blood flow to the lining there, and it allows the drug to be readily absorbed. It can also be easily washed out once it's had the desired effect."

"What does it do?"

"It's going to make him vomit."

"Oh…can we let him down?"

"Yeah, we'll take him outside now." I ducked into the back room for a garbage bag.

Shiloh was on the run before his feet hit the floor. Spinning madly, he pulled Jack toward the exit. Halfway to the door he stopped and lifted his foot to scratch at his eye.

"No, you don't," Jack said, grappling with him.

I grabbed a kidney dish from the counter in the lab and followed them as they charged through the door.

"Can you run the ethylene glycol test for me, Doris?"

"But…" My girl Friday looked a bit lost as I handed her the blood vial.

"Don't worry, just follow the instructions in the box. Everything's laid out on the counter."

At first, Shiloh led us around the parking lot sniffing here and lifting his leg there. I collected a urine sample as he sprayed the front wheel of my truck, then set the dish by the back door of the clinic. After a few minutes, he slowed down and stood glumly in one spot with his eyes closed.

"When does that pill do its thing?" Jack asked.

"It's working now. Unless I miss my guess, he's feeling like he wants to hurl."

Two or three minutes later he began to retch. The first time he produced a huge bolus of what had once been dry dog food. Over the next ten minutes, he made several smaller deposits.

"Let's take him inside now," I said after he heaved for a third time without bringing anything up.

Due to the sedating effect of the apomorphine, Shiloh was more subdued when we put him back on the table. He sat in a stupor while I flushed his eye with saline and clipped the hair from his forearm.

"We have to wait ten more minutes for the test results," Doris said authoritatively.

"Let's get the IV set up in the meantime," I suggested.

As she wheeled the IV stand to the exam room and readied the fluids, I mixed up a slurry of activated charcoal and water.

"I hope we're not doing all this for nothing," Jack said as he lay draped over his dog on the table watching the preparation. "How much would he have to drink to get himself into trouble?"

"My notes said that five millilitres per kilogram of body weight is a lethal dose...that amounts to three tablespoons for a dog that weighs ten kilos. Shiloh would be thirty-five kilos—that's about seventy-five pounds—so do the math. It wouldn't be too hard for a dog chewing on a gallon container to swallow enough. Even if what he got wasn't enough to kill him, it could leave him with major kidney damage."

"It's already turned a darker purple than the control," Doris announced. "That's what it said it would do if it was positive."

"Damn!" Jack muttered.

"I guess it's time for him to start hitting the bottle."

"What do you mean?"

"He's going on a three-day drunk."

"I don't understand," Jack said with a puzzled look.

"Within four hours of antifreeze being consumed it will all be absorbed—it's taken in almost as rapidly as alcohol. Apparently, ethylene glycol itself isn't very toxic. It doesn't hurt the gut or other tissues, and although it may make him a bit drunk, it doesn't damage the brain."

"Then how does it kill him?"

"It's the breakdown products from metabolizing it that are the big concern. There are lots of them, and they're all acids. If the dog drinks enough, the acidosis itself can cause a crash of both the kidneys and the cardiovascular system. If he survives that, then calcium oxalate crystals start forming in the blood vessels and the renal tubules—that's what shuts down urine production."

"So what's getting drunk got to do with all this?"

"Ethanol has a high affinity for the enzyme that metabolizes the antifreeze. If we keep him drunk enough, there won't be enough enzyme available to break down the ethylene glycol, and the kidneys will have the chance to excrete it from the body unchanged. Pile lots of fluids on top of that, and we should be able to chase it through more quickly."

"Makes sense," Jack said. "But three days—that's really tying one on."

"My notes say to administer a dose every four hours for five treatments, then every six hours for four more. After that, he'll be a good day sobering up enough to go home."

"Would any kind of booze work?"

"I don't see why not. I have some ninety-eight-proof grain alcohol in my drug cabinet, but vodka would do as well. I'll give him the grain alcohol intravenously in his drip so his blood levels stay steady."

"What's that stuff?" Jack pointed at the dirty-looking solution I had mixed up in a stainless steel bowl.

"Activated charcoal. As soon as his stomach settles down from the apomorphine, we'll get him to swallow some. Hopefully, it'll tie up the antifreeze that's still free in his gut and keep it from being absorbed."

The three of us were played out by the time we got the intravenous started on Shiloh. The effect of the apomorphine appeared to have worn off, and our patient could see no reason for us to stick holes in his body.

"It seems strange to be starting an IV on an animal that we can hardly hold on the table," Doris puffed. "Usually, they're half dead and more cooperative than this."

"I know…that's the problem. Even when people see their animals get into antifreeze, they just sit and watch to see if something develops. By then, it's often too late…It's a good thing your wife wouldn't let you do that, Jack."

"How long a window did we have?" Jack's face was still buried in the fur at the back of his dog's neck; he had literally been lying on Shiloh to keep him pressed to the table.

"It probably depends on how much he consumed, but my notes say somewhere between four and eight hours. Apparently, all of it's metabolized and excreted from the body within twenty-four."

I quickly calculated the recommended amount of alcohol and flushed it into the administration bag. "Bottoms up, Shiloh!" I joked as I massaged the bag to mix the alcohol with the fluids. "I hope you're going to be a happy drunk."

I retrieved a 35-millilitre syringe and drew up some of the charcoal sludge. Shiloh's blue eyes glared at me as I pried open his mouth and squirted the solution over the back of his tongue. I was aware that I was pushing my luck, but wanted to get the charcoal into him as soon as possible. After a third syringe, there was a low grumble in the back of his throat.

"Shilooooh…" Jack chastised. "Behave yourself."

"One more for the road, old boy," I quipped, trying to pry his mouth open an additional time.

The dog snapped and chomped on the syringe. Shaking his head with the syringe in his mouth, he effectively painted Jack and me and the wall with the sooty material.

"I guess you know what kind of drunk he is now," Doris remarked as she grabbed a cloth and began scrubbing the wall.

I quickly dipped a urine stick in Shiloh's sample. It was positive for protein and very acidic. I poured some in a tube and began spinning it in the centrifuge.

"Just one more thing before you sleep it off, Shiloh." I drew up some sodium bicarbonate and added it to the cocktail in his fluid bag.

"What's that for?" Jack asked.

"One of the big worries with this condition is a severe metabolic acidosis from all the breakdown products of the antifreeze. We'll try and keep it from getting out of hand by monitoring how acid his urine is and giving him bicarb."

"You can tell how acid he is from his pee?"

"Yeah." I pointed to the yellow square on the stick. "This little segment is sort of like the litmus paper you played with in chemistry class in school. It gives a rough idea what his acid base balance is."

The crowning indignation for Shiloh was the application of a plastic cone to keep him from chewing at his IV. He was not a happy camper when I slipped it over his head and anchored it firmly to his collar.

Thankfully, Jack stayed with his dog until half of the bag dripped into him. Even with his master at his side, Shiloh whined continuously and worked diligently but unsuccessfully to remove the plastic halo that encircled his head.

By six o'clock I was able to sit down at the microscope to catch up with the other lab work. It was hard to focus with the constant crashing, banging, and whining coming from Shiloh's kennel. Trying to tune him out, I removed the slide from the top of a fecal flotation that Doris had set up earlier. Laying it drop side up on the counter, I covered it with a delicate glass slip and mounted it on the microscope. I focused on the air bubbles at the periphery of the field, then moved to the centre in search of parasite eggs. The entire field was covered with the large dark-centred eggs of *Toxacara cati*. Sprinkled among them were the small thick-shelled eggs of a *Taenia* species.

"Doris! The Marshall cat has both tapes and roundworms. Give them a call and tell them they need to pick up some Droncit for the tapes. I already gave him Strongid when I vaccinated him."

I removed the test tube of malamute urine from the centrifuge and poured the liquid down the sink. I sucked up a dropper-full of Sedistain, dispensed a single drop to the remaining sediment, shook it aggressively, then applied a drop to a clean slide. I put on a cover slip and mounted it on the microscope.

"What were you hollering about?" Doris asked. "I was in the kennel room and couldn't make it out."

"Oh, I was just telling you about the fecal…the Marshall cat needs some Droncit. But take a look at this. It's Shiloh's urine."

I leaned back and Doris peeked through the eyepiece. "What are those shiny things?"

"They're oxalate crystals."

"They're kind of pretty."

"Yeah, I never thought about it, but I guess they are."

Doris stepped back and said, "I'll make up the prescription for the cat."

I glanced first at the slide, then back at the picture in my lab handbook. Both the needle-shaped oxalate monohydrate crystals and the envelope-shaped dihydrate crystals were present along with red blood cells and renal epithelial cells. There was no doubt—Shiloh's kidneys were under siege.

"Are you hungry, Doris?"

"Getting that way!" she chimed enthusiastically. "Don't tell me you're going to spring for Chinese."

"I think I'm suffering from a sweet and sour deficiency."

"Well…you do look like you could use some sweet, anyway."

I grabbed Button Vance's slide from the counter and slipped it onto the stage of the microscope. Setting it to low power, I perused the sample for approximate cell size and distribution. I applied a drop of oil to the slide and went to the emersion lens. For the next five minutes I lost myself studying the morphology of the individual cells. What a disappointment. There was a tremendous difference in red-cell size, indicating that the liver and spleen were busy munching away at them again. Thankfully, there were nucleated red blood cells, too—at least the bone marrow was battling to try and keep up. We weren't back to square one with Buttons, but we sure had slid a considerable way down the ladder.

As usual Doris and I pigged out at the Club Café. We reassured one another that Chinese food always vanished within the hour to leave you hungry, and crammed in more. By the time we left, our platters were polished clean and not a recognizable grain of rice had survived intact.

We were walking past Gordon's office on Canyon Street when I grabbed Doris's arm and stopped.

"Hear that?"

"Hear what?"

"Listen closely."

"Oh my word…it's Shiloh."

"OOOOOOOOOOOOOOOOOOOOOOO, OOOOOOOOO, OOOOOOOO, OOOOOOOOOOOOOOOOOOOOOOOO."

Doris was right. It was our resident malamute trying to communicate details of his plight to distant relatives in Alaska.

The next two days were absolute hell at the office. Shiloh was indeed a nasty drunk. For forty-eight hours he sang dirty songs punctuated with yips and piercing wails, twisted IVs into pretzels, and snapped at us whenever we tried to attend to him.

We discharged him the moment the final drop of alcohol

dripped through the chamber of his intravenous apparatus. He stumbled to the car, yipping, whining, and tugging at his leash. Jack said he kept the neighbours awake for that entire night with his serenading. It took him three days to recover from his hangover, but after that he was right back to normal. Shiloh lived a long and healthy life but always had a terrible aversion to anyone who had been drinking.

Laddie Come Home

"Quit it, Dave…you do that once more and I'm going to scream! That sound sends shivers up my spine—it's worse than fingernails grating on a chalkboard."

I daubed some more liniment on my forearm and moved my hand from side to side. Eeeeeeeee, eeeeeeeee…my tendon squeaked in protest as it slid through its inflamed sheath.

"Dave!"

"It's not my fault, Doris. It does that every time I move my wrist."

"Well then, stop moving your wrist…and quit swinging that stupid caveman's club. I couldn't believe it when I saw you using that thing."

"I can't…I've almost got my shakes split. A couple more days should do it."

"Suit yourself…" Doris wrinkled her brow to reprimand me and went back to the day page. "How's it going to work out now that you're living at the farm? A lot of people will be unhappy that they can't just give you a call and whip in to the office."

"They'll have to start keeping more supplies on hand instead of showing up here at ten at night expecting me to be waiting at the door. As far as the emergencies, I have to wait for most of them to get here anyway. Maybe I've been too handy for folks."

"We'll see." Doris looked skeptical. "Knowing you, you'll just burn up more profits in that truck of yours." She checked her watch. "You better get going, or you'll be late for Peggy Hawes at four o'clock. She told me to remind you that she works tonight…and Bill Herchmer phoned about the insurance for your house. He's supposed to be out there at five-thirty to take a few pictures…I thought that would give you enough time to get home after Peggy's."

"What am I seeing at Peggy's?"

"A horse. She says it's stumbling when she tries running it."

I went to the kennel room and slipped into a pair of coveralls. I was on my way out when Doris hollered. "I almost forgot! Jan Murray called in when you were in surgery. She wants to talk to you about her dog."

I glanced at my watch—quarter to four. I was going to be late again. I checked the day page, got the Murray number, and called.

"Hello."

"This is Dave Perrin from the vet clinic returning your call."

"Oh, thanks for getting back to me, Dr. Perrin…You may not remember me, but I'm the one who brought my dog in with the preschool class last summer."

"Yes…I remember."

It would be hard to forget trying to examine a dog in a room jammed full of four- and five-year-olds. As I recalled, most of the boys were far more impressed with my height than they were with what I was doing with Jan's dog. Three or four of them insisted on measuring themselves against my legs to see how far they came up. It was only after I got the needles out and began drawing up the vaccines that I'd gained everyone's attention.

"We're having dog troubles," Jan continued on the phone. "Our two males are fighting constantly. Do you think it would help if I neutered Gus? He's the older one, the one who usually starts things rolling."

"It might make a difference, but I can't guarantee it. Neutering will reduce his testosterone levels and make him less aggressive, but he'll still want to defend his territory...Did you just recently get the second dog?"

"No, we've had them both for a while now. Gus was here first. We got him as a pup. He was two when we brought Niki home. My six-year-old daughter came home from a birthday party with the story that she had won a St. Bernard puppy. Bob and I always liked the breed, so we went out to Lister and picked him up. Gus seemed to tolerate Niki when he was younger, but not anymore. It's crazy. They can be lying out in the yard as quiet as can be...a car comes up the driveway, they both run out barking, and the next thing you know, they're rolling around in the dirt fighting. They're big dogs and they really get into it. I have a devil of a time breaking them up. I'm afraid one of these days the kids'll get mixed up in the middle of it."

"I can appreciate that. Neutering one may help, but if the other one's aggressive, too, you may need to do both. It sounds like it's all about dominance."

Jan groaned. "That's not in the budget right now—I'm a stay-at-home mom and Bob's a teacher. He'll soon be off for summer vacation. We're adding on to the house and finances are really tight. Up until yesterday, we were both determined to work it out between them. We took them for walks on leashes together and even had neighbours drive in the yard when we were there to intervene. But yesterday took the cake. Bob was really annoyed by the time we got them pried apart. The poor guy...my being such a nut for animals has saddled him with a lot of pets and expenses we wouldn't have otherwise, and he's been great at accepting them all. He really likes the dogs but thinks we have to resolve this or find a home for one of them. The kids and I don't want to consider that."

"Well, we can certainly make you an appointment."

"The sooner the better," she said. "Yesterday was the breaking point. We have to do something."

"We can probably squeeze Gus in for tomorrow morning if that works for you."

"That would be great."

"Bring him in tonight before closing…You can feed him a bit before you leave home. After that he won't get anything until tomorrow night when he's recovered from his anesthetic."

At five minutes before four I pulled onto the main street and headed toward Canyon. It never failed that whenever I was running late, I ended up behind someone who insisted on following the speed limit through the Erickson orchards. I poked along behind a long line of vehicles and turned right at Little John's Fruit Stand. I slowed as I crossed the Goat River bridge.

The river was roaring at full force with spring runoff, and several carloads of people were lined up at the rail staring at the turbulent water in the canyon below. Lug growled as we passed and turned on the seat to watch the unsuspecting locals from the rear window.

Peggy Hawes was waiting in her front yard as I drove up the steep hill on 44th Street and turned into her yard. A sorrel Arab mare was at the end of a lead, picking at the new grass growing alongside the driveway.

Peggy led the animal over to me. "Hi, Dave."

"Hi, Peggy, sorry I'm late…"

"Vicky didn't mind getting a few extra blades of grass, and I don't have to be at work until seven."

"When did you get this mare? I thought maybe it was your son's pony you were having problems with."

"No, he's fine, but Vicky's got me worried sick. I've been around horses all my life but she's the first one I've ever owned. It'd be just my luck to have trouble with her. "

"What's up?"

"I don't know, that's why I called you. She's got me buffaloed."

"Tell me more."

293

"It's kind of hard to know what's really happening when she stumbles. She seems to lose control…"

"So she isn't limping constantly?"

"No, it's almost like her joint gives out on her or something. When it happens it really throws her off and she favours the leg for a few strides."

"It's not always the same leg?"

"No, that's the strange part."

Peggy clucked at her mare and ran her hand from hip to stifle. "I don't know where it originates…it's sort of like there's a clicking sensation that throws her off her stride."

"Is she stumbling with both front and back feet?"

"No…only the back. I'm sure of that. I had her over at Canyon Park last night. We were loping along when something gave out on her and she stumbled. She almost went down on me—it scared the heck out of me. I just walked her home."

I worked my way around Vicky as she munched on the grass. She was a beautiful specimen—fine-boned yet sturdily built, and more heavily muscled than most Arab mares. I ran my hands down one back leg then the other, looking for heat or swelling.

"Can you lead her back and forth up the drive, please, Peggy? Get her started, then let her have her head." I watched carefully for any hitch in the horse's gait as the pair walked back and forth in front of me on the gravelled surface. "Can you trot her?"

My client obediently picked up her pace and trotted the mare back and forth. Vicky showed her Arab ancestry by prancing proudly and holding her tail high.

"Do you see anything?" Peggy gasped after the second lap.

"Only that you're a bit hesitant on the right hind."

"You would be, too," she puffed, "if you spent all day running back and forth on those concrete floors at the hospital."

"When did you first notice this clicking, and what are you usually doing when you feel it?"

Peggy waited to catch her breath. She frowned. "I've really only noticed it this week. I bought her at the beginning of February, but with all the ice and mud around, I didn't get in as much riding as I'd have liked. When I did get out, I took it pretty easy with her, so I could have overlooked it. I rode her quite a bit before I bought her, though, and never noticed anything then."

"Who did you buy her from?"

"Jean Partington…she's out of her mare, Saiawna."

"Really?"

"Yes, why the sudden interest? Have you seen her before for this problem?"

"Not Vicky…but I sure had a go-round with her mother."

"I knew Jean had difficulties with Saiawna, but I never gave it another thought when I bought Vicky. Do you think it's something hereditary?"

"Let's take her over on that steep hill by your barn."

We walked past the house along a well-worn dirt path. Vicky followed closely at Peggy's heel without missing a beat. When we approached the barn on the top of the hill, I pointed to a steep embankment. "Try her down there."

Vicky hadn't taken three or four steps down the slope before her pastern gave out.

"There!" Peggy shouted as the horse quickened its pace and dragged her down the hill. For the next ten minutes, Peggy walked her horse up and down. Frequently, the pasterns clicked just like her mother's. Several more times, the mare stumbled and went careening down the bank.

"What do you suggest?" Peggy asked as we returned to the barn.

"Saiawna recovered within a couple months of starting her on the high selenium mineral mix, but I never did draw a blood on her. I've always regretted not doing a baseline panel on her first." Peggy nodded in agreement and I went on. "There are a lot of other minerals in that mix, so it may be that one of them made the difference—for all I know, it could be a combination of all of them.

What I'd like to do is draw blood to make sure that Vicky really is deficient, then treat her with only an injection of selenium and vitamin E. If we get a positive response, then we'll know for sure that's the remedy."

"That sounds sensible."

We returned to the truck and I drew a blood sample from Vicky.

"Why would you only see problems with Jean's horses?" Peggy asked.

"That's a good question, but it may be that some breeds or strains are less efficient at absorbing minerals. I think we're having more trouble with deficiencies of both copper and selenium since ranchers started importing bulls to the valley. It makes sense to me if you culled every critter that couldn't reproduce or that showed symptoms like this, you'd eventually get animals that could thrive on the conditions we have here. The problem is we select for other characteristics, like bone structure, speed, conformation."

"What about my other horse, Holly? You tested her last year when I was having trouble getting her pregnant. Her selenium was good then—she was only low on iodine and phosphorous." She handed me Vicky's lead shank. "Just a second, I have the report filed in the house."

Most of my clients had to struggle to remember when things were done for their animals. Nurse Peggy had everything at her fingertips—birth records, breeding dates, vaccination and de-worming histories.

"See." Peggy handed me the lab report. "Her selenium, copper, zinc, calcium, and magnesium were all normal—it was the iodine and the phosphorus she was deficient in."

I perused the information. "How long had you had Holly when we took this sample?"

"Only a couple of months...I had just made the deal with Judy Stead to lease her so I could get a foal out of her."

"Where did she come from before that? I've never seen her at Judy's."

"She bought her in Alberta a few weeks before I got her."

"Then I'd test her as well. If she's developed a selenium deficiency since you've had her here, then you may get in trouble with her foal…There's nothing more frustrating than struggling with a weak babe."

"Let's do her, too."

Before leaving, I administered an injection of selenium to Vicky. We decided to wait for Holly's results before treating her.

I drove directly to Lister from Peggy's. It was strange to be thinking of Lister as home now. Most people wouldn't have considered moving into my house at this stage of completion, but I convinced myself that I'd had enough of the chorus of Friday-night drunks, squealing tires, and roaring diesel engines. The night after the windows were installed, I began moving my meagre possessions south.

It took me almost a week to get used to the different surroundings. The first night I had tossed and turned in my cavernous bedroom, unable to handle either the silence or the utter darkness. Lug was insulted that I'd go to bed without him—I still hadn't built my stairs, and he couldn't quite figure out how to climb the ladder to the loft.

When I got to the farm, I studied the wiring map Gordon Veitch had drawn for me, pulled twenty feet of two-wire from the spool, and began threading it through the holes he had drilled. We had wired most of the main floor, and Gordon had tied in enough plugs and lights for me to get by upstairs. Of all the jobs I had tried my hand at, electrical wiring was the one I enjoyed the least. Moving the stepladder from one ceiling joist to the other, I pulled the wire to a box for a light receptacle in the far corner of the living room. Leaving an extra few inches at the switch box, I cut it off.

I checked my watch—almost six. Bill Herchmer was late; Doris said he would be here at five-thirty. I went back to work wiring another box.

When Lug ran barking to the door half an hour later, I was certain that Bill had arrived. I grabbed my mad dog's choke chain and opened the door. He growled when he saw the horse and rider. I stepped outside and closed the door on his antisocial behaviour.

"Good evening, neighbour." It was Phil McGraw.

"Hi, Phil...what are you doing in this neck of the woods?"

"I thought I'd ride past and see if you were here...wanted to let you see my new horse."

I looked to the horse with surprise. "Isn't that Gray?"

Phil grinned broadly. "Yeah, we just came back from a ride over to Canyon. We took one of those trails that goes way up on the mountain. He hardly broke a sweat—he's as good as new. Who'd ever believe it? Thanks, Doc."

Phil turned the animal sharply and gave him his heels; the horse took off from the yard at a gallop. I smiled as I watched them disappear from sight—another pearl from heaven. When I opened the door, Lug ran barking to the gate. For several minutes he stood looking down the road after them. "Come on, old man, we better feed up. Bill must have gotten busy."

We followed the path across the draw and through the pine forest. We were halfway to the hay shed when there was a woofing sound off to our right. I saw the streak of pink but before I could grab Lug, he was gone. That darned pig was out again.

"Lug! Lug, get back here!"

I broke into a run to try and catch him, knowing full well I was wasting my breath yelling. The dog was tolerable around cattle—he only loved to tease them. But he had decided to dislike hogs—especially Hogan. When he was on Hogan's trail, there was no reasoning with him.

Hogan had become the bane of my life. Constantly coming up with new and innovative ways of escaping his compound, he was always one step ahead of me. Jack named him after one of his favourite television personalities—Colonel Hogan, the American commander from the show *Hogan's Heroes*. Each week an inmate in the German prisoner-of-war camp planned an escape from Stalag 13.

When I sent twenty of my biggest hogs to market last week to complete the load Jack was sending, I had been determined to make sure Hogan was on board, too. But it didn't work that way; after two hours of chasing him back and forth in his run, I told the truck driver to leave without him.

I was huffing my way up to the cross fence when Lug started barking angrily. As I approached the hay shed, I couldn't see either him or the pig. As much as I couldn't abide Hogan's antics, I certainly didn't want him chewed up into bite-size dog food.

"Lug! Get over here!"

I was out of breath by the time I reached the lane on the edge of the farm. Although Lug's barking sounded close, he was still eluding me. It was the movement of his tail that gave him away. Hogan had dug a hole not more than a few feet from the last one I filled in.

"C'mon, Lug!"

Nothing protruded from the excavation but his tail. I looked over the fence at the insubordinate German shepherd. His front feet were buried in muck, and he barked ferociously at several hogs that stood in a semi-circle around him. In the middle of the throng, not six feet away from him, was Hogan.

"Get out of there!"

Lug's tirade stopped when I grabbed his tail and unceremoniously dragged him from the hole. I glowered at him as he cowered before me with his head on his filthy paws and his tail pulled tight to his butt. His legs and belly were covered in pig dung.

"When are you ever going to listen? Look at you!"

I spent the next twenty minutes gathering boulders in the barnyard. The entire time, the defiant Hogan stood watching the hole beneath the prison wall slowly fill with rocks. After feeding and watering the pigs, and throwing a few bales of hay to the cattle, I headed back to the house.

"You're not coming in like that, Lug…You stay outside."

I tied him to the pine tree in the backyard, then scurried up the ladder to grab the bar of soap from the bathroom. When I got back outside, Lug had curled up dejectedly. I turned on the garden hose and walked toward him.

"Stay put!" I ordered, as he slunk down at the end of his rope.

By the time I had finished bathing him, my hands had taken on the aroma of "poo de pork." I left him whining plaintively and went back upstairs. I ran hot water into the old claw-footed tub I had salvaged from a farmer's backyard and stepped in. It felt exquisite to relax and enjoy a few minutes of peace and quiet out of reach of my dog and my least favourite pig. I closed my eyes and slid down in the deep tub until only my nose was sticking out.

"Hello! Hello, Dave…are you around?"

I awoke with a start and whirled around in the tub. There at the top of the landing, not ten feet away, stood Bill. His wife Chris was about to step from the ladder. The only thing that separated us were the bare studs of what would one day be the bathroom wall.

"Uh, hi…I'm over here," I said meekly. "I guess I fell asleep."

Bill smiled broadly and gave his wife a hand to step up onto the plywood floor. He waved his Polaroid camera at me. "We're here for the pictures."

"I can see why that poor woman is at her wit's end with this dog," Doris said as Gus dragged her toward the exit. "He's like a bloody horse."

I grabbed a leash, snapped it on his collar, and helped convince the big hulk to come back to the surgery room. Even sedated, the dog was a handful.

"Mrs. Murray said he was an Irish setter / German

shepherd–cross but he looks more like an overgrown golden retriever," Doris said, turning on the oxygen tank.

The golden-red dog flopped his head back and forth in an effort to break free as I struggled to lift him. I plunked him on the table and lay on top of him while Doris put her hands on his butt to keep him from backing up. She traded positions with me as he settled down. Wrapping her hand around his elbow, she blocked off the vein in his front leg. I soaked his foreleg with alcohol, felt for the vessel, and popped in the needle. The dog slowly relaxed as I injected Biotal, and he slumped to the tabletop, yawning widely. I waited for a minute and checked his jaw tone; when he lolled his tongue, I injected what remained in the syringe. Doris pried open his mouth and pulled out his tongue, while I inserted an endotracheal tube.

Within a few minutes the dog was stretched out on the table with a large foot dangling over each corner. I grabbed the clipper and was about to prepare him for surgery when I noticed that there was only one testicle.

"Oh man, Doris, wouldn't you know it. The one time I don't look for the family jewels and I end up with a one-nutter." I pushed his testicle forward until it disappeared into the inguinal ring on the left side, then began palpating the groin on the right. After several minutes of searching, I gave up. "I can't find it."

"What now?" Doris asked.

"I better phone the Murrays." I dialled the number and waited. "Just my luck! Sounds like no one is home." I was about to hang up when Jan answered. "Hello, Mrs. Murray, it's Dr. Perrin calling."

"Is there a problem with Gus?" she asked breathlessly.

"Yes, I'm afraid there is…He's only got one testicle down."

"Do you think he only has one?" she asked hopefully.

"I doubt it. He probably has another one somewhere in his abdomen."

There was silence as we each waited for the other to speak.

"If I remove the one, he'll be sterile, but he'll produce testosterone—he'll still think he's a male and probably be just as aggressive. Besides that, a cryptorchid testicle is much more likely to develop a tumour."

I waited while Mrs. Murray absorbed the significance of the information. "Will it cost more?" she asked hesitantly.

"Yes, I'm afraid so…it's a much more difficult surgery—we'd have to open him up. It could be twice as much as a normal neuter. It all depends on how hard it is to find."

"Oh, there's no way…"

"We have Gus under anesthesia right now, but we can wake him up and I won't charge you for it. I should have noticed he only had one before we induced him."

"But then they'll be right back to fighting! I can't handle that any more…What if one of the kids gets hurt?"

There was a long silence. I glanced at Doris and raised my eyebrows. I felt like a highwayman holding this poor woman to ransom.

"Put him…to sleep," she said hesitantly.

"Sleep—you mean euthanasia?"

"Yes!" she blurted. "Giving him away would be impossible— he's such a big dog and he's a devil with chickens. I can't pass my problems off on someone else…that would be dishonest." There was the sound of unrestrained wailing, then the phone went dead.

I trudged to the surgery where Doris sat on her stool diligently watching her patient. I solemnly turned the halothane dial to maximum, shut off the oxygen, and turned up the nitrous oxide. Doris didn't say a word, but sadness was written all over her. The telephone rang; she answered it. I was hoping it was Mrs. Murray changing her mind, but from the sound of the conversation, it was someone wanting to book a spay. Doris went on to describe the merits of vaccinating and deworming pets even though they were only farm animals.

I went dejectedly to the kennel room for one of the heavy plastic bags we used for cadavers. It was too morbid to stand there watching for the poor dog's last breath. I drew up the Demerol and atropine to premed my next patient. The telephone rang again.

"Dave...it's Jan Murray!"

I shut the door and bolted to the front. Doris held the phone for me at arm's length. All I could hear when I took the receiver was uncontrolled sobbing. "Hello."

"Have you done it yet? Is he dead?"

I dropped the phone and rushed to the surgery. Shutting off the nitrous oxide and halothane, I cranked up the oxygen and deflated the bag. As it rapidly distended with oxygen, I closed the valve, slowed the flow, and started compressing the bag.

"Doris, come take over!"

There was no movement to Gus's chest; his tongue was blue, his membranes grey. I hesitated for a moment with my hands on either side of his rib cage, searching for a heartbeat. As Doris continued to compress the bag and expand the dog's lungs, I untied the ropes holding his legs and flipped him onto his right side.

"Let the air out, Doris."

When she unscrewed the valve to the anesthetic machine and his chest collapsed, I placed the heel of my hand on his rib cage just behind his elbow, placed my other hand on top, and sharply depressed ten times running.

"Again, Doris."

I watched impatiently as the huge dog's lungs expanded and collapsed, then repeated the procedure. After the third round, I stopped and checked. The heart was beating.

"Keep it up, Doris."

I grabbed a stethoscope and listened intently. Lub-dub, lub-dub, lub-dub...his heart was faint, but definitely beating. Within a few minutes it was contracting strongly and the dog was attempting to breathe on his own. I went back to the phone.

"Hello? Are you there, Jan?"

"I'm here," she answered anxiously. "Is Gus still with us?"

"He is—"

"Oh thank God…I was sure I was going to be too late."

"You almost were."

"After I talked to you, I went into the bathroom and cried myself silly. I kept visualizing Gus running up the drive with his long golden hair blowing in the wind—just like on *Lassie Come Home*. That's when I ran to the phone to call you. I dialled and dialled, but it kept ringing busy."

"I can understand how you feel. I'll call you when I finish…I better get back to him."

Gus recovered quickly from his ordeal. Throughout the surgery, his breathing was as regular as clockwork. After twenty minutes of searching, I found his wayward testicle halfway between its origin at the base of his kidney and its intended destination in his scrotum. Gus and Niki settled their differences, and Jan got to watch Gus run up the driveway with his long golden hair blowing in the wind.

"Is This Guy Really a Vet?"

"Beautiful day for the truck to be coming," Father grumbled.

It had been raining for three days straight and the hog runs had turned into a sea of mud. I watched as one of the feeders left the shelter of the hay-shed roof and ambled to the edge of the concrete. Standing for a moment in the pelting rain, he stepped chest deep into the mire, plowed his way ten feet from the concrete, and stopped to take a poop.

"What's the plan?" Father asked ruefully.

I wasn't looking forward to this any more than he was. I had been standing under the shelter of the hay shed for the last several minutes trying to think of some alternative—there wasn't one. We simply had to drive the pigs through this muck to the hole in the fence at the other end.

"What time's it coming?" he asked.

"Gary Koebel said around two-thirty...He and I are sharing the load."

"We better get more planks nailed on in that holding pen—we don't need another escape."

I trudged into the pasture, dragged a slab from the pile, and held it in place while Father drove the spikes into the railway ties we used for uprights. Rain pounded down, matting my long hair to my face and neck.

"Do you think that'll hold him?" Father asked after we nailed one more on.

"God knows with him…"

It was always a question of "him," not them. Every time I shipped, the priority was the same—get rid of Hogan. Two weeks ago I had gotten him this far. He was right here in the enclosure with twenty-five others; the whole pen had been jammed full. The other hogs were filing up the loading ramp into the truck as calmly as kids shuffling to the gymnasium for assembly. Hogan had been halfway up the ramp when he scrambled over the gilt in front of him and squeezed out between the upper bars.

"We did build this for cattle," Father reasoned. "Those planks were a bit far apart."

After spending an hour plugging every possible avenue of escape, we could delay the inevitable no longer.

"Should I get Jack?"

"I guess…I can't see anywhere that blamed critter could get out unless he really is superpig and can fly."

While I removed a few slabs from the corner of the first run, Father went in search of Jack. Only nine of the slower growing finishers and Hogan remained in this pen…the others would have to be sorted out of the second one.

"So what do you want me to do?" Jack asked, squinting through the driving rain.

"Let's get the rest of these planks off, then we'll start sorting."

I pounded off three more slabs, and Father leaned them against the outside railing.

"We need fifteen or sixteen of the biggest hogs from there." I pointed to the second pen. "Then we'll take these nine."

"It'll be a bugger sorting them in all that muck," Jack said. His voice had that tone of surrendering to an unavoidable chore. "How do you plan on doing it? That crap is way over your boots."

"I think I can walk on that two-by-six." I pointed to the cross member the slabs were nailed on.

"What do you want me to do?" Father asked.

"How about if you chase them from the shed. I'll sort them, and Jack can work the gate in the holding pen. Leave Hogan for now. The longer we wait to get him involved, the less likely we are to have trouble with him."

"That's wishful thinking," Jack replied. "It'll just give him longer to come up with a plan."

While Father rousted the most robust of the feeders from their straw bed and chased them out into the soup, I grabbed the long maple stick I had cut as a prod for the previous load, and ventured out on the narrow ledge. Using the stick as a supporting crutch, I moved cautiously along the slippery surface holding onto the slab fence with my free hand. I prodded the hogs along the now submerged path to the end of the pen, and drove them through the opening. Within half an hour we had all of them out and safely locked in the holding pen.

"Well, that went a lot better than I thought it would," I said, congratulating myself.

"It did," Jack agreed, looking at his watch. "We made good time…Why don't we sneak over to the house for a coffee and get out of this rain for a bit. We've got a couple hours before the liner gets here."

"Sure, sounds good to me. It shouldn't take long to get those others out."

I shed my rubber boots in the stairwell and followed Jack and Father through the mudroom into the kitchen. I shivered as I stepped through the porch door and felt a blast of warm air. What a treat to get out of the weather and smell fresh coffee instead of hog manure.

"I put on a new pot as soon as I heard you guys come in," Sandra said.

We all sat around the kitchen table watching the last of the coffee drip through the filter into the pot. I was taking my first sip of the strong brew when we heard it.

"Damn!" cursed Jack. "That sounds like the truck…they must have finished at Gary's quicker'n they thought."

A semi with a double-decker trailer lumbered past the kitchen window. We all jumped into our boots and evacuated the house. Jack helped the driver turn around in the confines of his yard while Father and I went into action with the remaining pigs.

"Chase them all out, Dad!" I was already perched on the side rail halfway into the pen.

"Yah! Get out of here!" Father yelled, knocking on the end of the pen with a shovel.

The hogs reluctantly trundled to the end of the slab and took the plunge—all but one, that is. Hogan stood on the edge of the concrete watching me as I poked and prodded his pen-mates toward the other end.

"Go on, you fat bugger! Get out there!" Father shouted, banging his shovel on the concrete.

Hogan jumped in and headed straight for the hole at the other end. I was beside myself with anticipation as he passed the others to spearhead the drive along the path through the mud. He got to the hole before the others, then turned broadside to it and looked at me impudently.

"Get up there, Hogan!"

I poked the pigs behind him and two scrambled around him and up the bank onto solid ground. The driver and Jack were busy loading the feeders from the second pen on board.

"Get up there, Hogan!" I bellowed again.

I swung the stick at the stragglers at the back of the log-jam and lost my balance. My foot slipped off its mooring and I plunged into the mud. By the time I hit bottom, I was knee-deep in the mire. Hogan turned toward me, then plowed past his fellows. By the time I dragged myself onto the path, the remainder of the animals were all back on the concrete waiting for instructions.

I stood dejectedly in front of the hole safeguarding the two animals we had trapped in the alleyway, while Jack and the trucker finished loading the first bunch. I glared across the moat at the fat porker standing proudly at the other end.

"So much for staying clean!" Jack hollered gleefully as he opened the gate and I chased our two captives into the holding pen.

"Not now…" I growled.

The rain picked up to a deluge as I climbed back onto the cross member and edged my way to the middle of the pen. Huge drops pounded on the tin roof of the shed; water cascaded from the eaves.

"Okay, Dad, chase them out!"

Father banged on the boards with his shovel and the group scattered like a flock of turkeys. Every pig, save one, jumped off the concrete and trekked through the muddy waters toward me.

Father was losing it. "Get going, Hogan! I've had about enough of you!" He lunged at him with his shovel, but the rotund porker ran right back in the shed for cover.

"Just leave him for now, Dad! Get these guys to come a little further."

"Okay!" he yelled. "Go! Go!"

The pigs' momentum stalled before they reached me, and they all stood staring up at me. I inched my way past them as Father pelted them with the chunks of crusted manure he pried from the inside corners of the shelter. When he struck the first feeder on the back, it lunged forward down the water-filled trench. I began hollering and banging my stick as the whole group sloshed down the trail in single file. I followed in hot pursuit as the string of them climbed the bank and trotted out of the pen. Jack quickly chased them to the holding area, and he and the trucker kept them moving up the ramp into the liner.

"Okay, Dad, get him moving!"

I was drenched to the skin and shivering with the cold—all I could think of now was to get this over with and immerse myself in a tub of steaming water.

Father chased Hogan back and forth across the concrete pad. With each lap his curses got louder and the swinging of the shovel more animated. A sharp crack to the backside with the flat of the shovel sent the stubborn pig lurching into the mud. As if convinced the slop granted him immunity, he tripped just far enough down the submerged path to avoid the shovel and stopped. Father rained dried chunks of manure upon him, but Hogan stood his ground.

"Are we going to call that a load?" the trucker hollered.

"No bloody way!" I replied adamantly. "This SOB is going on your truck one way or another—he's already going to grade as a fat."

"Make it quick," he said, adjusting his yellow slicker. "I'm not about to stand around in the rain all day waiting for one pig!"

"You'll wait for this one!"

I sidled my way along the slippery ledge, taking longer and longer steps. I wasn't sure what I was going to do when I got to him, but I wasn't about to be defied yet again by this obnoxious porker.

"Hogan, get your ass out of here!" I bellowed.

The pig remained eerily still. What happened next was my undoing. When I swung my stick in a wide arc to whack him, a portion of the slab I was anchored to broke loose. There was a raucous cheer from the trucker before my butt even entered the pig-poo soup. I landed with a splat next to Hogan.

Still clutching my stick, I struggled to get my feet under me in the channel the pigs had worn in the Lister clay. My heart was pounding and I was holding my breath to keep from cursing. Driven on by hoots of laughter from the trucker's corner, I slogged after Hogan. He seemed surprised that I had joined him in his soggy playground and took several strides toward the opening. I was sure he was going to go all the way this time.

"Okay, up you go, Hogan!"

I went to prod him, but the moment my stick touched his

backside he turned and charged directly at me. I grabbed for his ears, and wrestled to push him back to the hole. With a piercing squeal, he planted his front feet on my chest and ripped himself free. By the time I regained my footing, he was halfway across the swamp to the concrete pad.

"Maybe we better leave him, Dave," Father reasoned as I continued in pursuit.

Without saying a word in reply, I forged on. I had lost my stick, so it was more difficult to keep my balance in the narrow trench. Water sloshed in my boots, and each time I took a new stride they threatened to bog down in the mire.

"Jack! Do you think you could stop laughing long enough to get me a pig board?"

I worked my way to the side of the pen and waited for him to return with the strip of half-inch plywood he had fashioned for moving his sows. It was a full sheet of plywood lengthwise, but only two and a half feet wide. With handles cut out of either side, it was easy to jog back and forth to help maneuver a hog. For some reason, when it was plunked in front of them, they almost always changed their direction.

By the time I had dragged the board the third time for the length of the pen, I was plastered with muck. I was convinced that my only hope was to corner Hogan in front of the exit hole for long enough to push him out. Each time I thought I almost had him there, he lunged away before I could get in position. The rain continued to pelt down, and both Hogan and I were reaching the point of exhaustion. Father kept trying to reason with me, but there was no way I was going to quit until that annoying critter was on the truck and out of my life. The guffaws from the trucker's corner diminished; the smirk on Jack's face faded and was replaced by a frown.

"Is this guy really a veterinarian?" I heard the trucker ask.

I finally edged Hogan toward the hole in the corner. While he paused for a rest and looked longingly to the pasture beyond the fence, I dug the board into the mud behind him. "Up, Hogan! This is it. We've both had enough…"

By this time, Father had made his way to the communal end of the pen; the moment I pinned Hogan in place he, Jack, and the trucker rushed in to help me. I pushed forward on the top of the board with every ounce of strength I could muster while they grabbed desperately for a purchase on some portion of the pig's slippery anatomy. Jack grabbed a leg, the trucker and Father each caught hold of an ear. Thrashing his head wildly, Hogan let out an eardrum-piercing squeal.

"Get up there, you stubborn SOB!"

Just when victory seemed inevitable, the incorrigible critter got his hind feet against the boards of the fence. Shaking his head defiantly, he gave a mighty heave, broke free of his antagonists, and sent me reeling backward into the muck. Sprinting for freedom, he ran the length of the pig board, which now rested on my chest. I saw a flash of his underbelly before a hind foot landed on my forehead and drove my head into the mud. I dug deep with my arms in an attempt to keep my face out of the slurry. With my feet and arms totally mired, I struggled frantically to be free. My heart was racing; blood pounded at my temples. I was so consumed with rage that I feared something might actually explode. In total frustration, I released an unintelligible scream.

The only thing I could move was my eyes. I shifted them furtively in Father's direction. At that moment we both broke into uncontrollable fits of laughter. I gave up the struggling and lay passively where Hogan had left me. Father waded in to my rescue. He managed to pry me loose in time to see the tail end of the liner disappear down the drive past Jack's house. Hogan had won again.

Father awoke the next morning feeling queasy. Declining breakfast, he decided to go home to Riondel to rest for a few days. That evening my mother called, so beside herself that she had trouble relating her story. Between sobs, she informed me that Father hadn't been feeling well for most of the afternoon, and she had convinced him to visit the local doctor. Dr. Savory had sent him directly to Nelson by ambulance. She called my mother to explain his malady, but Mom had trouble understanding the medical terminology and wanted me to phone the doctor for clarification.

"Hello, Dave, I've been expecting your call...I suspected you would want to know more."

"Thanks for taking my call, Frances...I know what it's like trying to get a few minutes of peace."

"It's actually not bad at all here in Riondel—certainly not like my city practice was." She hesitated for a moment, then went on. "About Marsh...he came in this afternoon complaining that his stomach was upset. He was feeling nauseous and tired. I discovered an aortic aneurysm—quite a large one really, very readily palpable. They're most commonly seen in men your dad's age—I don't suspect you'd get this sort of thing very often in animals."

"As a matter of fact, they're quite common in horses. How long do you think Dad's had it? He hasn't complained of anything like that in the past."

"It's hard to answer that...usually I'd have expected to detect it at a smaller size and monitor it over time. I saw your dad six months ago for a cough and didn't pick it up then. They're much more common in overweight men in their sixties. It's unusual to see one in someone who's in such good shape—your father has the body of a much younger man."

"What are the odds of its rupturing?"

"It's uncommon for them to rupture when they're less than five and a half centimetres wide. However, Marsh's is much larger than that, so it worries me. It could be that it's been slowly growing, but it's also possible that it was more sudden."

"What will they do for him in Nelson?"

"I expect they'll arrange for transport to Vancouver General Hospital."

I was in a quandary when I hung up the phone. My experiences with aneurysms hadn't been good. In humans, the bulging was almost always the result of arteriosclerosis and high blood pressure. In horses, it was because of parasite migration. The larvae of *Strongylus vulgaris* drilled through the walls of the major vessels and weakened them. Although I had picked up several of the buzzing bubbles on rectal palpation, it was the horse that had dropped dead while being worked in the arena that flashed to mind. I vividly remembered pulling the tack from the animal with the assistance of its very distraught owner, and dragging it out to the pasture to perform a post-mortem. The dorsal aorta had simply blown out—like a tire that had bulged with weakness then perforated. He had bled out more quickly than if his throat had been slit. Most of his blood lay free in his abdomen.

As I imagined the worst for Dad, Lug sidled up to me and plunked his head in my lap. Flipping his nose under my hand, he insisted on being recognized. How did he always know when I needed his support? I hugged him tightly and buried my face in his coat. I had never once hugged Father—and I wasn't ready for him to die. We had so much to accomplish together. It was only since working with him on the farm that I felt we could become friends. There were so many things I needed to tell him—so many things he needed to tell me.

. I called the Nelson hospital, but all they could let me know was that he hadn't been admitted and must still be in transit. I rushed out to the truck and drove across Lister to Veitches.

"I can't believe it, Gord. I always thought Dad was invincible…I mean I've noticed him getting older and slowing down a bit, but I sure wasn't expecting something like this—not now. Hell, he was out wrestling pigs with me yesterday, up to his waist in the mud. What if it had ruptured then? I'd never have forgiven myself." I could feel the mantle of self-pity settling gently on my shoulders. "We were just starting to understand one another."

"You're lucky…I never got to understand my dad." Gord

315

frowned. "After Dad had his stroke, it seemed he was mad at the world...he told me I'd never amount to anything. Maybe that's why I keep coming up with new projects—to prove him wrong."

"I know that feeling," I replied melancholically.

"Hell, old Pop thinks the sun rises and sets on you."

"I don't ever see that..." I quickly wiped away a tear and turned away from my friend.

"Then you must be blind. If he were any prouder, he'd burst his buttons."

"Whenever we did anything together when I was younger, it was always the same—I couldn't do it right and I couldn't do it fast enough."

Gordon nodded knowingly. "Hell, that part of being a father... I probably do a lot of that with my own kids. It's easy for you to sit here as a judge now—just wait 'til you have children of your own."

"I don't have to wait for my own kids—I treat Dad like that now. What if he dies before I see him again? There are so many things I want to tell him."

"He already knows a lot of what you want to say."

"I never once told him I loved him...I don't remember ever hugging him."

"That's a man thing, Dave. There are things a man doesn't need to do or say."

Tears pooled. I looked away from Gordon and said nothing.

Two days later at the office, I could see that Doris was concerned. "What are you going to do, Dave?"

"I should fly out so I can be with him when he's in recovery. I've got a call in to his doctor to find out how the surgery went. I'll probably have a better idea once I've talked to him."

She gave me a motherly look. "That would be a good idea. Your dad's probably worried sick out there all by himself...it's been two days now."

"I can't understand why it took them so long to get him into surgery...especially after flying an air ambulance all the way to Nelson to get him there. The nurse told me they already had him premedicated and waiting before they bumped him at the last minute. Apparently, someone in worse shape showed up."

"Maybe you should call again," Doris suggested.

It was three o'clock in the afternoon. Surely, they'd have news by now. I went to the phone and dialled the familiar number.

"Vancouver General Hospital...how may I direct your call?"

"Intensive care, please."

"Intensive care, can you hold please?" Before I could reply there was a click and then familiar bars of Beethoven.

I shook my head in frustration at Doris. "More classical music."

A few minutes later a nurse came on. "Can I help you?"

"This is Dr. Perrin calling. Can you give me information on how my father's surgery went? He was slated for ten and I thought I'd have heard something by now."

"I'm sorry, Dr. Perrin, but your father's surgery was rescheduled until tomorrow."

"Tomorrow! How could that be? You bumped him yesterday, too!"

"I'm sorry, but there was something more urgent that tied up the operating room. There was no way they could possibly fit him in today."

I bit my tongue to fight off the mounting anger. What right did they have to leave my father with a time bomb ticking in his abdomen? He'd probably been bumped by a politician with a sprained toe.

"Would you like to speak to your father?"

"You can get him to the phone?" I asked incredulously.

"Oh yes...let me see if I can arrange it." There was a click and Beethoven was back. I stood at the front desk looking over the messages scratched in the margin. If I had learned anything from

317

this episode with Father, it was how I didn't want to be treated as a client. I had spoken briefly to his doctor in Vancouver after he'd been admitted, but he hadn't answered a call since. I could understand his being busy, but surely there had been five spare minutes in his day.

"Hello?" It was as if Father's voice were speaking to me from the grave after all the fretting I'd been doing.

"Hi, Dad...how're you feeling?"

"Not good..." He sounded stressed. His speech was slurred and there was an element I wasn't familiar with in his voice—fear. "I'm afraid it's all over, Dave. It's going to bust...I know it is."

"Don't talk like that." I was struggling to keep my voice level. "You're going to make it! You're tough and you've got a lot to do here yet."

"It's driving me nuts, Dave—the buzzing—it feels like somebody's tied a thousand bees in a plastic bag and stuck 'em in my belly. I just know it's going to break."

"Try to settle down, Dad. Quit being so negative."

"I'm tired...I can't sleep. I was ready when they gave me that shot in the ass this morning. I wanted it over, one way or the other. I waited and waited, then they told me it was put off again until tomorrow...maybe it'd be better if it broke so I could get this over with. I can't keep my hands off my gut—I want that damn buzzing to stop."

By the time I finished talking to Father, I was more distraught than ever. It was as if someone were intentionally tormenting the poor guy. Getting psyched for the knife once would be hard enough; three times was torture.

"Doris, could you call Paul Haines and see if he can get me on a flight to Vancouver tonight...I think I better get out there."

"Okay. Have a quick look at the book, though...you have some calls to make. And check out the lab reports that came in today. The results for those horses of Peggy Hawes are finally here."

I ran to the lab and flipped through the sheets until I got to

Peggy's. A flush ran through me as I read the comments. *Severe selenium deficiency…*

"Peggy, it's Dave Perrin calling. The samples are finally back. They're both selenium-deficient. Normal levels should be well over 0.1, but Vicky's is only .086, and Holly's is even worse—it's .058. We better get a shot into her as well, then start both of them on the mineral mix. If we don't, you could end up with terrible problems with that foal of hers."

"Oh, I'm so glad we decided to check her, too," said Peggy. "I was out for a ride on Vicky last night…Connie Kolthammer and I were all over Canyon. We raced full out on the track at the park, and she was as good as gold. It looks like you were right."

I hung up the phone with a smile on my face and ran upstairs to start packing my bag. Lug was constantly underfoot as I grabbed clothes from my closet and stuffed them into my suitcase. How did he always know when things were up?

"Paul said he's got you on a flight!" Doris yelled up the stairs. "I'll run down and pick up the tickets—you don't have much time! Catch the phone while I'm gone."

I was running around the office trying to get caught up on the last-minute details. I was so used to letting other people call the tune of my daily dance that making decisions for myself felt foreign. I dragged my suitcase downstairs, then picked up the phone in one last effort to call Father's doctor. He was unavailable.

"You better get out of here or you'll be missing that plane. It leaves at 7:10."

The telephone rang. I stopped on my way to the door and stared at Doris as she answered it. She frowned and was obviously debating whether or not to pass it over.

"Just a second, Bob." She held her hand over the mouthpiece. "It's Bob Vance…they're having problems with Buttons. Should I tell them to call Cory?"

I stood there for a moment, frozen by indecisiveness. Finally, I glanced at my watch and set down my bag. "Tell him to bring him right in."

I loaded my suitcase in the car and came back to sit in the office. I checked my watch for the tenth time and went back to my job of scratching Lug's ear.

"Cory could handle this, Dave...you know that," Doris scolded.

"Yeah, but I know Buttons' history, and I'd feel I had cheated the Vances if I walked out now."

I was standing on the street as Bob's car pulled up. Kevin was out of the vehicle with Buttons in his arms the moment they came to a stop. "He's really bad this time," the boy said as he rushed past me through the open door. The dog's head was hanging; his mouth was open wide, and he was gasping for breath.

"In here, Kevin." I diverted him to the surgery.

I quickly turned on the oxygen tank and attached the mask to the anesthetic machine. Before Kevin could even lift Buttons onto the table, the dog stiffened in his arms and arched his head back in a seizure. I slapped the mask over the dog's mouth as he relaxed, and grabbed for my stethoscope. I couldn't hear his heart.

"Doris! I need you—quick!"

I grabbed a tube and opened the dog's mouth. Even as I pulled out his tongue I knew it was hopeless; his membranes were totally blanched. I slipped in the tube and inflated the cuff. Breathing into it, I watched the dog's chest rise. I puffed into it again as Doris readied the hoses for the anesthetic machine. I flipped Buttons onto his right side and started compressing his chest, stopping briefly to let Doris work the bag and expand his lungs with oxygen. We worked for several minutes before giving up. Kevin stood through the entire procedure, waiting in anticipation. He stared at me in disbelief when I finally quit.

"I'm sorry, Kevin."

The boy ran from the room and crashed out the door. His father slumped against the wall in defeat. I slipped Buttons into a cadaver bag, but when I turned to ask Bob what he wanted to do with the body, he was gone. I ran to the door to see his car pulling away from the curb. I flopped in a heap on the waiting room bench and buried my head in my hands. All I could see was the look in Kevin's eyes as he fled the room. The boy had been so certain I'd be able to bail Buttons out one more time. I had failed him.

Doris sat down beside me. "Sometimes there are things you just can't change."

"I'm always stuck under this big black cloud," I moaned. "It hangs over everything and refuses to let a ray of light through."

"Dave, look around you!" Doris scolded me again. "There's lots of light…but you don't see it. How many people do you know who have never had anything bad happen to them? I get really frustrated with you when you get in one of these moods. You can't afford to take a dive when something negative happens. Sometimes life gets in the way of your plans, but there are a lot of good things going on for you right now. I think you often just push them all away. How do you think my husband felt when he found out he'd have to be on a kidney machine for the rest of his life? How do you think I felt when he died in the middle of dialysis?" She looked at her watch with a frown. "Get up and get out of here—you've got a plane to catch."

I drove the seventy miles to Cranbrook as if my truck were a Formula-One race car. I glared at the clock on the dash as I poked my way through the city's downtown traffic. By the time I reached the airport turnoff, I had resigned myself to missing the flight. The plane was taxiing down the runway when I pulled into the parking lot. I sat back with cold resignation and watched the jet lift off and bank out of sight.

The return drive to Creston and the ten-hour trip to Vancouver gave me lots of time to think. Doris was right, as usual. Even with all the unpleasant things that had happened over the past year, I had a lot to be thankful for. Maybe I had missed opportunities to better my relationship with Father, but I had taken a lot of them, too. Building the house together and working on the farm had created a bond that was never there in my childhood.

I thought back to Swami Radha's words when I left the ashram. *Unless you change your thinking and your habitual patterns of reaction, you'll be sent one situation after the other to try you until you finally learn your lesson. There are no accidents in life, Dave—only different experiences.*

I checked into a hotel in downtown Vancouver at five the next morning. I picked up the phone in my room and hesitantly dialled.

"Vancouver General Hospital."

"Intensive care, please."

"Just one moment."

"Intensive care."

"Can you tell me how Marsh Perrin is doing? It's his son calling."

"He's resting comfortably. His surgery went well and there don't appear to be any complications."

"His surgery? He's already had it?"

"Yes, he was given priority last thing yesterday."

"How soon can I see him?"

"You should be able to visit for a few minutes later in the afternoon."

A sudden flood of relief came over me as I pulled off my shoes and crawled into bed. I couldn't believe it—Father was going to make it!

"You can see him now."

I reverently got up from my seat in the waiting room and followed the nurse down the corridor. Another nurse was finishing with Father as I arrived. I approached the bed with humility. A tube protruded from his nose, an IV dripped, monitors flashed. The moment my father saw me his eyes brightened, and he threw open his arms. I bent and hugged him, wires and all.

Father slowly released his grip on me and slumped back onto the bed. He smiled. "I didn't think I'd ever get the chance to do that."

"I know, Dad...I know."

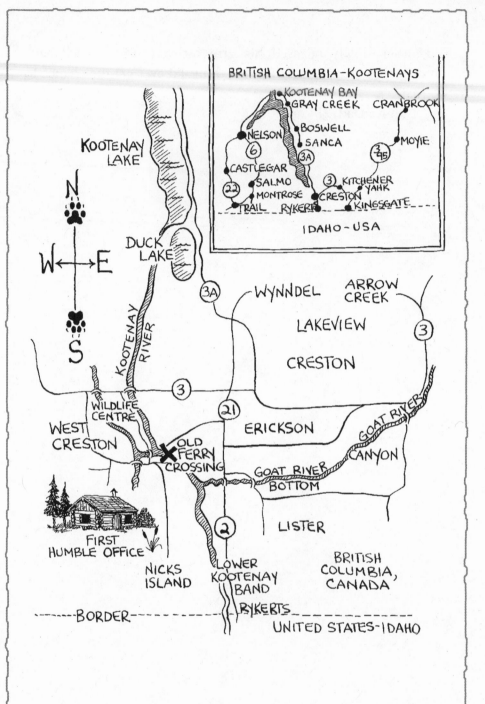

About the Author

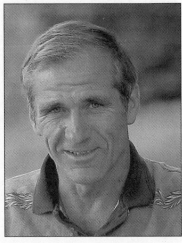

Photo by GERI BUCHANAN

Dave Perrin was raised in Casino, a small town nestled in the hills near Trail, British Columbia. He attended Selkirk College in Castlegar, the University of British Columbia, and the Western College of Veterinary Medicine at Saskatoon, Saskatchewan.

He graduated as a veterinarian in 1973 and practised in the Creston Valley until 1998. After a year in Hawaii where he began writing the first book about the profession he loved, he returned to his farm in Lister, BC. He established Dave's Press and has published three previous books on his veterinary adventures: *Don't Turn Your Back in the Barn* (2000), *Dr. Dave's Stallside Manner* (2001), and *Where Does It Hurt?* (2003). In 2004 Dave's Press published a book about a young girl growing up in the fundamentalist Latter-Day Saint community of Bountiful, called *Keep Sweet: Children of Polygamy*.

Dr. Perrin continues to write and practise veterinary medicine as a locum in British Columbia and Alberta.

Find Dr. Dave's veterinary adventures at your local bookstore

For more information, for comments,
or to order autographed copies of

Don't Turn Your Back in the Barn,
Dr. Dave's Stallside Manner,
Where Does It Hurt?
and
Never Say Die.

Visit our Web site at:
davespress.com
Phone: 250-428-3931
E-mail: dave@davespress.com
or write to:
Dave's Press Inc.
Box 616, Lister
British Columbia
Canada V0B 1Y0

Dave Perrin's books are distributed by
Sandhill Book Marketing Ltd. of Kelowna, B.C.